FOREWORD

This study was undertaken as part of the Development Centre's programme on the theme of Changing Comparative Advantages in Food and Agriculture. It provides a synthesis of the International Interactions research. It was carried out by Ian Goldin, who heads the programme on agriculture at the OECD Development Centre, and Martin Brown, of the OECD Directorate for Science, Technology and Industry.

ALSO AVAILABLE

Development Centre Seminars

Restoring Financial Flows to Latin America *edited by Louis Emmerij, Enrique Iglesias* (1991)
(41 91 06 1) ISBN 92-64-13476-X FF130 £17.00 US$31.00 DM50

Development Centre Studies

Agricultural Policies for the 1990s *by Sartaj Aziz* (1990)
(41 90 01 1) ISBN 92-64-13350-X FF120 £14.50 US$25.00 DM47

Agriculture and Economic Crisis. Lessons from Brazil *by Ian Goldin, Gervasio Castro de Rezende* (1990)
(41 89 09 1) ISBN 92-64-13392-5 FF90 £11.00 US$19.00 DM35

Rebalancing the Public and Private Sectors: Developing Country Experience *by Olivier Bouin, Charles-Albert Michalet* (1991)
(41 91 04 1) ISBN 92-64-13440-9 FF150 £18.00 US$32.00 DM58

Biotechnology and Developing Country Agriculture: The Case of Maize *by Carliene Brenner* (1991)
(41 91 14 1) ISBN 92-64-13595-2 FF100 £13.00 US$24.00 DM39

Prices charged at the OECD Bookshop.

THE OECD CATALOGUE OF PUBLICATIONS and supplements will be sent free of charge on request addressed either to OECD Publications Service, or to the OECD Distributor in your country.

OF AGRICULTURE:
DEVELOPING COUNTRY IMPLICATIONS

by
Martin Brown
and
Ian Goldin

DEVELOPMENT CENTRE
OF THE ORGANISATION FOR ECONOMIC CO-OPERATION AND DEVELOPMENT

ORGANISATION FOR ECONOMIC CO-OPERATION AND DEVELOPMENT

Pursuant to Article 1 of the Convention signed in Paris on 14th December 1960, and which came into force on 30th September 1961, the Organisation for Economic Co-operation and Development (OECD) shall promote policies designed:

— to achieve the highest sustainable economic growth and employment and a rising standard of living in Member countries, while maintaining financial stability, and thus to contribute to the development of the world economy;
— to contribute to sound economic expansion in Member as well as non-member countries in the process of economic development; and
— to contribute to the expansion of world trade on a multilateral, non-discriminatory basis in accordance with international obligations.

The original Member countries of the OECD are Austria, Belgium, Canada, Denmark, France, Germany, Greece, Iceland, Ireland, Italy, Luxembourg, the Netherlands, Norway, Portugal, Spain, Sweden, Switzerland, Turkey, the United Kingdom and the United States. The following countries became Members subsequently through accession at the dates indicated hereafter: Japan (28th April 1964), Finland (28th January 1969), Australia (7th June 1971) and New Zealand (29th May 1973). The Commission of the European Communities takes part in the work of the OECD (Article 13 of the OECD Convention). Yugoslavia has a special status at OECD (agreement of 28th October 1961).

The Development Centre of the Organisation for Economic Co-operation and Development was established by decision of the OECD Council on 23rd October 1962.

The purpose of the Centre is to bring together the knowledge and experience available in Member countries of both economic development and the formulation and execution of general economic policies; to adapt such knowledge and experience to the actual needs of countries or regions in the process of development and to put the results at the disposal of the countries by appropriate means.

The Centre has a special and autonomous position within the OECD which enables it to enjoy scientific independence in the execution of its task. Nevertheless, the Centre can draw upon the experience and knowledge available in the OECD in the development field.

Publié en français sous le titre :
L'AVENIR DE L'AGRICULTURE :
Incidences sur les pays
en développement

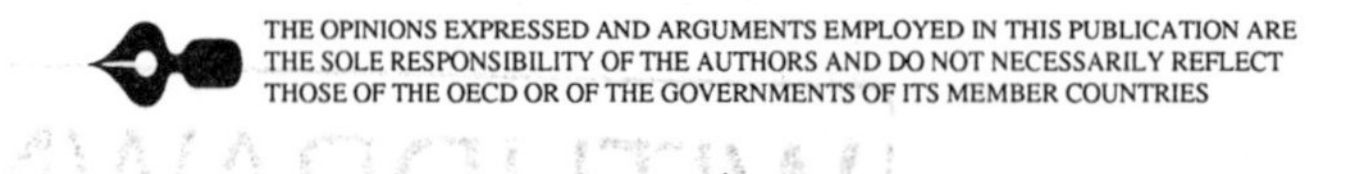

* * *

TABLE OF CONTENTS

LIST OF TABLES

ACKNOWLEDGEMENTS

The research project on which this study is based has depended on collaboration and interchange with a wide range of institutions and experts. Particular thanks are due to Irma Adelman, Kym Anderson, Sartaj Aziz, Carliene Brenner, Ron Duncan, Guillermo Flichman, Yair Mundlak, James Pickett, Suthad Setboonsarng, Ammar Siamwalla, Bernardo Sorj, Wouter Tims, Alberto Valdés, John Wilkinson, and, especially, to Nikos Alexandratos and Albert Simantov, for their contributions and comments to the research and its synthesis.

The project as a whole depended on the generous support of the Finnish and Swiss Governments, to whom much credit is due. Neither they nor any other institution or expert is however responsible for the errors, interpretations and conclusions of the study: these are the responsibility of the authors alone.

PREFACE

The Development Centre's 1987-90 research on food and agriculture was guided by two different but inter-related preoccupations. The first aimed at examining the impact of developing countries' macroeconomic, trade and sectoral policies on their agricultural development; and the second focused on developments outside the control of the developing countries: OECD Member countries' policies, technological trends, changes in food processing, and developments in trade.

This study provides a synthesis of the "international interactions" element in the research programme. It provides policy perspectives on trends in global food product markets, identifying the factors which are expected to impinge on developing countries' production, consumption and trade over the coming decade. The consequences of these trends for nutrition are examined. The pessimistic outcome — the number of malnourished is expected to approach a billion people by the year 2000 — stands in sharp contrast to the optimism over global food balances. World production will exceed consumption growth, and food prices are consequently expected to continue to drift downwards.

Developing countries are expected to account for much of the new consumption growth, and OECD Members for much of the production growth. OECD Member exporters, even under liberalisation scenarios, thus gain most from consumption growth in the developing world. Global market developments will have a sharp impact on food security.

Innovation is expected to transform world agriculture, but for developing countries there are major concerns. Technological changes need to be relevant to their needs and capacities for implementing them, rather than widening the productivity gulf between and within countries.

Developing countries' agricultural and macroeconomic policies have been the subject of a series of country studies commissioned by the Development Centre and synthesised in a volume by Sartaj Aziz. Martin Brown and Ian Goldin's synthesis reinforces the conclusion of the Aziz book in highlighting the importance of both national and international policy responses. Macroeconomic policies which provide adequate infrastructure for agriculture are seen as essential ingredients of sustainable development. So, too, are international policies, not least on the part of the OECD Member countries, whose exporters stand to gain most from developing country growth. At the very least, they should provide an even playing field and allow developing countries access to markets and technology.

This study provides clear indications of likely developments and the policy options, presenting important new perspectives.

Louis Emmerij
President of the OECD Development Centre
Paris, September 1991

EXECUTIVE SUMMARY

Introduction

This report brings together broad policy concerns about global markets in food products and global nutrition. It examines the impact on food production, consumption and trade of trends in technology, ecological developments, the industrialisation of the "food system", production costs and comparative advantage and the role of agricultural policies. The policy discussion of issues is situated in the context of a medium- or longer-term quantitative framework of projections of demand, supply, trade and prices. The important shifts in the projected quantities of basic foodstuffs (essentially cereals) consumed, produced and, especially, traded and the expected price trends inform the policy discussion and the research agenda.

An overview of the projections to the year 2000

All the projections show a major sustained rise in world trade in basic foodstuffs even within the present protectionist world trading system. Net world trade in cereals could rise from some 60 million tons in 1984 to between 100 and 200 million tons in the year 2000. Developing countries' share of global imports would rise above 50 per cent. OECD countries would be the major source of world exports, with net exports doubling. World prices for major foodstuffs are projected to fall. No plausible policy changes would significantly reverse this underlying downwards drift. It is difficult to overstate the importance of these conclusions for the discussion of agricultural policies and world trade.

Likely **consumption** trends for basic foodstuffs (annual average growth rates in volume terms) are:

	World	OECD	Developing
1970-84	2.5	1.2	3.6
1984-2000	2.2	1.6	2.6

Clearly, a deceleration is in prospect, especially in the developing countries. The corresponding deceleration in **production** projections will occur primarily in developing countries. Thus, while total world cereals production growth may decelerate from 2.8 per cent in the 1970-84 period to 2.0 per cent in the 1984-2000 period, the corresponding decelerations would be from 2.8 per cent to 2.1 per cent for the OECD countries, and from 3.4 per cent to 2.0 per cent for the developing countries.

Consumption and nutrition

Trends in global consumption of food over the past three decades show two major trends. First, in regional terms, consumption growth rates for most foodstuffs are now much higher in developing countries than in OECD countries. They are also somewhat higher in Eastern European Economies. Second, there has been a shift in the pattern of demand for food away from traditional basic staples towards other cereals, and especially towards animal products.

The higher growth rates for developing countries reflect their higher population growth rates, higher income growth rates and higher income elasticities of demand for food. These differences are likely to persist. The product shift will have significant effects on international markets, since it favours more internationally traded products. Developing countries will be increasingly dependent on world markets. Conversely, global market trends are likely to have an increasing impact on food consumption trends and policy issues in developing countries. The shift towards animal products implies a greater role for world markets.

The world in 1980 still had somewhere between 340 and perhaps even 730 million **undernourished people** and this number increased further during the 1980s. Hunger is primarily an Asian and rural problem. The projections imply some improvement in relative nutrition and food security, although an actual increase in the number of hungry people. Most undernourished people already depend on global markets trends: hunger-related policies will have global market implications, and, conversely, global market developments would have impacts on the global hunger problem. On the other hand, the actual "deficit" is very small in relation to the total and national food availabilities. Thus hunger is primarily a question of economic policies in the countries with hungry people.

Non-food uses for some food products are potentially important. There would be no serious technological or industrial problems about the massive substitution of agricultural for petroleum-based products. The major constraint on non-food uses of agricultural products, especially in the energy sector, reflects relative price differentials, rather than technical constraints.

Prospects for basic food production

For most of the developing world, food production has risen relatively rapidly over the past two decades, but a deceleration is now expected. Continued productivity increases in food production depend on a number of interdependent factors. The key question regarding technology developments in developing country agriculture concerns the extent to which it will reduce costs. Lower food prices to consumers generate more economic development than higher agricultural prices to farmers. If technology can continue to be cost-reducing, there is a "virtuous circle" in which increased food production leads to increased rural incomes, including non-food-production incomes, which stimulate further rural development. Domestic prices do not need to move out of line with international prices. However, only through fairly egalitarian land exploitation will the necessary rural incomes be generated to promote self-sustaining rural development. Thus, a rural-based development strategy is the only one that has any chance of success for most developing countries. The central issue thus is the extent to which the additional incomes must be generated from food production itself and, in particular, from higher farm-gate prices.

Raising producer prices may yield disappointing medium-term output responses. Governments in low-income countries face competing uses for scarce budget resources. One may contrast the financial costs of producer price supports, subsidies for inputs and cheap credit with public infrastructure expenditures. The former tend to be regressive and self-perpetuating, and may ultimately lead to economic distortions and inefficiencies. However, they may yield fairly rapid production increases. Requirements for public investment in physical infrastructure, control of environmental degradation, and the development and distribution of "new technology" innovations are crucial.

Historically, most of the world's food production growth has come from increasing *areas* under cultivation, but more recently most additional output has come from **yield** increases. This trend is expected to continue. In most important food producing regions, **water control** is the key constraint on both area under basic food crops and on yields. The development of controlled water systems is integrally related to public finance policies with profound equity and food entitlement implications. Major **technology** advances are under way. At the same time, current productivity is well below levels obtained by efficient farmers. Conclusions about **employment** generation in basic food agriculture are relatively pessimistic. The share of agriculture in the total labour force will fall significantly. The **financing of agricultural development** is a central concern: if associated investments are included, water control probably represents at least 30 per cent of all agricultural investment required in the coming decade. The total investment requirement for 93 developing countries (excluding China) over this period would be some (1980) $1 500 billion.

The food system

"Off-farm" activities are increasingly dominating food production and consumption, even for poor people in developing countries. The most important developments are likely to be "downstream", in the processing of basic foods, while technology developments seem likely ultimately to reduce agriculture's dependence on agro-chemical inputs. While most of the "off-farm" activities are "informal" and "unorganised", an increasing share is in the modern sector. World-wide turnover in 1980 in the seeds industry is estimated at $20-30 billion, compared with 1982 $13.3 billion sales of agro-chemicals. Organised, industrial activities **downstream** had a world-wide turnover of more than $1 000 billion already in 1981, of which developing countries accounted for around 14 per cent. The organised food system has an international dimension, which is comparable to that of other manufacturing industries. The degree of concentration is surprisingly high, with an estimated one-third of all food production in the market economies controlled by the one hundred largest agro-industrial companies.

Technology issues

Technology innovations, especially involving the use of information technology and bio-technology, will transform world agriculture producing a new "revolution", more radical than the agro-chemical revolution of the 1960s and 1970s. The effects of information technology advances are already widespread. The potential impacts of bio-technology are difficult to judge. In the 1990s, there will certainly be some significant effects on livestock product markets, in plant protection, and in developing cereal varieties better adapted to "more hostile" geographical and climatic environments. However, there is uncertainty about the major break-through in plant genetics — nitrogen-fixing in basic cereals. Lastly, there could be developments in industrial use of agricultural raw materials, for energy or chemicals, which would significantly affect global markets for basic foodstuffs.

There is a contrast between the developments in prospect and the agro-chemical-based "green" revolution of the past two decades. That revolution was dominated by the R&D and industrial characteristics of bulk chemical "process" industries. It led to standard products not always adapted to the needs of particular, nutritionally vulnerable groups of people. Applications of the next generation of technology innovations will seem more various and "diffuse" than earlier ones. "Start-up" costs, especially for R&D but also for some manufacture, will be less dominating. This is a source of optimism for developing countries and their poor people. However, there are worries. Technology developments tend to promote international trade around a few cereals (especially maize) with substantially falling real prices.

Trade and food security

Very large increases in international food trade are in prospect. Global food markets have traditionally been very "narrow", with major fluctuations in quantities traded and (especially) prices. Recently, much discussion has been about the effects of OECD country agricultural policies and, more recently, about the corresponding effects of developing and Eastern European countries' policies. Undoubtedly, the policies are currently dominating global markets, with very obvious effects on prices. However, these short-term policy concerns should not be exaggerated, given the prospect of large increases in world trade and a massive shift towards developing countries as food importers.

The key question for **food security** is about its compatibility with greatly increased imports of food and agricultural raw materials. Thus imports will be constrained by foreign exchange availabilities with major consequences in Asia and Africa.

Agricultural policies and strategies

The Development Centre commissioned a quantitative analysis of the effects of agricultural policy reform for temperate zone food products, involving Producer Subsidy Equivalents (PSEs) and Consumer Subsidy Equivalents (CSEs). The results are presented in terms of year 2000 outcomes which compare various policy reform scenarios for OECD and developing countries with a base case.

Elimination of OECD agricultural protection would yield modest price increases for wheat and rice, somewhat stronger price increases for beef and sugar, and price falls for coarse grains and soya. The projected price changes would generally be small in relation to underlying longer-term price trends. For volumes, the overall results are also very modest: developing country net cereal exports would be little more than 1.0 million tons higher with OECD liberalisation than the approximation of 200 million tons trade projected for year 2000. There would also be important "indirect" macroeconomic effects.

Policies and developments in the **Eastern European Economies** could have a considerable influence on world markets for basic food products, both because they are potentially large "swing" traders and because their trading activities have not always been predictable or transparent.

Developing countries' policies relating to agriculture have had more important (negative) effects on developing country production and world trade for major basic foodstuffs than the policies of OECD countries. World markets would be considerably disturbed by developing country policy reform, but developing countries' own situations would be considerably improved.

Policy analysis should consider the diversity of developing countries and the different groups within them. There will be losers as well as winners. The nutritionally most vulnerable people in food importing countries could be losers from OECD policy reform, but possible winners from developing country reforms, notably in their own countries.

Comparative advantage

Due to distortions arising from interventions in domestic and global markets, one cannot draw practical conclusions on international competitive advantage. Existing major global food markets are very narrow and do not reflect international competitiveness. Tropical product markets are more competitive, but even here the measurement of comparative advantage is fraught with difficulties. The most difficult problems concern the valuation of labour, land and capital employed. For the tree crops (cocoa, rubber, oilpalm, coffee), these factors may not be mobile in the short run and this further complicates the analysis. Comparative advantage is thus seen to be useful conceptually, but practically difficult or even impossible to evaluate.

Governance

In the OECD countries, it is accepted that agricultural policies are driven by "lobbies", which reflect a complicated range of economic and social interests. In the Eastern European countries and, still more, the poor developing countries, the problems of "governance" are pervasive and dominating. Most of the present analysis of agricultural trends and policies assumes that national governments can implement macroeconomic and food and agricultural policies, and even "strategies": to many observers, this is visibly not true. At this very general level of preoccupation, there are further, heterogeneous concerns which are of great importance, but which cannot easily be integrated into a coherent discussion of food and agriculture. These include: political and military conflicts, agriculture-based narcotics, smuggling, the AIDS epidemic, the role of women in food and agriculture, and, more generally, religious and cultural traditions. Most food and agricultural analysis proceeds as though these problems cannot explicitly be taken into account, although it would hardly seem plausible to assume that their impact should be ignored.

Environmental and ecological issues

Environmental concerns are becoming dominant. They will have implications for developing countries, both directly in international discussions of global environmental issues, and through changes in international food and input product markets. Given the projections of greatly increased world trade in cereals, the biggest uncertainties concern OECD food production. On balance, the conclusion is that market and institutional forces within the OECD countries will ensure that they do produce (or over-produce) the basic foods "needed" in the 1990s. Nevertheless, there are longer-term concerns, essentially about "global warming", which could affect the economics of production of basic foodstuffs for global markets in the 1990s and beyond. In the medium term, changed attitudes towards fertilizer and other chemical-based products may also lead to a scaling down of OECD production trends.

Policy conclusions

Prospects for global basic food product markets suggest an increasing self-sufficiency deficit for developing countries and deteriorating nutritional standards for poor people in poor countries. While efforts to promote developing country food production are crucial and structural reforms and redistribution of income could generally eliminate food deficits, the reality is greatly increased international trade in basic food products at falling real prices, essentially from OECD countries to developing countries, and, perhaps, to Eastern European Economies.

OECD agricultural policy reforms would lead to more rapid growth in the OECD countries, as factors were reallocated to more efficient uses and the dead-weight losses arising from distortions reduced. Reduced support for agriculture is expected to lead to higher prices, temporarily offsetting the downward drift in world prices. Perhaps more importantly for developing countries, liberalisation will spell more stable prices and greater market access, not least for non-traditional products. The main losers will be developing country importers, and special measures may be required to ensure that these countries do not suffer adverse nutritional consequences.

Developing country macroeconomic and agricultural policy reforms are necessary to ensure that the benefits of international liberalisation are reflected in improved developing country agricultural production. Macroeconomic reforms, including the realignment of overvalued exchange rates, should ensure that farmers enjoy higher prices, even if there is not OECD liberalisation; indeed the evidence suggests that their own reforms are most important to developing countries. Reductions in the levels of net taxation in agriculture need to be associated with the provision of appropriate infrastructure and inputs (including technology). The focus should be on the establishment of sustainable rural-urban-international balances. Food self-sufficiency is neither a desirable nor feasible national target for most countries. The target should be rural-based (but not exclusively food-based) development to generate rural incomes to meet food "entitlements".

Chapter 1

INTRODUCTION

In 1987, the Development Centre initiated research on changing comparative advantages in food and agriculture. It was decided to develop initially two types of research. On the one hand, eight country case studies have been undertaken, which analyse the domestic interactions between food and agricultural sectors and the rest of the national economy, against the background of trends in global markets[1]. On the other hand, it was decided to undertake an overview of the major "international interactions" in food and agriculture. A synthesis of the country studies has been conducted by Sartaj Aziz and is available as a Development Centre Study. Our intention in this volume is to present a synthesis of the "international interactions" element in the research programme, and wherever applicable to integrate into this synthesis the findings of the country studies.

The issues identified as affecting "international interactions" are exogenous to the national policy measures examined in the context of the country case studies. They include: developments in bio-technology and in the food system and the global balances which emerge as a result of the cumulative impact of individual countries' policies.

Research into "international interactions" was conducted by the Centre's staff in collaboration with external consultants. A series of discussion papers were produced and reviewed at expert meetings. The present report draws on those findings[2].

A central focus of this report is the interaction between trends in international markets, on the one hand, and national developments in food and agriculture in poor countries, on the other hand. The report stresses the role of non-economic developments, and the difficulty of integrating them into economic analysis. Linked to this is the growing importance of issues and research which are not primarily focused on agriculture in a traditional, narrow sense: the role of technology (especially "new technologies"), the increasing upstream and downstream linkages (the "food system") and the national economic interactions which influence the basic food sector.

The report brings together: the longer-term trends and issues (Chapters 2 — Consumption and Nutrition; 3 — Production; and 6 — Trade and Food Security); the Food System (Chapter 4); the technology and institutional issues (Chapter 5 — Technology); the issues about costs of production and international comparative advantage (Chapter 8); and the issues about the effects of changing policies towards food and agriculture (Chapter 7).

Global balances

The different available longer-term projections of global trends (reviewed in Chapters 2, 3 and 6) produce widely differing results and suggest conflicting conclusions on the principal policy issues. They partly reflect the optimism or pessimism of their authors, and are heavily influenced by the most recent events[3]. This report seeks to show that such views are mistaken: first, there is sufficient consensus on some of the trends for them to be taken seriously, and, second, it would be unwise to base policy discussions on the recent unsettled situation.

That is not to deny the importance of recent international macroeconomic trends. This report is directly concerned with interactions between these trends and the food and agricultural prospects and problems of developing countries. However, the discussion below of the various specific aspects of these prospects and problems suggests that the difficult economic experience of the 1980s and the associated threat of protectionist policies in agricultural trade should not be exaggerated. The longer-term trends are more important.

There is now a very large body of research and writing about "food security" for developing countries and poor people. Food security implies adequate and secure levels of food intake for all people, based essentially on national (or local) production. In addition, it refers to international obligations to underpin the national self-sufficiency efforts. A key question for this report is the extent to which food security is compatible with greatly increased imports of food and agricultural raw materials.

More generally, there are issues about global macroeconomic trends and their relevance to developing country food and agriculture. Most of the uncertainty (in the available literature) seems to be about the demand (food consumption) side of national and global food balances. The available consumption projections, reviewed in Chapter 2, are primarily driven by population growth, with a great deal of uncertainty about the possible effects of per capita income developments and about income distribution.

However, one of the key issues for this report is about the role for food imports, and it is plausible to question the extent to which these may (for both developing and Eastern European countries) be constrained by foreign exchange availabilities. How far will increased food import possibilities be constrained by foreign exchange problems? What does or should the trade-off look like between food and other imports? How far are there feasible trade-offs between agricultural exports and food imports, and how far are these conditioned by overall macroeconomic prospects? To what extent will the debt problems of developing countries constrain the food import possibilities over the longer term?

On the supply side macroeconomic policies are also of vital importance. Macroeconomic developments affect the profitability of agriculture and production levels, especially the balance between different crops and livestock products. For some developing countries, longer-term production prospects depend greatly on public investment in physical and human infrastructure. Foreign trade and exchange rate policies greatly influence agriculture, with changing policies reflected in input policies — most obviously fertilizers.

In spite of the undoubted global success of food agriculture over the past thirty years, nutritional concerns remain dominant for low-income groups in large parts of the globe. While, statistically, many of these "gaps" could be met by redistribution of incomes and existing food availabilities, realistically, any strategy for meeting basic food needs and aspirations requires continued rapid growth in food consumption and production (including of livestock products) in most developing countries, and especially in the large, low-income countries of South and East Asia.

Technology

Food agriculture world-wide has shown a surprising capacity to raise productivity and output over the past four decades. This has been most visible in the OECD countries, but has equally applied to many important developing countries and, much more modestly, to the Eastern European Economies. It has been associated everywhere with a shift of agriculture towards commercial markets: increasingly, productivity growth has come from improved yields (rather than increased acreage or livestock numbers) associated with increased commercial inputs.

As shown in Chapter 5, an increasing part of agricultural growth is associated with "technology" innovations. Again, this has been most obvious in OECD countries, but is nevertheless very important in many developing countries. While great technological advances have been promised for the coming decades, the extent to which these will be diffused and applied to the advantage of developing country agriculture requires careful consideration.

Technology analysts argue that the generation of technology innovations which are now in the pipeline could have as radical implications for productivity as those of the past thirty years, although their rate of adoption will be influenced increasingly by economic conditions. Some of these innovations, and notably those associated with bio-technology, require careful consideration by developing countries, who are faced by "institutional" and "technological" capability constraints. Others, particularly those associated with information and materials technology, seem likely to have pervasive effects on developing country food and agriculture on almost any institutional assumptions. However, their effective adoption is dependent on the economic environment and on interactions between agriculture and the rest of the national economy.

These "technology innovations" are broadly favourable to world food prospects and to developing countries. An analogous, but more pessimistic, growing awareness concerns ecological and environmental threats to longer-term "sustainable development" of food and agriculture[4]. This is taken up in Chapter 3.

Food security

The quantitative projections reviewed below suggest that international trade in basic food products, which has been rising rapidly over the past decade but which remains very small in relation to world consumption, may emerge as a major factor in food and agricultural policies of developing countries.

Trade and food security questions are examined in Chapter 6. Some projections assume that most developing countries will aim for food self-sufficiency. World trade then becomes almost a statistical residual — world import requirements — which is shared out between traditional food exporters. OECD countries as a group will largely remain the "swing" producers, adjusting their production to the growth of their own domestic markets and the "requirements" of world trade. Other projections have no implicit self-sufficiency assumptions.

To a large extent, this may reflect the practical complexities of making longer-term projections for a large number of commodities which are partial substitutes in demand and supply. The FAO and World Bank projections are rich in terms of their technical (country and product) content, but this at times is at the price of fairly simple policy assumptions.

The various projections reflect the assumption that developing countries' policies will not change greatly over the medium term (except in sub-Saharan Africa, where they should become more rational) and that OECD countries as a group will not greatly restructure their own agricultural markets. The analysis in Chapter 7 suggests that while the projections are very sensitive to the policy assumptions for developing countries they are not as sensitive to policy changes in OECD countries.

Comparative advantage is at the core of the debate concerning the relationship between development and agricultural production, consumption and trade. In Chapter 8, the theory and practice of comparative advantage is analysed, with a view to providing perspectives on future trends in agricultural production. The examination in Chapter 9 is extended and concluded by introducing all the differing perspectives into the argument, thereby offering a final evaluation of the role of "international interactions" in developing country agriculture.

NOTES

1. The countries studied and the authors concerned are: Argentina (Mundlak, Carvallo and Domenech), Brazil (Goldin and Rezende), Mexico (Adelman and Taylor), Ethiopia (Pickett), Ghana (Pickett and Shaeeldlin), China (Anderson), Pakistan (Hamid and Tims) and Thailand (Setboonsarng, Werakarnjanapongs and Siamwalla). These country studies and the synthesis volume by Aziz have been published by the OECD Development Centre; the full references are provided in the bibliography to this report.
2. Staff discussion papers were prepared by Martin Brown (food trends), Ian Goldin (comparative advantage and factor costs — see Goldin 1990b) and Carliene Brenner (bio-technology — see Brenner). Consultant reports were prepared by Alberto Valdés and Joachim Zietz (on the implications of trade liberalisation — see Zietz and Valdés), Guillermo Flichman (on engineering cost comparisons of production costs — see Flichman) and John Wilkinson and Bruce Traill (on the food system).
3. For a discussion of these sources of bias, see Carter *et al.*, Chapter 5.
4. For a discussion of "sustainable development", see World Commission on Environment and Development (the "Brundtland Report"), Parikh 1988b, Davis and Schirmer, and Mellor 1990.

Chapter 2

CONSUMPTION AND NUTRITION

Introduction

Patterns in global consumption of food over the past three decades show two major trends. First, in regional terms, consumption growth rates for most foodstuffs in volume terms are now much higher in developing countries than in OECD countries. They are also somewhat higher in Eastern European Economies, although with these countries the product pattern is more mixed. Second, in all the major country groupings, there has been a shift in the pattern of demand for food away from traditional basic staples (which vary from region to region) towards other cereals, other crops, and especially towards animal products.

The much higher growth rates for developing countries reflect their higher population growth rates, higher income growth rates and higher income elasticities of demand for food. These differences are likely to persist for all three of these factors, and available medium- to long-term projections, reviewed below, indicate continued deceleration in consumption growth rates in volume terms for OECD countries, contrasted with continued relatively rapid growth in developing countries. Thus, the developing countries' share in world consumption of most important cereals has risen significantly over the past two decades and will continue to rise in the period to year 2000. Details for individual products are presented in Tables 2.1-2.4.

The shifts in the pattern of products consumed will have important effects on international markets. First, the shift between staple cereals, including tubers, has generally been in favour of products which are more internationally traded, and developing countries' increasing dependence on these products is likely to increase their role in world markets, both as importers and, to some extent, exporters. Conversely, global market trends are likely to have an increasing impact on food consumption trends and policy issues in developing countries.

Second, the shift in consumption patterns both in OECD, Eastern European Economies and developing countries towards animal products clearly implies a greater role for world markets, both because these products are increasingly traded in world markets and, much more importantly, because their (competitive) production is increasingly based on traded feed materials.

As suggested above, these two trends — higher growth in aggregate demand in developing countries and important shifts in the product composition of food consumed — are likely to increase their influence on global markets over the period to year 2000. Several, more specific, factors or issues will be important in influencing the trends. These would include:

i) demographic trends;

ii) global and regional macroeconomic trends, which will have little effect for the OECD region but major effects in developing countries and, potentially, in the Eastern European Economies;

iii) trends in international prices for major agricultural products;

iv) trends in technology, which will certainly influence consumption trends both by their direct effects on products consumed but also by their effects on supply conditions;

v) the pervasive influence of government policies in OECD, Eastern European Economies and developing countries (this is taken up in Chapter 6);

vi) political responses to food security trends;

vii) non-food demand for some major food products.

Trends and prospects

Food consumption in volume terms is now rising considerably faster in developing countries than in developed countries. Thus, total world grain consumption (Table 2.1) rose during the 1970-84 period at an annual average rate of 2.5 per cent, with corresponding rates of 1.2 per cent for the OECD countries, 1.8 per cent for the Eastern European Economies and 3.6 per cent for the developing countries. Since total grains include feed grains and the trade in livestock products is rather low, these growth rates may be taken as a proxy for the growth of basic staples and livestock consumption.

For basic staples/**food** grains, the divergent trends are even more striking. Taking wheat and rice together, the average annual growth rates in the 1970-84 period were (per cent):

World	2.9
OECD	1.8
Eastern European Economies	0.7
Developing countries	4.0

As a result, developing countries' share (Table 2.1) in total world grains consumption (food and feed), which may be taken as a proxy for cereals and livestock products, increased significantly (per cent):

	1969-71	1979-81	1986
World	100	100	100
Developing countries	43.7	48.5	50.2
OECD	35.1	30.6	30.1
Eastern European Economies	21.2	20.9	19.6

Again, the shift in consumption shares was most striking for *food* grains, and especially for wheat, for which the developing country share in world consumption rose by 10 percentage points to almost 44 per cent.

Total food consumption is projected to grow much faster in developing countries than in either Eastern European or OECD countries. Table 2.5 shows seven different sets of projected growth rates for the period to year 2000. FAO projects total food consumption in volume terms rising over the 1983/85-2000 period at an annual rate of 3.1 per cent for developing countries as a whole, of 0.8 per cent for developed market and 1.2 per cent for Eastern European Economies[1]. The other projections shown are of cereals consumption. One comes from the International Food Research Policy Institute (IFPRI) and with a 1980 base is for "major food staples"[2]. Another comes from the World Bank: it takes 1986 as base year, and makes use of econometric models[3]. The International Wheat Council (IWC) projections[4] take 1985 as base year and use *ad hoc* projection methods. The International Institute for Applied Systems Analysis (IIASA) projections[5] use 1980 as base year and are generated within a general equilibrium modelling framework. Lastly, Zietz and Valdés have prepared a set of (partial equilibrium) projections in the context of the policy analysis undertaken for the Development Centre[6].

The projections imply a deceleration from consumption growth over the past two decades. For the developing world, the various projections for cereals consumption show annual average growth rates over the period to year 2000 of 2.5-2.7 per cent. There is considerably more disagreement in the corresponding projections for the industrialised countries, between zero growth (IWC) and 1.6-1.8 per cent (World Bank). Since this group still represents about half of total world consumption, one could conclude, slightly surprisingly, that most of the uncertainty about world cereals consumption concerns the developed world. The projected deceleration for developing countries is noteworthy. It mainly concerns Asia, and especially China, which is examined in greater depth in Chapter 6 below.

FAO projections for developing countries (shown in Tables 2.6 and 2.7) show some shift between basic food staples. This is partly due to greatly increased animal food use of cereals and roots and plantains. However, with China excluded, the projections (Table 2.7) imply significant per capita increase in direct food consumption of roots, tubers and plantains, especially in sub-Saharan Africa. As expected, consumption growth rates for oilseeds, sugar and livestock products are much higher than for basic cereals and tubers.

Cereal use as animal feed will grow considerably faster than direct consumption as food. Thus, for the developing world as a whole, FAO projects feed use rising over the 1983/85 to 2000 period at an annual average rate of growth of 5.5 per cent (as against a corresponding 1.9 per cent for direct food consumption), lifting the feed share in total cereal consumption from 15 per cent to 24 per cent. Details are shown in Table 2.6. This would represent a deceleration from the corresponding 1969/71 to 1983/85 rate of 6.5 per cent. IFPRI projects significantly lower feed use growth rates, with a 4.6 per cent rate over the 1980-2000 period, to lift the year 2000 feed share to 23 per cent.

The FAO data show that developing countries' cereal feed use overwhelmingly (90 per cent) involves coarse grains, principally maize (for which less than half of total "disappearance" is directly consumed as food). Thus, developing country consumption of maize rises much faster than that of other cereals: the FAO projections yield 1984-2000 annual average growth rates of developing country consumption of (per cent): 2.7 for total cereals, 2.4 for wheat, 2.1 for rice and 3.8 for maize. Thus, maize would account for more than one quarter of all cereals consumed in the developing world in year 2000. Moreover, animal feed use of cereals is confined (98 per cent) to middle-income countries and China. More than 40 per cent of Latin American cereals consumption is now as animal feed, and this share could rise (according to IFPRI) to 47 per cent in 2000.

The uncertainties in these projections and the differences between them should be noted. While the projected growth rates are very similar for total developing world cereal consumption, they vary considerably for particular regional groupings, especially Africa. Of course, the product definitions vary between the different projections (as noted in the footnote to Table 2.5) and, to a lesser extent, differences result from differing country groupings and base years. Nevertheless, to the extent that they are assumed to be comparable, the gap between higher and lower projections of developing world food consumption would represent some 50 million tons of annual cereals consumption by year 2000.

The greatest uncertainty concerns China. Indeed, both FAO and IFPRI present their projections both **with** and **without** China, so that Chinese data do not distort the overall results. The different projections imply the following average annual growth rates in Chinese cereals consumption over the period to year 2000:

	Products	Base year	Growth rate (%)
FAO	Cereals	1983/85	2.3
IFPRI	"Major foods"[a]	1980	3.0
World Bank	"Total cereals"	1984	2.9
IWC	Cereals	1985	2.2

a. Livestock products are represented in feed grain equivalent.

It is interesting to take a glimpse at a much longer future. In a study conducted at Resources for the Future, Sanderson[7] has developed an indicator — primary food energy (PFE) — which expresses demand for specific food products on a common basis. This is especially important for livestock products, whose PFE equivalent can be as high as eight times their final calorific value. PFE cannot be taken as a proxy for cereals, of course, because of the importance of other crops, which were estimated in 1975 to represent in grain equivalent about 25 per cent of total food crop production. There are also important unaccounted-for discrepancies, for example livestock forage and waste products. Nevertheless, PFE can give an indication of likely trends for consumption of basic foodstuffs, and therefore for cereals.

On this basis, world demand for PFE might increase at an average annual rate of 1.6 per cent over the period between 1975 and 2050, as against a corresponding 2.6 per cent rate in the 1975-2000 period. Most of this growth will be in the developing world, since consumption per head in the industrialised countries (including the Eastern European Economies) should have levelled out before year 2000. Corresponding growth rates to 2050 might be 2.8 per cent for the middle-income countries, as higher incomes boost demand for livestock products, but only 1.9 per cent in low-income countries, in spite of their faster population growth rates. However, on this national average basis, the diet in the poor countries will be roughly comparable to current levels in Mexico and Brazil.

Determinants of demand growth

Consumption growth may be analysed in terms of: population growth, income (and, therefore, income per head) growth and income elasticities. To illustrate the influence of the different main quantifiable factors on aggregate demand growth for cereals, a composite table (Table 2.8) has been prepared. It brings together different estimates of growth in population and income per head, and of income elasticities.

Income distribution, which is highly skewed in most developing countries, should be relevant to consumption growth. The quantification of this effect remains, however, illusive. First, while we know intuitively that income distribution is highly skewed, the quantitative data is poor, and particularly so when it comes to an analysis of food consumption. Second, estimates for income elasticities for different income groups within different groups of consumers, and of share of different foods in total food consumption are not available[8]. Third, an evaluation of the effect of income redistribution on total demand for cereals needs to take into account the evidence that livestock products (for which the relatively rich have high income elasticities) are very cereal-intensive. More equitable income distribution in developing countries would increase total cereal demand, but the extent and form of the changes which would arise require further analysis. This uncertainty notwithstanding, it remains true, as we emphasize in Chapter 6, that a redistribution of income and, more generally, increased "entitlements" for the poor would go a long way towards eliminating undernourishment in most countries.

There is comparatively little divergence in the different projections about **population** growth assumptions, although (as argued below) the overall food projections are very sensitive to population assumptions. Most projections are based on UN population projections, with the differences resulting more from the use of different versions of these projections, which are revised from time to time.

World population growth is slowly decelerating. As shown in Table 2.8, over the 1980-2000 period the annual average rates of growth are likely to be: total world — 1.6 per cent; Asia — 1.6 per cent; sub-Saharan Africa — 3.10 per cent; Latin America — 1.8 per cent; OECD — 0.4 per cent; Eastern European Economies — 0.5 per cent. The greatest uncertainty concerns China. It now seems plausible that the official projections of Chinese population understate the likely year 2000 population by as much as 10 per cent (120 million people).

There is more disagreement about **income per head** growth prospects, and it should be noted that growth per head prospects used in the projections reflect any divergencies in population growth assumptions. The projections shown in Table 2.8

are broadly based on World Bank projections[9]. They are fairly pessimistic, with an annual growth rate over the 1980-2000 projection period of some 2.3 per cent for the developing world and 2.1 per cent for the industrialised countries. Moreover, between the World Development Reports for 1988 and 1989, the pessimism seems to have grown. However, in both cases, it is argued that growth prospects could be raised significantly by appropriate policies for "adjustment with growth", perhaps by as much as one percentage point. This is the figure used in the sensitivity analysis below. As shown in the table, the projections may understate the scope for more accelerated growth in the second half of the 1990s. Again, the biggest uncertainties concern China, for which a growth rate of 3.0 per cent is assumed.

Considerable uncertainty also exists regarding the **income elasticities** of demand for basic foodstuffs. The estimates shown in Table 2.8 were made on the basis of the conflicting and fragmentary assumptions articulated in the various projections. A central problem is that national averages reflect assumptions about (or past trends in) income distribution. Income elasticities in developing countries are high for cereals at both the bottom and the top ends of the income profile: at the bottom end because of the desire to increase consumption, and at the top end because of strong demand for livestock products, which are very cereal-intensive, and the substitution of foods. The determination of income elasticities in longer-term projections poses an even greater challenge as they should capture the "underlying" shifts in consumer tastes, including the effects of urbanisation, together with the effects of technology change on the food system.

The "composite" elasticities in Table 2.8, based on the indications from the various projections, appear to be low. They are, for the volume response of cereal consumption to per capita income growth: world — 0.20; developing countries — 0.24; China — 0.20; S. Asia — 0.30; sub-Saharan Africa — 0.50; Latin America — 0.30; industrialised countries — 0.10. By comparison with the (crude) indicator of growth in cereal consumption in relation to income per head over the period since 1970, around 0.7 for the developing world, they imply an important deceleration, especially for the industrialised countries.

Table 2.9 lists some (FAO) estimates for basic food staples in developing countries used in the IFPRI projections, which distinguish between direct food consumption and feed grain elasticities. If one leaves aside China (elasticity: 0.17) and India (0.27) which because of their size would dominate the results and whose elasticities are, interestingly, very much higher than those for other countries, the results suggest average income elasticities of demand of 0.07 for food grains, of only 0.12 for low-income countries, about zero for middle-income countries and 0.15 for sub-Saharan Africa. For feed grains, the averages are, as may be expected, much higher, although still, as compared to the estimates of others, rather low — around 1.0 for low-income countries, including China, India and sub-Saharan Africa, and only about 0.6 for middle-income countries.

The IIASA analysis assumes higher elasticities for direct human consumption of cereals. These are:

OECD	0.08
Developing countries	
Total	0.53
Middle-income	0.19
Low-middle income	0.32
Low income	0.75
World	0.43

Other estimates suggest still higher elasticities, especially for rural areas. Kilby and Liedholm[10] have reviewed available evidence on expenditure elasticities, which suggest that in sub-Saharan Africa, rural population food expenditure elasticities could be above 0.9, with a corresponding estimate for Malaysia (a middle-income country) of 0.57. The income elasticities used in the Development Centre's (Zietz and Valdés) policy projections are shown in Table 2.10.

In relation to the estimates of Table 2.8, an increase in the projected **population** growth rate in the developing world of 0.1 percentage points, from 1.9 to 2.0, would raise year 2000 world cereal consumption by around 40 million tons, almost 2 per cent. Even if this is a conservative margin of error for likely population growth, it is, in terms of world consumption, a rather modest amount.

An increase in the rate of growth of **per capita GDP** in developing countries by 1.0 percentage point would raise year 2000 world cereal consumption by almost 100 million tons. This might be taken as a representation of the World Bank's "growth-oriented structural adjustment" scenario[11]. It could also be taken as an indication of the margin of error in this type of projection.

The political implications of the different projections are considerable: a developing world GDP per head growth rate of less than 2.0 per cent annually is likely to imply that the downside projections carry considerable risk. It is desirable to have higher income growth rates, but it has to be recognised that these will have a substantial impact on world cereal consumption, and probably on world cereal markets.

The convenient figures of 100 million tons of world cereal consumption for a 1.0 percentage point change in the developing countries' GDP growth rate illustrate the effects of more optimistic growth prospects on food consumption. If the increase were across the board, more than half of the extra consumption would be in South Asia and China. Roughly one quarter would be in sub-Saharan Africa.

Raising the rate of growth of GDP per head in the industrialised countries, from 2.1 per cent to 3.1 per cent, would raise year 2000 world cereal consumption by slightly over 30 million tons, about 1.4 per cent.

Changing the **income elasticities of demand**, however, would have considerable effects on world cereal consumption, in spite of the obvious trade-off referred to above between upper-income livestock consumption and lower-income basic food consumption. Raising the developing country income elasticities uniformly to 0.5 would raise year 2000 world cereal consumption by more than 200 million tons, approaching 10 per cent. Most of the additional consumption would be in China and South Asia. This would bring the assumed income elasticities in line with the IIASA assumptions, but well above those of most other projections.

Somewhat surprisingly, as Table 2.8 indicates, the consumption growth forecasts are driven by population growth. In spite of low sensitivity to possible population variations, population growth remains the main determinant of food consumption growth. In the "base" case, population growth contributes almost 75 per cent of total consumption growth. In none of the income-related variations considered above does this share fall below 60 per cent. Moreover, for individual main developing regions, the share does not fall below 50 per cent, except marginally for China.

Food **prices** are increasingly recognised as an important determinant of food demand, especially among poor people and especially in developing countries. This recognition reinforces the links between food policy in developing countries and international markets. However, the issues are not straightforward, primarily because there can be gaps between domestic consumer (food) and producer (farm gate) prices and between domestic and international prices. More generally, even when food products can be considered as relatively homogeneous, quantitative analysis is still frustrated by questions concerning the representativeness and meaningfulness of official price series.

In the analysis of the determinants of food consumption and, therefore, of the projections, the data ambiguities are compounded by assumptions regarding the choice of price indicators, the assumptions regarding price transmission mechanisms and price elasticities of demand. These issues are taken up in Chapter 6, where the implications of longer-term price trends and the diverging estimates of own price elasticities are highlighted.

While it is generally accepted that international prices are unlikely to increase much in relation to the average of the past decade, the most reliable specific projections (from the World Bank) point to sharp falls for all the major cereals. More uncertainty exists about trends in rice prices, which are expected to rise in relation to other cereal prices, and perhaps in real terms.

On the basis of the World Bank price forecasts of a 50 per cent fall in cereal prices, and the demand price elasticities, presented in Table 6.4, developing world basic food consumption could be higher by between 5 and 10 per cent in year 2000 (very roughly 100-200 million tons) because of falling prices.

Nutrition

In nutritional terms, FAO's conclusion is:

> The past quarter-century has brought extraordinary achievements in food and agriculture. One measure stands above all others: the successful response to the challenge of feeding 1 800 million more people in the 25 years to 1985, at levels of average per caput food consumption which have been constantly improving, in terms of both quantity and quality. Fears in the 1960s and early 1970s of chronic food shortages over the larger part of the world have proved unfounded[12].

This overall nutritional improvement is reflected in Table 2.11, which comes from the FAO study. FAO's analysis suggests that world food availabilities for human consumption, measured in calories per head per day, rose from 2 450 in 1969/71 to 2 660 in 1983/85, with a corresponding increase for 94 developing countries from 2 110 to 2 420.

This nutritional improvement still leaves very many undernourished people. In terms of calories per head of population, the number of countries with an intake below 1 900 calories per day fell from 23 in 1961-63 to 9 in 1983-85 (Table 2.12). On this basis, the number of people involved fell from 985 million in 1961-63 to 196 million in 1983-85.

The analysis suggests that the world in 1980 still had somewhere between 340 and perhaps even 730 million undernourished people. These figures exclude China. The upper figure denotes people unable to lead a normal life, the lower, people clinically at risk of serious disease and death. The numbers are staggering, and the World Bank estimates are more pessimistic than FAO's[13], which are shown in Table 2.13. However, the differences between the two sets of estimates are also very large, and they do raise issues about the credibility of the analysis.

The number of hungry people in the world increased during the world recession of the 1980s. The World Food Council, basing itself on FAO analysis, claims that, following an increase of 15 million in the 1970-80 period, there was an increase of about 40 million in both halves of the decade of the 1980s. This would bring the total for the WFC to about 550 million in 1989, of which about 17 per cent was added in the 1980s[14].

Assuming that these figures of hunger are indicative of the real situation, the decade of the 1980s has indeed been ghastly. It would be difficult to question that this is due to the global economic recession and associated policy responses of developing countries. Nevertheless, two points should be made. First, although the number of hungry people increased by almost 17 per cent in the 1980s, most of the total were already hungry at the end of the "good" years of the 1960s and 1970s. Second, although there is some evidence to suggest that the debt crisis and "structural adjustment" packages have been associated with a deterioration in indicators of nutrition, it is clear that the problem preceded and will persist beyond the debt crisis. The difficult conclusion is that while the world's hunger problem certainly has an international dimension, it cannot simply be laid at the door of global macroeconomic performance or national protectionist policies. These issues are taken up in more detail in Chapter 6 and in other Development Centre publications[15].

It is important to note that both the FAO and World Bank analyses show that hunger is primarily an Asian problem. The World Food Council claims[16], basing itself on FAO data, that in the mid-1980s, 57 per cent of the world's undernourished people were in South and East Asia, 27 per cent were in Africa, 11 per cent were in Latin America and 5 per cent were in the Near East. The estimates are reproduced in Table 2.13. While the African numbers square with the available evidence, the estimates appear to understate Chinese undernourishment, estimated at 6 per cent of its population (less than 70 million) as against 22 per cent for Asia as a whole (some 290 million). Very probably, the Asian share in total hunger is around two thirds.

It should also be stressed that hunger is a rural phenomenon. IFPRI estimates suggest that the rural share in total hunger is 80-90 per cent in Asia and Africa (where most are located) and more than 60 per cent in the rest of the developing world[17]. There is much which still needs to be learnt about the distribution of hunger within the rural areas and the issue cannot be divorced from the question of the changing nature of employment and ownership in the countryside. Nor should it be forgotten that within the countryside, it is particular groups of people, especially women and children, who are most at risk. Furthermore, while the health risks involved are much more varied than simply access to an adequate supply of calories from basic foodstuffs[18] an adequate supply of basic foodstuffs is a necessary condition for survival and the ability to lead an active life.

The FAO projections imply (using FAO/5th World Food Survey methodology) some improvement in relative nutrition and food security, although an actual increase in the number of hungry people (see Table 2.13). The relative improvement involves a fall in the calculated percentage of clinically undernourished, from 14.6 per cent to 10.5 per cent, and of people unable to lead a normal life, from 21.5 per cent to 15.6 per cent. The absolute deterioration involves 5 million more people who are clinically at risk, taking the total to 353 million in year 2000. The extra undernourished people would be in sub-Saharan Africa, although in absolute terms there would remain more hungry people in Asia. The other projections would produce roughly comparable results. The FAO projections exclude China.

These undernutrition projections are plausible. It should be noted that the available food in the year 2000 would adequately feed the world's population if it could be redistributed to those in need. However, this would imply some shift in product composition, especially from feed to food grains. Given the massive prevalence of undernourishment in developing countries, how far might policies to deal with hunger affect world markets? The data and arguments reviewed below suggest that the food price (and availability) policies mentioned above are fairly marginal to the hunger issues, which are primarily about "entitlements", which, in turn, are primarily about jobs and incomes.

The many millions of undernourished people in the world are mainly located in countries which are already active in global markets: this would suggest that hunger-related policies would have global market implications (and, conversely, that global market developments — for example prompted by OECD policy changes — would have impacts on the global hunger problem). On the other hand, the available data and analysis indicates that the actual "deficit" (the amount of food that would be needed to stop people going hungry) is very small in relation to the total food availabilities in most of the countries concerned (and insignificant in relation to world availabilities). This would suggest that world hunger (however real and dramatic) is primarily a question of economic policies in the countries with hungry people.

The key to this important problem, and apparent paradox, may be partly a generally high income elasticity of demand for food in the countries with hungry people. It is difficult to implement policies which address hunger which do not also raise demand for food in the rest of the economy. These issues are addressed directly in the Centre's recent case study on Mexico[18]. The results suggest that in Mexico it would not be difficult, provided that petroleum prices do not collapse, to make policy changes that would make most people better-off and poor people better-fed.

Technology and the food system

Trends in technology (reviewed further in Chapter 5) and, particularly but eventually, bio-technology, will certainly have a major impact on consumption trends for particular food products. These trends are, at present, most obvious in the OECD countries. Their increasing application in the next few years to developing and Eastern European countries seems likely, but because demand in general is rising so much more rapidly in these countries than in the OECD region this represents a major uncertainty for global trends for some food products. The most affected major product is sugar, whose soft-drink and confectionary uses are threatened by natural (HFCS) and synthetic substitutes: these uses are very important in the dynamic urban markets of developing countries. [It should be noted that HFCS substitution has occurred mostly in the United States and depended on high (protected) sugar prices and low prices for maize. These price relationships are not typical of LDC markets, so that at present the substitution is mostly an OECD phenomenon. Technological developments which lower HFCS production costs may however make HFCS more competitive in LDCs.]

More generally, technology trends in food processing industries — primarily in OECD countries but increasingly elsewhere — will affect global markets through their effects on the consumer preferences between food products and on the choice of intermediate inputs in the livestock sector. In the OECD region, over the past few decades, technology-induced productivity changes within the animal husbandry sector have led — via price changes — to marked shifts in consumer preferences between different products (most obviously in favour of poultry and pig meat). Further shifts are likely in the near future. The already-acquired technology changes in the OECD region are likely to have major impacts in some important developing country markets over the coming decade, but some of the impacts of the "new" technologies in animal breeding may begin to come in at the same time.

Technology innovations which extend "shelf-life" or reduce waste in food processing may have significant impacts on global food consumption (in volume terms) within the medium-term future. In general, these would tend to reduce the volume of food "consumed", but the effects on particular products and particular geographical sources could be expansionary.

Most projections of future demand assume that these technology effects are captured in longer-term correlations between income and food consumption and/or make intuitive assumptions about the likely effects of particular innovations (e.g. assume HFCS captures x per cent of a particular soft-drink market). With the "new" technologies and, especially, current bio-technology developments, one may wonder whether sufficient attention has been paid to this problem of projecting the demand effects of technology innovations on global food markets.

Non-food uses

Non-food uses for some food products are potentially important. Clearly, the most important potential uses are as a source of biomass for conversion to products which would replace petroleum-based products[19]. Present experience, especially in Brazil and the United States, indicates that there would be no serious technological or industrial problems about the massive substitution of petroleum-based products. The problems are economic: most studies show that at any likely international prices for the raw materials and for petroleum, the substitution would not in general be economically viable. However, there could be economic (and non-economic) reasons which would allow local prices in particular countries to diverge from international prices (or would justify some corresponding subsidy or tax relief). Moreover, conversion costs will certainly fall both because of economies of scale (learning by doing — as in the Brazilian case) and from advances in bio-technology.

The question for this present overview is about how far such energy uses of food staples (including sugar) could become important enough to influence world food markets. In 1986, some 8 million tons of maize (3 per cent of national production) was converted to ethanol in the United States, the only major OECD producer, and until the 1990 Gulf crisis, indications were that this would remain roughly stable.

Conclusions

There is general agreement that in volume terms world consumption growth for basic cereals is decelerating. The deceleration in the OECD countries is not surprising. The even greater deceleration expected in developing countries is, however, a matter of great concern, given both the extent of hunger in the world and the shift in consumption tastes (towards more cereal-intensive livestock products) as incomes rise.

The extent of divergence between the projections is noteworthy. Differing assumptions regarding livestock developments in the OECD countries are important in determining the different projections, and the implications for international trade and prices are also of great significance, not least for the developing countries themselves.

The projections of world consumption of basic foodstuffs are unlikely to be too low. The developmental challenge needs to be met in order that consumption growth confounds the pessimistic projections. These demand implications, as we show below, pose massive challenges to developing countries' agricultural production and, above all, to world trade.

NOTES

1. Alexandratos (1988), Table 3.5, p. 70.
2. Paulino.
3. World Bank (1989a).
4. International Wheat Council.
5. Parikh *et al.* See also Fischer *et al.*
6. Zietz and Valdés (1989).
7. Antonelli and Quadrio-Curzio, Chapter 9. See also Crosson, Chapter 4 in Clark & Munn.
8. See e.g. Alderman.
9. World Bank (1989b), Table 1.2, p. 21. The World Bank's growth rates to 1995 are extrapolated to 2000.
10. Kilby and Liedholm.
11. World Bank (1989b), p. 21.
12. World Bank (1986a), p. 1.
13. Alexandratos, Table 3.4, p. 66, based on FAO (1987a).
14. WFC (1989), p. 4.
15. See Aziz for a synthesis of the national studies, and Goldin and Knudsen for an analysis of the implications of protectionism.
16. WFC (1989), p. 4.
17. Mellor, quoted in WFC (1989), p. 5.
18. Behrman *et al.*
19. Adelman and Taylor.
20. See e.g. Schliephake (Chapter 11) and Hall and Coombs (Chapter 12) in Antonelli and Quadrio-Curzio.

Chapter 3

PROSPECTS FOR BASIC FOOD PRODUCTION

Introduction

For most of the developing world, food production has risen relatively rapidly over the past two decades. However, most projections foresee a deceleration over the 1990s and perhaps beyond. What are the factors involved?

Continued productivity increases in developing countries' food production are dependent on a number of interdependent factors:

i) "technology" factors (continued innovation and the successful diffusion of both recent and prospective innovations);

ii) "ecological factors" (especially degradation of intensively farmed arable land);

iii) "institutional" factors ("human resource" developments, the social organisation of agriculture, the efficiency of government and parastatal organisations);

iv) the "industrialisation" of agriculture through the rapid development of the "food system";

v) "economic" factors (profit incentives to farmers, including the prices of purchased inputs and marketed outputs).

The projections based on the extrapolation of historic trends aim to capture the longer-term impacts of these different factors. In the case of the economic factors, the projections tend to assume that price incentives will be adequate in future to support whatever production projections seem otherwise to be plausible. However, this is not a totally satisfactory approach to the discussion of longer-term trends and possibilities.

It has been persuasively argued by Mellor[1] and others that the key questions about further technology developments in developing country agriculture are about how far they will reduce costs. This goes to the heart of the development process.

Lower food prices to consumers generate more economic development than higher agricultural prices to farmers. If technology can continue to be cost-reducing, we have the "virtuous circle" in which increased food production leads to increased rural incomes, including non-food-production incomes, which, with high income elasticities for wage-goods (including agricultural products), stimulate further rural development. And, importantly, to the extent that technology innovations can be cost-reducing, domestic prices do not need to move out of line with international prices for major traded food products. It is also clear that with this "optimistic" scenario, the issues of "food security" and "sustainability" become much less serious. It is not necessarily important for this process that the initial innovations in food production technologies be employment-intensive. The employment and income creation may come from secondary farm and off-farm activities.

This discussion needs to be related to the other familiar discussion about the need for "land reform" or, at least, for structures of land use which are fairly egalitarian. This assumes that only through fairly egalitarian land exploitation will the necessary rural incomes be generated to promote self-sustaining rural development. The two lines of argument are not incompatible. Both imply that a rural based development strategy is the only one that has any chance of success for most developing countries. (Morris and Adelman have argued that this was also the experience of the now developed countries[2].) However, the key question concerns the extent to which the additional incomes must be generated from food production itself and, in particular, from higher farm-gate prices.

The following section reviews different available supply projections over the period to year 2000. This is followed by a discussion of some of the issues. This discussion is not intended to be exhaustive, and is linked to more detailed discussion in subsequent chapters. It is concerned with the relevance of the issues to the plausibility of the longer-term supply projections. It is important to note the uncertainties about national production data, even for major crops and major developing countries. Longer-term "trends" in the available data are less uncertain than the absolute magnitudes.

Trends and prospects

FAO data indicates that world gross agricultural production increased at an annual average 2.5 per cent over the 24 years to 1985. Corresponding rates for different groups of countries, shown in Table 3.1, show that growth was in general much faster, at 3.2 per cent, in the developing countries, than in the developed countries 2.0 per cent. However, within the developing world there were wide divergencies, between a 1961-85 average annual rate of growth of 3.5 per cent in Asia, but only 2.0 per cent in sub-Saharan Africa. More than 25 per cent of FAO's 94 developing countries had growth rates below 2.0 per cent.

Over the 1970-84 period, annual average production growth of total cereals (Tables 3.2 to 3.5) was considerably higher in developing countries (3.4 per cent) than for the world as a whole (2.8 per cent) or for the OECD countries (2.8 per cent). The corresponding growth rate for the Eastern European Economies was strikingly low (1.0 per cent). Within the developing world, however, performance varied widely, with 1970-84 annual average growth rates of 3.6 per cent in Asia, 3.3 per cent in Latin America, but only 1.6 per cent in Africa.

The performance of different major cereals varied considerably (Tables 3.3 to 3.5). The annual average growth rate over the 1970-84 period was significantly lower for coarse grains (2.1 per cent), than for wheat (3.4 per cent) or rice (2.9 per cent), whose production was boosted by the Green Revolution. These Green Revolution effects were particularly strong for wheat, with developing world production rising by 6.5 per cent annually.

FAO projections suggest a small deceleration in developing world agricultural production over the period to year 2000. Total agricultural production, which rose at an average annual rate of 3.2 per cent over the 1961-85 period, would rise by a corresponding 3.0 per cent rate over the 1985-2000 period. However, with China excluded, the corresponding deceleration is very small, from 2.9 per cent to 2.8 per cent. FAO projects an acceleration in output growth for sub-Saharan Africa, although from very low 1983-85 levels.

Projected developing world growth rates for cereals production are significantly lower in the five main sets of projections shown in Table 3.6. However, for sub-Saharan Africa and for Latin America, cereals production is projected by FAO to rise faster than total agricultural production, although in both cases the FAO cereals projections are substantially higher than the IFPRI or IWC projections.

All the projections imply a significant deceleration in world, and especially developing country, cereals production from the 1970-84 period to the 1984-2000 period. For the developing world as a whole, cereals production would decelerate from an average annual growth rate of 3.4 per cent to 2.6 per cent (FAO) or 2.3 per cent (IWC). Of the major regions, only Africa would see an output acceleration. For the developed world, output growth would slow sharply in the OECD countries, although FAO still projects some modest (0.9 per cent) annual growth. Prospects for Eastern European Economies are most uncertain.

Sustained production growth: sources and issues

The economic climate for growth

It is important to situate the projected trends in a discussion of the underlying sources of growth and of the constraints. The representation of these sources and constraints is necessarily schematic and simplified in the global projections. This section considers some of the key issues to which the projections seem sensitive.

Price elasticities of demand and supply are a central mechanism driving most of the projections. Different estimates are presented in Tables 6.4 and 6.5 and are discussed in the context of longer-term price trends. It is noted that demand price responses over the medium term to the projected major international price shifts may prove relatively important (i.e. higher than the historically derived elasticities used in most models). This — together with likely response asymmetries — could lead to major demand shifts between products.

On the supply side, there are also reasons to expect some rather large shifts. The relatively low elasticities of Table 6.5 for low-income countries (China and India) probably reflect too much the historical constraints of land (and more recently, controlled water) supply with relatively stable traditional technology. There is evidence that with Green Revolution technologies, supply price responses have been significantly high[3]. Similarly, in sub-Saharan Africa (especially West Africa) supply response seems to be constrained by seasonal labour shortages and traditional cropping practices.

The cautious conclusion from this line of argument would be that raising producer prices may yield disappointing medium-term output responses, or more pessimistically, the prospective international price trends may pose very severe financial and fiscal problems for producer price policies, in low-income countries in both Asia and sub-Saharan Africa. For the poorest countries, these macroeconomic (and political) problems could prevent the implementation of stimulatory producer prices incentives.

Even within the agricultural sector, governments in low-income countries face important competing uses for scarce budget resources[4]. Very broadly, one may contrast the financial costs of producer price supports and subsidies for inputs (especially for fertilizers and irrigation water) and cheap credit with public infrastructure expenditures. The former tend to be regressive in practice, for both economic and political reasons, and tend to be self-perpetuating, and may ultimately lead to economic distortions and inefficiencies. However, they may yield fairly rapid production increases in situations where the physical and human constraints are not too binding. It is argued below that, over the longer period, these constraints are becoming more important. Requirements for public investment in physical infrastructure (especially roads and water control), control of environmental degradation, and the development and distribution of "new technology" innovations

are likely to become worrying. Similar requirements for social i
— especially in female education — may be even more important
intractable.

The following sections outline some of the constraints and possibilities for sustained basic food output growth over the longer term. The outlook is not very promising, given the exhaustion in Asia of major prospects for arable land expansion, the likely continuing fall in international prices, the intractable problems in the provision of public infrastructure and, more generally, the "governance" problem, and the growing ecological threats.

However, there are grounds for cautious optimism coming from continued technology innovations, especially from the "new" technologies. Moreover, since the prospects are that these will be input-reducing and, more generally, "cost-reducing", they should ease the fiscal burden of producer price supports and input subsidies. However, they reinforce the priority for public infrastructure investment.

As noted elsewhere in this report, the optimism can be partly characterised as "technology optimism". Moreover, an emphasis on public infrastructure investments, especially in the social sphere, and on the social structure of basic food production, raises very severe "governance" doubts — about the ability and political commitment of national governments to implement the required priorities. Indeed, the current enthusiasm for producer and input price incentives may reflect "governance scepticism".

Areas and yields

For arable crops, production growth is normally analysed in terms of areas and yields. Historically, most of the world's food production growth has come from increasing areas under cultivation, but more recently, and especially since the Second World War, most additional output has come from yield increases. This trend is very significant for developing countries. Over the two decades to 1980, three quarters of additional developing country staple food production came from yield increases (Table 3.7). Even if China (which has faced extreme constraints on area expansion) is excluded, more than 60 per cent of the 1961-80 increase came from higher yields. Moreover, the yield contribution accelerated over the two decades: in the later, 1971-80, period, as much as 80 per cent of all additional staple food production came from yield increases. With China excluded, the acceleration is even greater.

This trend is expected to continue. FAO projections imply that some 60-75 per cent of increases in major food grain production (wheat and rice) in the developing world (excluding China) over the 16 years to year 2000 will come from yield increases[5]. For coarse grains, the yield effect will be even more important as cultivation shifts from lower to higher yielding crops. The IWC projections show a stronger dependence on cereal yields as the engine for developing country production growth. With China included, the contribution of yields growth to developing country production growth over the 1985-2000 period would be 74 per cent for wheat, almost 80 per cent for rice and more than 86 per cent for coarse grains[6].

There is still, potentially, considerable scope for increasing crop areas under staple food crops. Thus, Table 3.8 shows both the share of total potential arable land in arable use (36 per cent in 1982-84 for developing countries, excluding China) and the share of total cultivated land under cereals (a corresponding 54 per cent).

In most developing countries land that is suitable for food production with today's technology and today's world market prices is already producing food. There is, of course, some competition for land between food staples and other agricultural crops. However, in general, any further production from additional land would need to be linked to yield increases which brought marginal land into food crop production. Conceptually, therefore, there may not be a need for a strong distinction between areas and yields as a source of production increases. Nevertheless, it is striking that most observers are looking to yields rather than areas to raise world food production.

Average yields, even for a particular crop, vary enormously from country to country, as is illustrated in Table 3.9. Although these data are the important starting point for most production projections (FAO, IFPRI, IIASA, IWC), they may not in themselves tell us much about country performance or the scope for output growth. These national averages reflect a whole range of climatic and soil conditions (especially irrigation possibilities) within a country as well as varying cropping patterns. They also, of course, reflect the "efficiency" of crop production in particular countries, and, therefore, the scope for production increases.

Particular attention needs to be given to "coarse grains", which contributed as much as 30 per cent of developing world cereal production in 1986. Yields vary considerably between the different crops, with world averages in 1986 of (tons per hectare): barley — 2.3; maize — 3.7; millet — 0.8; oats — 1.9; rye — 2.1; sorghum — 1.5. Moreover, although maize is the preponderant coarse grain, contributing about 60 per cent of all coarse grain production, average yields vary enormously between different growing areas, from little over 1 ton per hectare to around 7 tons per hectare in the United States. Clearly, "average country yields" for coarse grains should be used with caution.

Controlled water availability

In most major food producing regions, apart from sub-Saharan Africa and Latin America, water control is the key constraint on both area under basic food crops and on yields (especially choice of high yielding varieties, and the use of fertilizers). As is illustrated in Table 3.10, there is a clear deceleration, especially since 1980, in the rate of growth of total irrigated area, and this is primarily due to a slowdown in growth in Asia, which has more than 60 per cent of the world's irrigated areas. Rice is the most affected product.

The causes of the deceleration are diverse, and are both technical and financial in nature. The World Bank[7] has emphasized the need for research on the determinants of the spread of irrigation. Such research is required in order to derive a better understanding of the factors accounting for the slowing of irrigation growth trends and its implications for future agricultural production.

The development of controlled water systems is integrally related to public finance policies and, as evident in our Pakistan case study[8], points to the need to recognise a continued role for the public sector. Irrigation systems in general have profound equity and food entitlement implications, so that the role of the public sector cannot simply be confined to that of financial allocation: irrigation investments have important developmental significance both in terms of growth and distribution. Here, a recurring concern is with the implications on the balance between small and large farmers and between food and export crops.

The issues here can be seen as both economic and physical. Unit costs of irrigation and flood control can be assumed to be rising, because the least-cost projects are being taken up first, because specific environmental protection costs are rising and because developing country capital costs in general have moved up sharply (as the negative real interest rates of the 1970s have been replaced by relatively high positive rates).

On the "benefits" side, various methodological issues need to be considered. First, most water control investments have important "benefits" (flood control, electricity generation) which cannot simply be imputed to agriculture. Second, assumptions must be made about cropping patterns (both desirable cropping patterns and the patterns that the planning/political process are likely to try to enforce). Third, assumptions about the returns to different crops, which are ultimately related to their effective prices, need to be considered, including trends in international prices and their linkages to domestic prices. Beyond these, are questions about who receives the benefits, and about how irrigation water is allocated between different users.

Since much developing country water control investment is in the public sector, the issues tend to appear less about social costs and benefits and more about government budgets and fiscal resources. This is true both for the financing of infrastructure investment and for the problem of international/domestic price linkages. These economic issues tend to be absent from discussions of both the social implications of different investments and aggregate water control trends, and thus the scope for further increases in controlled water acreage. Hence, the discussion is much more in terms of physical constraints.

Technology

Informed discussion about "new" technologies suggests that major technology advances are under way, involving principally bio-technology, information technology and materials technology. These developments and the associated policy issues are discussed in Chapter 5. Bio-technology developments will go "qualitatively" beyond the innovations of the Green Revolution or the livestock technology developments of the 1960s and 1970s. In particular, it will be possible to reduce drastically the period required to breed and test new seeds or animals, while the scope for mass reproduction is greatly increased. Developments in "materials" technology could transform traditional techniques for supplying water and bulk chemicals and for preserving food.

Very little quantitative analysis has been made (or, at least, published) of the likely or possible effects of "new" technology innovations on supply trends for major food products. One fairly general conclusion that is drawn is that there will be, on the most optimistic assumptions, relatively long delays before "new" technology innovations can have any significant effect on aggregate supply trends. Given this, any quantitative assessments are likely to be problematic.

One comprehensive "delphi" study for maize produces relatively optimistic results for the United States[9]. Average maize yields should continue to rise over the 1980-2000 period at annual rates above 1.5 per cent. Significantly, the growth rate would rise to almost 2.0 per cent for the 1990s, and more than 75 per cent of this growth would come from bio-technology developments. Importantly, these developments would increasingly be "built into" the seeds and be very relevant to developing country agriculture — including nitrogen-fixing, better photosynthesis and reduced water requirements.

Clearly, however, most current developing country productivity ("yields") with today's technology is well below levels obtained by efficient farmers and still more in laboratory conditions. In many countries, raising average yields to levels achieved in comparable physical conditions elsewhere could sustain aggregate production growth for major products through the medium term without the introduction of "new" technologies and with no increase in unit production costs. Critically, the constraints on higher yields in the medium term may be primarily about information and its management and diffusion, and, more generally and importantly, about human resource development ("skills") and the social structure of agriculture.

Undoubtedly, a very wide range of information technology developments offer scope for greatly increased efficiency in the management of today's technology. These could lead to lower variability in yields, lower input costs, less off-farm crop losses and the mitigation of the effects of natural disasters.

Employment, human resources and incomes

The projections imply relatively pessimistic conclusions about employment generation in basic food agriculture. In fact, the FAO projections are implicitly pessimistic for the whole of agriculture[10]. In spite of relatively rapid growth in total output, the agricultural labour force would only rise on average over the 1982/84-2000 period by 1.3 per cent annually, with corresponding growth of 1.8 per cent in sub-Saharan Africa, 1.2 per cent in Asia (excluding China) and 0.3 per cent in Latin America. The share of agriculture[11] in the total labour force would fall significantly, as follows (per cent):

	1985	2000
World	49	42
Developing countries		
Total	63	53
SSA	74	66
Asia	67	57
Latin America	29	21

These projections suggest that even rapid agricultural growth oriented towards basic food production will not generate sufficient employment in agriculture itself to absorb the growing rural labour force. However, this does not in itself mean that there will be a worsening employment or income outlook, since agricultural growth generates employment and incomes upstream and downstream and, more generally, through expenditure multiplier effects. The available evidence on these effects is reviewed below.

Financing agricultural development

The discussion above has pointed to the importance of controlled water supply as a key determinant of future food production in most of the developing world. In investment terms, securing additional irrigated area is proving increasingly expensive. Table 3.11 presents the FAO estimates of developing country investment requirements needed to meet the FAO production projections for year 2000. Several features deserve emphasis. First, investment in irrigation is, by a long way, the major item, representing 16 per cent of all gross agricultural investment: if associated investments are included, water control probably represents at least 30 per cent of all agricultural investment required in the coming decade.

This investment requirement associated with water control would be of the order of $450 billion (1980 dollars) 450 billion over the 1983-2000 period. The total investment requirement for the 93 developing countries (excluding China) over this period would be some $1 500 billion (1980 dollars). In 1988 dollars, this is of the order of $2 000 billion. These financing requirements are not fully reflected in total investment and financing projections for developing countries. In part, this is because they have yet to be debated upon. Given the magnitude of the investments involved, such a debate would be of far-reaching significance and imply a shift in development strategies towards a rural-development based policies.

In the context of discussions on public investments, attention needs to be paid to how far these investment "requirements" need to be in the public/government sector. Most observers assume that the irrigation/water control component will be in the public sector and are thus principally concerned with public finance requirements. However, there are observers who argue that a greater share of these investments could be in the private sector. Given that most of the interest concerns low-income Asian countries, research is needed to explore the potential for private investment or joint ventures. This should also focus on the implications for land-tenure, income distribution and nutrition.

To the extent that these financing requirements are not met, what are the alternatives? It should be remembered that the FAO projections imply a 1983-2000 financing requirement of $1 500 billion in 1980 prices and, perhaps, $2 000 billion in 1990 prices. It should also be noted that these projections must primarily concern Asian, low-income economies (although they exclude China). The extent to which increased world trade — essentially cereals imports of these Asian countries — may in the future substitute for the investment requirements outlined above will be pivotal in determining patterns of growth, nutrition and trade in the coming decades.

Rural social structures

There is considerable agreement that both growth in agricultural production and poor people's food consumption are linked to ownership and exploitation patterns in agriculture. More egalitarian systems of land ownership and exploitation tend to produce better output performance and a better distribution of income and, therefore, more assured food "entitlement". It is a small further step to argue that effective land reform is, therefore, an important determinant of future global trends in food demand and supply.

It is a somewhat bigger step to argue that strategies to promote food production and food security cannot work without effective institutional reforms. Griffin, for example, suggests[12] that "green revolution" strategies have failed even to increase growth rates for aggregate agricultural **production** in countries which did not have preceding land reforms (e.g. Philippines, India), let alone to raise incomes and nutrition of the rural poor.

Ecological threats to continued production growth

There is increasing concern about the medium-term "sustainability" of agricultural production. This comes partly from environmental degradation of currently relatively high-yielding land. There are also fears about pests, plant diseases and genetic variety. Moreover, in the densely populated OECD regions, there are growing concerns about the polluting effects of intensive use of agro-chemicals. The land concerns are both about some of OECD's "breadbasket", especially in North America, and, potentially much more seriously, about intensively cultivated land in high population-density areas of Asia. Lester Brown argues[13] that the outlook is alarming in important food producing regions for largely technical reasons. Worldwatch Institute rough estimates suggest that the world is losing an additional 14 million tons of grain production each year due to environmental degradation. Most of this (9 million tons) would be from soil erosion[14]. Globally, the greatest concern is for parts of the North American breadbasket, the USSR, and for China, where the water table is falling as more water is pumped than is being replaced. Elsewhere, excessive or ill-managed water use is leading to salinity and water-logging.

So far as the OECD countries are concerned, these concerns are likely to be met partly by policy-induced shifts towards the removal of more "fragile" land from arable farming. There is also growing public interest in the OECD countries in a shift away from the agro-chemical-intensive and mechanical-intensive technologies developed over the past three decades. This Low-Input Sustainable Agriculture (LISA) would not be a fully "green" or "organic" agriculture, and would not necessarily be much more labour-intensive than present agriculture. Research and development directed towards the LISA path could greatly increase its economic viability, and some funding in OECD countries has already been steered in that direction. However, the development of LISA requires more than research: it requires shifts in factor or product prices to be widely adopted. Other things being equal, these trends would point towards a rise in world prices for major temperate arable crops (especially wheat and maize).

A significant part of these shifts (the US "set-aside" policies) are already discounted in the World Bank projections of substantial falls in cereal prices over the period to the year 2000, although the complexities of the livestock sector in the OECD countries mean that these projections, about the world price effects of specific measures on particular products, are speculative in nature.

Longer-term concerns, which may already begin to be felt in the 1990s, are becoming more pressing. It is increasingly accepted that the planet is facing man-made climatic changes, coming largely from burning fossil fuels and deforestation. The resulting "global warming", the "greenhouse effect", which could be in the range of 1.5-4.5°C by 2030, would influence major wind patterns and, thus, rainfall, sunlight and crop yields over a large part of the globe. Temperature induced expansion of the oceans and the associated progressive melting of the polar ice-caps could raise global sea-levels by 0.3-0.5 metres by 2030, and could devastate some low-lying and densely populated areas. From a global food point of view, the most worrying case would be Bangladesh, neighbouring coastal states in India, and Java in Indonesia.

There is much uncertainty about the pace of the global temperature increase (and the pace is probably more important than the eventual extent), the climate implications, and the consequential agricultural implications[15]. The climatic uncertainties largely concern the effect on oceans and on cloud cover in different regions. In itself, a rise in mean temperatures and an increase in the density of atmospheric CO_2 would increase the rate of photosynthesis and shorten crop cycles, allowing the possibility of increased yields and, in some higher latitudes, a shift towards higher yielding crops. However, these output-increasing effects would be largely offset by water constraints. The rainfall implications of global warming seem likely to affect some major (semi-arid) cereal producing regions. In addition to the possible implications for mean temperatures is the concern with possible changes in the range of the daily or annual temperature cycle and the possibility that the process of change will be associated with increased instability. Both agronomically and economically the implications are important. In developing countries, risk management may be expected to become more significant, affecting both the choice of crop and the patterns of ownership and investment in agriculture.

To date, these considerations have hardly come into discussions of agricultural trends or policies, on the implicit grounds that the effects are too long-term and speculative. None of the available published long-term supply/demand projections reviewed in this report makes explicit assumptions about global warming. Nor could global warming be captured in statistical analysis of long-term historical trends, since the physical causes (deforestation and fossil fuel burning) could not have produced significant climatic effects so far. However, the recent (1988 and 1989) North American droughts (and, perhaps, other unusual climatic patterns elsewhere) focused popular attention, leading to suggestions that we may already be seeing evidence of long-term climatic shifts. If so, then even though recent sharp weather shifts may reflect rather severe short-term fluctuations, the underlying shifts should be taken into account in longer-term projections.

Most observers expect global warming to have adverse effects on crop yields in the major (Northern Hemisphere) exporting regions, although the extent to which this may affect global markets and the time-scale have not been specified. Analysis of the implications of global warming implications for developing country agriculture is in its infancy.

Cereal production in monsoon areas of South and East Asia (which represents some 12-15 per cent of world cereal production) is already highly sensitive to the timing (and quantity) of annual rainfall. To the extent that "global warming" produces greater climatic variations around average levels[16] this production will be affected, especially if, as is also suggested, there may be an increase in natural climatic catastrophes, with more hurricanes and cyclones interacting with higher sea-levels.

To the extent that these possible threats are taken seriously, they could prompt agricultural policies in low-income developing countries towards greater self-sufficiency and to promote crops which are less climatically sensitive. Greater instability may mean that a greater emphasis will be placed on "food security", both globally and in the more threatened low-income countries. (It seems unlikely that OECD countries will feel "threatened" for some years yet.)

There is as yet no certainty that the more negative effects will happen, and the most threatened countries and regions already have major "food security" and balance of payments problems. There is, however, an important case for greatly increased R&D, with two thrusts. First, we need to know more about what will actually happen with "global warming". Second, the global community could take out insurance against the worst outcomes by developing the capability to produce the crops that would be appropriate. This implies the maintenance of genetic variation and the development of bio-technology capabilities in seed production[17].

There is currently great international interest in checking the pace of global warming essentially through limiting the growth in global greenhouse gas emissions. Since the major source of these emissions is the use of fossil fuels, policies adopted (e.g. a "carbon" tax) would have some direct effects on global agriculture through raising the international price of (hydrocarbon) energy. This might be felt primarily in increased fertilizer, irrigation and international freight costs, and would tend to promote higher prices for basic foodstuffs. It is important to note that these effects would be transmitted to developing country food and agriculture, whether or not the countries concerned participated in the international efforts or were "compensated" for their participation.

Conclusions

The projections suggest a significant deceleration in world production of basic foodstuffs over the coming decade, after a period of two and half decades in which world agricultural production expanded by more than 2.5 per cent annually, and by 3.2 per cent in the developing countries. The aggregate deceleration in basic foodstuffs growth is likely to be modest — around 0.3 percentage points — but could be much higher (even 1.0 percentage points) in the developing world.

Most further growth in developing country food production must come from rising yields rather than increasing area under cultivation — probably as much as 60-75 per cent of increased output. This is the challenge to technology in developing countries. However, it is important (to anticipate the conclusion of Chapter 6) that this is a challenge to introduce more technology while reducing costs in real terms, because international prices in real terms are likely to fall dramatically. It is also a challenge to world trade.

NOTES

1. See e.g. Antonelli and Quadrio-Curzio, eds., Chapter 8, and Mellor (1988a, b and c).
2. Morris and Adelman.
3. See Ranada, Jha and Delgado (Chapter 11) in Ahmed and Mellor.
4. See e.g. the concluding chapter of Ahmed and Mellor.
5. Alexandratos, Chapter 4.
6. IWC, Appendix Tables IX-XI.
7. World Bank (1989a).
8. Hamid and Tims.
9. Hamid and Tims.
10. Alexandratos, Table 4.9. Note that the agricultural labour force projections are exogenous in the FAO (Alexandratos) analysis. They refer to availability, based on ILO projections, not necessarily to employment. In the FAO year 2000 projections, labour input use (only in the crop sector, not livestock) is used to derive implicit employment indicators.
11. Alexandratos, Table A.1.
12. Griffin (1987 and 1989).
13. Brown (1988, 1989 and 1990).
14. L. Brown (1990). Note that as no good data exist on the extent of soil erosion, the data presented are truly estimates.
15. For recent reviews of the state of our knowledge, see e.g. IPCC, Parry *et al.*, German Bundestag (a relatively pessimistic assessment) and Isaken.
16. See e.g. German Bundestag.
17. This is a classic "free-rider" problem which limits the extent of research (or developing a research "capability") on a subject which may never become commercially viable. It is not obviously an "access-to-technology" problem.

Chapter 4

THE FOOD SYSTEM

Introduction

This report's concern is with longer-term trends. The projections reviewed in Chapters 2 and 3 suggest that, by the year 2000, there will have been a massive shift for basic foodstuffs towards internationally traded cereals (essentially, wheat, rice and maize). Moreover, they suggest that developing countries, and particularly low-income countries, will become more dependent on food imports. This will be expressed in Chapter 5 in terms of self-sufficiency ratios: sub-Saharan Africa's self-sufficiency ratio for cereals may fall to around 50 per cent. At the same time, the projections reviewed above suggest that basic food production, even on optimistic assumptions, will not generate sufficient employment in basic food agriculture itself to employ the growing rural labour force. This does not mean that the "food system" cannot feed the people or employ them, but rather that the focus should shift to the off-farm activities and their organisation. Finally, with a year 2000 focus, technology (and, particularly, the new technologies) must be expected to have important structural implications for the food system, as well as for basic agriculture.

The notion of "food system" in this report refers to activities associated with basic food that are "off-farm". It thus concerns upstream and downstream activities associated with basic food agriculture. Our central hypothesis is that these "off-farm" activities are increasingly coming to dominate food agriculture, even among poor people in poor countries.

The notion is imprecise for various reasons. What counts as "on-farm" or "off-farm" varies in different situations for reasons that have little to do with economics or agricultural policy. In the OECD countries, it has much to do with accounting and fiscal practices.

There is a serious shortage of data about this "food system", both in OECD countries, and, especially, in developing countries. Some of the activities are in the "informal" sector. Thus, they tend to escape from any official statistics, and are only very partially captured in surveys (e.g. of household incomes and expenditures).

This data problem is compounded in two important ways. First, within the developed countries, a considerable part of these off-farm agricultural activities are now in the "organised", even "industrial" sector, and they raise the familiar and important questions of industrial organisation, especially in relation to technology. The upstream, input industry is well-documented in terms of agro-chemicals and farm equipment. The downstream, food-processing industry is less well-documented, particularly in relation to small-scale activities, but nevertheless, there are relatively good statistics which have allowed a whole body of economic analysis about the "food processing" industry.

In developing countries, the methodological problems are more severe and make it difficult to assess the significance of the activities of international firms. Much of the available analysis concerns Latin America, because on average the countries are economically more advanced and more urbanised, and because the activities of international (and national) firms have been extensively studied.

Hypotheses about the food system raise wider issues. Some concern the interactions between technology, and particularly "new" technologies, and the food system. Others are "institutional": the central concern about the "food system" is that one passes from rather small producers, who are "price-takers" in their purchases and sales, towards "business" or "industry" agents, who may not be price-takers within particular markets, and whose access to technology may not be an "arms-length" one[1]. A central concern is with the effects of urbanisation on food consumption patterns, and thus on basic food agriculture. Thus, ultimately, we are looking in agricultural terms at shifts between crops and between different groups of producers. There may also be consequent shifts within regions.

The gradual, seemingly inexorable pattern of the "industrialisation" of agriculture and its consequent importance in international markets and competition is conceived by Goodman, Sorj and Wilkinson, as the outcome of parallel trends of "appropriationism" and "substitutionism"[2]. In accordance with their proposition, discrete elements of the agricultural production process, originally a totally natural production system, have gradually been "appropriated" by industry (horsepower has been appropriated by the tractor, for example, and manure by synthetic fertilizers) but reincorporated into the production process as inputs. Similarly, the growth of the food processing industry represents the gradual "substitution" of agricultural raw materials by industrial products of both agricultural and non-agricultural origin. In the process, industrial activity accounts for a steadily increasing proportion of value added in final food products. Furthermore, agricultural raw materials are reduced to industrial inputs and, increasingly, substituted by non-agricultural components.

Those agricultural and food production systems which are at the frontiers of technology are increasingly science-based, dependent on R&D, on technological innovations and on basic scientific research. In these systems in particular, bio-technology research and bio-technology-related innovations will play a strategic role.

Much of the "food system" discussion is concerned with technology and institutional trends. It is important, however, to link the debate to the analysis of food and agricultural policies. The OECD's analysis of economy-wide effects of agricultural policies suggests that much of the effects of overall policies have their impact in the food processing sector[3]. This suggests, as a corollary, that much of the structural shifts resulting from changes in OECD food and agricultural policies might be absorbed off-farm.

From the point of view of the present report, this suggests two avenues for further exploration. First, if changes in OECD agricultural policies had important implications for the structure of food processing, these would be likely to affect developing countries. Second, the OECD policy analysis conclusions about the important role of food processing industries could suggest that shifts in developing country food and agricultural policies will have food processing implications: most of the available published analysis has focused primarily on the on-farm implications.

The dearth of comparative analysis means that much of this chapter draws on an (unpublished) report prepared for the Development Centre by Traill and Wilkinson, which is very much oriented to developments in Latin America. Latin America is different from Asia and, still more, Africa in that average income levels are much higher and the degree of urbanisation is much greater. Nevertheless, there is great interest in looking at the historic experience of Latin America as a pointer to possible developments in Asia and Africa towards year 2000.

Upstream activities

For "upstream" activities, an indicator of the share of off-farm activities in the total value of food sales would be the share of purchased inputs in farm-gate sales. Chapter 7 introduces some country averages for major food crops estimated by FAO staff. These suggest that these shares vary considerably — from 20 per cent to 80 per cent — between countries, and that disparate factors influence the differences, most of which have little to do with the "food system". The most important of these factors, and the most intractable, concerns the level of farm-gate prices. However, even in typical subsistence food production, bought-in farm inputs now represent at least 20 per cent of farm-gate prices, and that share rises fairly rapidly with rising yields associated with improved seeds and farm practices. It is important to note that the cost of hired labour is not included in these estimated shares.

FAO projects a rather modest increase in the share of the value of inputs in the value of gross output[4]. Between 1982/84 and 2000, the share would rise by around 3 percentage points for most broad regions, to reach around 30 per cent. The increase and the projected level (11 per cent) in sub-Saharan Africa would be much smaller. These shares in principle include the cost of irrigation and bought-in services, but not the cost of hired labour.

To pre-empt the discussion in Chapter 5, it can be argued that the development of "new" technologies may in certain circumstances lead to a fall in the share of purchased inputs. The development of seeds (or livestock innovations) which will be input-reducing is particularly important for poor farmers. Nevertheless, the purchased input share is expected to remain significant, even for poor farmers, and to continue to rise rapidly as agricultural productivity rises. With hired labour excluded, most of the purchased inputs are tradeable products coming from the modern sector (essentially from modern industry).

Downstream activities

The "downstream" activities are more difficult to characterise and quantify. Even within the rural areas, most agricultural products have to be processed, although this processing need not involve the "organised" or "modern" sector. Apparently, an increasing share does, and a significant and increasing share of the rural population is only partially directly involved in agriculture. Thus, in Thailand, it is estimated that in 1978/79 only 43 per cent of "farm households'" income came from their direct agricultural activities. Almost 9 per cent came from off-farm agricultural activities, which could be broadly allocated here as "upstream", leaving almost 35 per cent from other sources: much of this would concern "downstream" food activities[5]. Nevertheless, most of the focus on the downstream "food system" is about urban food consumption.

The downstream food chain normally more than doubles the price between farm-gate and the consumer of processed products. Even without the transport costs from rural to urban areas, it seems likely that the share of on-farm costs (value added) in consumer prices is below 20 per cent for an urban consumer, and that the ratio of value added upstream of farming to downstream is probably around 1 to 2. Of course, not all the off-farm value added is in the "modern", "organised" sector, and this varies from country to country and product to product. However, one can conclude that even "basic" food production is increasingly driven by the food system and that it is the downstream activities which are increasingly the most important.

Institutional issues in the developing country food system

Our focus here is on the modern food system in the context of development. The present situation reflects a mixture of influences coming from comparative advantage, the structure of demand and the pattern of industrialisation (primarily) in the developed countries.

Upstream, in the inputs industry, institutional issues seem much less important than they did in the 1970s. However, there are trends in the seeds industry relevant to longer-term concerns about the new technologies.

The seeds industry is not well documented, but has been characterised by a high incidence of takeovers and acquisitions in recent years. World-wide turnover in 1980 has been estimated at $20 billion, of which OECD countries would represent about half and developing countries about 15 per cent[6]. However, a FAO estimate in 1987 put current world-wide seeds turnover much higher, at $30 billion[7]. This would put seeds well ahead of the estimated 1982 $13.3 billion sales of herbicides, insecticides and fungicides, of which developing countries represented about 20 per cent[8].

The seeds industry is oligopolistic, with a few firms accounting for large shares of particular seeds markets in certain countries. It has been estimated that in the international seeds market, the 14 leading seeds groups (listed in Table 4.1) accounted for a share of approximately 20 per cent of the world market in 1982. Seven of these 14 groups together account for 10 per cent of world seeds sales. Such sales represent less than 15 per cent of their consolidated turnover[9]. International restructuring in the world seeds industry, which involved almost 300 firms between 1965 and 1980, was mainly in favour of the established international seed firms (almost one third), but also involved the chemicals industry (23 per cent) and agro-industrial firms (20 per cent)[10].

Competition among the major seeds groups is based principally on product differentiation and, more particularly, on the marketing of improved varieties, especially hybrid maize. Major firms market many different varieties, bred for specific geographic areas or growing conditions. The two leading hybrid maize firms, for example, each market more than 100 varieties, a dozen or so of which are replaced each year by new products.

As argued above, there is no clear frontier **downstream** between organised and informal activities in food processing, and between industrial and service activities. The organised, industrial part is estimated to have had a world-wide turnover of more than $1 000 billion in 1981, of which developing countries accounted for around 14 per cent[11]. Around this estimated $150 billion developing country industrial activity, there is a large service activity of storage, transport and retailing, although what is counted as "service" depends on how the industry is organised.

It has been estimated that as much as one third of all food production in the market economies is controlled by the 100 largest agro-industrial companies[12]. Of these, two thirds are based in either the United States or the United Kingdom. Even allowing for all the imprecision in the concepts and statistics, it is clear that while most of the concentration is in the OECD countries and may apply less to "basic" food than to convenience foods and beverages, this world-wide organisation of the industry is increasingly relevant to developing countries. We have noted that the trends are most advanced in Latin America, and that these may be followed in Asia and Africa.

The modern food system: its implications for Latin America

Little attention has traditionally been paid to the industrialisation of the food system in developing countries. Much of the existing work has been informed by concerns regarding the implications for national identity and for income distribution. The focus has been on agricultural modernisation and the transnationalisation of agricultural production. Two apparently contradictory tendencies of modernisation have been singled out. On the one hand, they involve the marginalisation of peasant production in favour of exports from enclave agro-industrial complexes for developed country food systems, leading to a crisis of the domestic food system on the supply side. On the other hand, the peasant economy suffered new forms of integration into domestic urban food markets. These two processes worked in tandem directed respectively to world and domestic markets.

The consequence of both trends is seen to be a squeezing of the traditional peasant sector as resources were switched from the supply of basic food to satisfy the demand patterns of the urban elite in developing countries or the growing demand for an animal protein diet in developed countries. Hunger, according to this argument, is not the result of a lack of agricultural modernisation, but the product of integration into the modern food system. The resulting domestic shortfall of supplies is increasingly met by imports, involving at the same time a shift from local grains to the commodity grains of the world food system — especially wheat and maize.

"Food security" in this context is conceived in terms of a strengthening of the traditional peasant sector, emphasizing agrarian reform and/or political reforms. According to this view, the modernisation of the developing country food system represented a distortion oriented to minority luxury interests.

A less polarised view, accepting the agro-industrial character of the food system as a necessary corollary of urbanisation, draws attention to the increased dependence on imports not only to service the modernisation of agriculture, but directly as food industry inputs bypassing the domestic agricultural sector. This is seen to result from the dominance of multinational firms with their international network of inputs and services. Food security strategies in this case have a clearly agro-industrial component, attempting to supplement or supplant imports with a national agro-food sector oriented to a domestic input supply base. According to this view, the modern food system is the product of urbanisation and industrialisation rather than an outside imposition sustained by exports and elite markets.

While sophisticated brand products may dominate the image of the modern food system through publicity, the latter's consolidation has been premised on the transformation of mass consumer habits. For example, in Latin America, over the past twenty years, local grain flour has largely given way to maize and wheat. Modern agro-industrial complexes have replaced locally produced poultry and eggs as the basic source of animal protein. New consumption patterns have led also to a shift in cooking from boiling to frying, leading to mass demand for new vegetable oils, stimulated also by the substitution of bread, complemented by margarine, for local starch products. These new sources of animal and vegetable proteins have become mass products of urban consumption, representing the backbone of the modern food system in developing countries.

To the extent that the industrialised food system represents a substitution of traditional food consumption patterns in response to urbanisation/industrialisation, we are dealing with mass or potential mass markets. The canning industry, one of the earliest industrial food sectors, has become a dynamic component of new catering branches — pizza and hamburger chains — proliferating in Latin America as a cheap commercial lunch. At the level of home consumption, however, canned products must compete with a modernised fruit and vegetable agricultural sector.

Products which are not clear substitutes for traditional basic foods — milk products, especially yoghurts and cheeses — conform more to the "elite" characterisation. (Fresh milk has, however, frequently been subject to administered pricing, and in developing countries is often marginal to traditional food systems.) Even in these cases, we are dealing with items with a typically mass vocation both in terms of production patterns and marketing strategy, particularly in Latin America.

The stigma often attached to the modern food system in developing countries derives from the regressive income distribution and the low level of economic and technological development which leads to the equation: modern food system = transnationals/luxury products. In fact, the industrialised food system represents an uneven but comprehensive transformation of mass food consumption patterns which very much parallels urbanisation. The consolidation of such a system in many developing countries represents a shift from the public to the private sector, which poses problems of effective policy intervention.

In Latin America, the peculiarities of the modern food system derive essentially from the velocity and intensity of urbanisation combined with an industrial structure largely deficient in equipment and intermediate goods, and unable to incorporate important segments of the urban population into the formal industrial or service sectors.

Such speed of change implies that instead of an organic expansion of small-scale retail outlets, supermarkets have a dominant presence in major cities. The weakness of the productive structure, both in agriculture and processing, implies pressures towards imports of intermediate and finished goods and technology, together with direct foreign investment. The model of economic development in most developing countries has led to a regressive income distribution pattern which poses unique problems of access to the modern food system.

The food system is different from other sectors in that it must be directly accessible to the whole population, in contrast to consumer durable industries which can be based on limited markets. So, its modernisation must be compatible with its universal availability. A further difference is that food is generally perishable.

While the industrialisation of the food system in Latin America was a response to urbanisation, it also represented an opportunity for multinational food companies. Earlier patterns of food industry investment had generally been stimulated by export strategies. However, beginning in the 1960s, and accelerating in the 1970s, the domestic markets of the Third World became the principal attraction. Stagnation in the industrialised countries had as its corollary a slowdown in the export markets of the Third World.

A combination of high economic and demographic growth combined with rapid urbanisation made developing countries' domestic markets an attractive alternative to the increasingly saturated markets of the industrialised countries. Third World markets, therefore, provided an "after-life" for the product cycle of a consumption model apparently reaching saturation.

In the same way, exports or direct investment provided outlets for a generation of mature food technologies. These technologies represented a major break from the artisan base of the food industry in the Third World and allowed for the rapid oligopolisation of specific market sectors.

Multinational capital installed itself both in the new staple products and brand markets. Import substitution policies in relation to finished goods favoured such a development, but at the same time opened the way to import dependence for agricultural products now incorporated as inputs for the food industry. In countries with non-agricultural, especially oil and other raw material exports, such imports often became substitutes rather than complements to domestic production.

The sharp increase in imports can be more readily understood once the substitution implications of the modern food system are taken into account. Of the basic staples of the new food system — wheat, maize, soya, sugar, milk — wheat and soya are virtually unknown in many countries and milk has a traditionally weak productive base. In many countries, the lack of complementary advantages, the lack of an infrastructure capable of adapting new crops, the speed of the changes in consumption patterns following urbanisation, all lead to heavy dependence on imports. Peru as one extreme case exemplifies this trend most clearly, with a dependence coefficient for wheat of over 85 per cent during the 1970s.

In the 1960s and 1970s, therefore, foreign food investment shifted from the export to the domestic sector of Latin American countries. While investment for export often led to the physical displacement of pre-existing agricultural production patterns, investment in the domestic sector paradoxically led to greater dependence on agricultural imports now incorporated as industrial inputs. Rapid economic growth in developing countries during this period made such an option, while vulnerable, apparently sustainable.

Within the modern food system, we have distinguished between the new basic staples and brand products, although the dividing line is often difficult, since marketing strategy continuously extends the scope of brand products. While transnational investment covers both these sectors, national capital is stronger in the new basic staples and brand products based on long established technologies, as in the case of the canning industry.

A decisive feature of the modern food system in Latin America has been the presence of multinational enterprises both in the basic foodstuffs and brand sectors. Brand items should not be equated with luxury products in developing countries. Rather they are products with a potentially mass market in a buoyant growth context, as was the case in the 1960s and 1970s. Foreign investment in these sectors was premised on the potential for expanding mass markets in the context of high growth rates.

Multinational presence in specific food sectors quickly reproduced the oligopoly market concentrations of the industrialised countries. While in the non-food sectors, multinationals rely on proprietary technologies or the need for prohibitive investment levels, industrial food processing technology is by and large in the public domain and generated outside the food industry. Similarly, for many product lines, plant investment is relatively modest. Market dominance, therefore, has depended on the ability to differentiate products through brand names, projected through heavy advertising and packaging costs.

Implications for low-income countries

Trends emerging from the middle 1970s are modifying the patterns of Third World participation in the internationalisation and modernisation of the food system. In the industrialised countries, the slowdown in overall growth apparent from the middle 1970s has been accompanied by two major trends which are at the heart of the current restructuring of the food industry on a world scale. One concerns the impacts of "new" technology innovations on food preservation and transformation. The other concerns the slowdown in food aggregate expenditure growth, which has shifted emphasis to "up-market" products. We can expect an increasing disengagement from the basic products sector of the industrial food system in developing countries, accompanied by a more general freezing or even reversal of investment trends, even in the brand sectors. These trends apply especially to Latin America.

Many multinationals are now exploring the Asian and South East Asian domestic food markets, where the Japanese import strategy has lent itself to an increasing adoption of Western style food habits. China exerts a particular attraction due to its immense size and the "apparent" satisfaction of basic food needs. Consolidation in these new markets, however, will be a long-term challenge. The important question is the degree to which a strategic investment reorientation is already under way.

Conclusions

For most developing countries (to anticipate the conclusions below) the problem is not technology itself or the conditions for its transfer. It is rather the infrastructure — physical and human — and the financing implications. It is also, and perhaps most intractably, organisational and institutional.

Even in low-income countries, an increasing share of food-related activities is "off-farm". The "downstream" share is much larger than the "upstream", inputs share, although the share of purchased inputs is expected to increase.

Much of the "off-farm" activity in developing countries is "informal" and "unorganised". Nevertheless, an increasing share is in the modern sector, especially in Latin America. Increasingly, also, the modern sector share structures the informal activities.

Given the projected increase in international trade in basic foodstuffs, one would expect that the role of the "organised" food system will increase over the period to year 2000. Important developments in technology, reviewed in Chapter 5, also point to a growing role for this organised food system, in relation both to inputs (especially, seeds) and to food processing. These will feed back into "on-farm" basic agriculture.

This organised food system has an international dimension, which is comparable to that of other manufacturing industries. The degree of concentration is surprisingly high, and while this at present mainly raises issues within the OECD countries, it already poses "institutional" problems in Latin America. Indeed, it can be argued that the stagnation of basic food markets within the OECD countries and the technology developments are pushing the international firms towards greater involvement in developing countries. Hitherto, most of the interest has been in Latin America and has involved North American companies. Increasingly, however, the focus is shifting to Asia and away from the established North American firms.

NOTES

1. See FAO (1987b) and Maunder and Renborg for a review of the institutional issues.
2. Goodman, Sorj and Wilkinson.
3. See *OECD Economic Studies*, Special Issue, "Modelling the Effects of Agricultural Policies", No. 13, Winter 1989-90. The Economy Wide Walras "*W*orld *A*gricultural *L*iberalisation *S*tudy" Model.
4. Alexandratos, Table 4.5.
5. World Bank estimates.
6. Brenner.
7. FAO (1987b), p. 52.
8. FAO (1987b).
9. Brenner.
10. Ducos and Joly.
11. IAMM. See also Oman and Rama in Oman *et al.*, Chapter 6.
12. IAMM.

Chapter 5

TECHNOLOGY ISSUES[1]

Introduction

As noted above, a central issue concerns the extent to which we shall see continuing cost-reducing technology innovations introduced into developing country agriculture. If a continuing stream of cost-reducing technology innovations can be introduced into low-income agriculture, many of the problems of international competitive advantage, global markets, national interactions, and domestic price structures for food can be avoided.

Ranged against the optimists are those concerned with "institutional" issues, and, of course, those concerned about environmental degradation and the ability of governments to follow technologically sound policies. There is a major strand in development thinking which associates problems of technology development, transfer and effective utilisation with "institutional" questions about who-owns-what and who-does-what. Behind these questions, there are, for the economists, questions about imperfect competition, and the development of perspectives informed by "games theory" and the interactions of small numbers of agents.

In the case of agricultural technology, the question of intellectual ownership is frequently regarded as central. Here, the primary concern is the relationship between the producer and user of an innovation. As noted, there are also serious concerns about ecology and the environment, affecting, not least within the OECD countries, perspectives on high-productivity agriculture. At the same time, there is considerable evidence of environmental degradation in developing countries, associated with intensified food production, particularly in the large population low-income countries of South and East Asia (China). Beyond these concerns are the issues about the implications of technology for income distribution and nutrition.

In the discussion below, the following issues are taken up:

— what is different about the "new" technologies?

— what products and what time horizon?

— what induces innovation in agriculture?

— institutional issues;

— conclusions.

"New" technologies: what is different?

Agricultural technology development can be characterised as passing from primarily "land-related" technologies, through mechanisation to bio-chemical technologies (associated with new varieties and relatively large amounts of agro-chemicals). It is now moving towards a "bio-technology" phase. The transition is, of course, continuous, but there are important differences between the different stages. The central question is about how far the latest, "bio-technology", phase is qualitatively different from earlier phases. The most obvious suggested answers are that it will be less resource-intensive and more "knowledge-intensive". It is also likely that once the innovations are achieved their use will be more pervasive and rapid than in the past, with more radical implications for economic and social structures and for world trade[2].

There is a considerable literature about technology innovation and "new technologies" and about their economic and social implications, which is not primarily concerned with food and agriculture. A key question concerns the extent to which "new technologies" lead to "technology paradigm shifts" and new "technology trajectories", and the resulting implications. These notions are recent but go back to Schumpeter, in the sense that they look for "creative waves of destruction"[3]. It is argued that a "paradigm shift" occurs if it results in:

i) a new range of products accompanied by an improvement in the technical characteristics of many products and processes;

ii) a reduction in costs of many products and services;

iii) social and political acceptability;

iv) environmental acceptability;

v) pervasive effects throughout the economic system[4].

Two broad categories of "new" technology seem relevant to food and agriculture — bio-technology and information technology. As indicated above, bio-technology seems likely to give its name to the next phase of agricultural technology. ("New materials" technologies may also be relevant to future food and agricultural trends.)

Information technology (IT) is much more problematic to analyse than bio-technology, and therefore much less discussed, but arguably will have a greater influence over food and agricultural trends in the medium term. The problem with IT is its pervasiveness. The final user — for example, a poor farmer — may be unaware that he is using IT when he acts on the basis of a weather forecast or market price report.

Even if one moves back from the ultimate user in the chain of providing the results of IT, analysis is not straightforward and predictions are hazardous. One can identify some major clearly agriculture-related IT applications, including weather forecasting, irrigation and pest management, but it is still difficult to analyse their likely progress, and it is important not to neglect either the links between the identifiable projects and technologies and the ultimate users, or the many day-to-day applications which cannot be linked to specific projects or technologies. The importance comes partly from the risk that focusing on identifiable activities may bias our assessment of who can or will benefit from the innovations and their diffusion. (It may also bias our assessment of the institutional requirements.)

To the extent that one accepts the arguments about "paradigm shifts", bio-technology is still problematic, largely because of doubts about the pace of its effects on costs of production and its social and environmental acceptability[5].

It is important to note that food and agricultural possibilities are only part of our preoccupations, although an important part. It is likely that the "acceptability" concerns will be met, leading to a major acceptance of bio-technologies, and leaving the primary concern about the pace of introduction of the innovations. The key questions then relate to the effects on costs of production in the using sectors and on economic and social structures. Because much of the dynamics of bio-technology development is not primarily about food and agricultural applications, one should not expect that the effects on costs of production and structures will be captured by traditional analysis of agricultural trends. How far this points to a further reinforcement of the "industrialisation" of traditional agriculture remains to be seen.

Bio-technology involves the manipulation of living organisms to alter their characteristics and produce specific products, which may ultimately be used in large-scale production processes. Traditional bio-technology depended largely on natural selection to obtain desired traits, especially through plant breeding and fermentation. "New" bio-technology is based on enhanced understanding of the genetic structure of organisms, and thus offers possibilities of short-circuiting traditional processes and of circumventing the conventional barriers of genetic incompatibility. However, recent developments in bio-technology for agriculture have mainly concerned livestock rather than plant production.

Plant-related bio-technology has focused on the insertion of genes with particular characteristics. These could include: resistance to disease and natural pests; adaptation to arid and saline soils; resistance to chemical pesticides; and, ultimately, nitrogen-fixation. While some developments should lead ultimately to less agro-chemical-intensive food production, others could give plants greater built-in pesticide and herbicide resistance, leading to greater agro-chemical intensity. There have been some fears expressed in this context about the motivations of agro-chemical firms, which (as noted above) have moved heavily into seed production. These firms could seek to gain or retain market power in bulk agro-chemicals by marketing seeds which are "dedicated" to particular agro-chemical products. These fears are largely discounted by FAO[6].

Cell fusion and culture techniques are expected to be used for the large-scale production of enzymes and other proteins to be used for livestock or human consumption, or as food additives. Research effort is also expected to lead to cell culture techniques for the industrial production, from plant cell cultures or from parts of plants, of natural chemicals, flavourings or perfumes which are traditionally extracted from whole natural plants. An even more radical prospect in view is that of cell culture techniques applied to the industrial production of whole plants or plant parts. This could have dramatic consequences for location-specific competitive advantage.

More generally, bio-technology offers the scope for industrial use of agricultural products or residues as biomass feedstocks. In principal, it will be possible to produce most bulk chemicals from biomass feedstocks such as starch (from cereal grains such as maize or roots such as cassava) or cellulose (from crop residues)[7].

What products with what time horizon?

In the most comprehensive study on new technologies for agriculture to date, the US Office of Technology Assessment (OTA) in 1986 attempted to determine the probable timing of the commercial introduction of a total of 127 technologies in the United States. The method used for this purpose was the Delphi technique[8].

Genetically engineered pharmaceuticals, techniques for the control of infectious disease in animals, super-ovulation, embryo transfer and manipulation with cows, and control of plant growth and development are, in fact, already available. The estimated timing for the introduction of genetic engineering techniques for farm animals and cereal crops extends to the year 2000 and beyond. Of 57 animal technologies, it was estimated that 27 would be available commercially before 1990 and 30 between 1990 and 2000. In plant agriculture, 50 of the 90 technologies examined were expected to be available commercially by 1990 and the other 40 between 1990 and 2000. No systematic follow-up data is available, but there seems to have been slippage in the projected time path[9]. Nevertheless, most of the identified specific new technologies are likely to come into commercial use during the 1990s.

The impact of these emerging technologies is difficult to forecast since a single "new" technology may constitute a minor, incremental change introduced into an existing, mature, widely diffused technique or a major innovation or scientific breakthrough. Furthermore, given the pervasive quality of new technologies, technological change in one area may create a "ripple effect" or synergies across a whole set of supporting or related technologies.

The OTA study concluded that the combined effect of information technology and bio-technology will reinforce long-standing trends in United States agriculture. While the new technologies will significantly increase yields, the impact will be felt in livestock before plant production. They will tend to be adopted more rapidly by large farmers who have easier access to information and greater financial resources. It is therefore anticipated that diffusion of the new technologies will reinforce the trend towards a reduction in the number of farms and towards a growing share of total output contributed by the largest farming units[10].

The pace of development and introduction of the new technologies will be determined by economic, social and political factors. Depending on the interplay of these factors and on the consequent nature and direction of technological change, the future "bio-technology" phase of technological change in agriculture implies both continuity and change. Clearly, it offers opportunities to reinforce and possibly accelerate technological complementarities and synergies across the seeds, food-processing and agricultural chemicals and pharmaceuticals industries. In this scenario, it could stimulate the "bio-industrialisation" of agriculture discussed in the previous chapter[11]. However, at the same time, it offers the prospect of input-reducing agricultural production, greater diversity rather than standardization of food products, and alternative agricultural production systems which are more sustainable from an environmental point of view.

Technology innovation

There is a considerable literature on the causes of innovation in agriculture[12], but very little of it has so far been concerned with the radically different characteristics, outlined above, of the "new" technologies. A strand has concerned the role of shifts in factor endowments and, therefore, relative factor prices, and has been illustrated by the effects of labour shortages in promoting mechanisation in North America, and of land shortage in improved rice varieties in Japan. It is not clear how well this approach will help us to assess the mechanisms driving the introduction of bio-technology and, still more, information technology in the coming decade.

The theory has been extended with some credibility to explain the role of public sector institutions in innovation, since these have hitherto played a major role. Nevertheless, critics have argued that the "induced innovation" theories do not intuitively explain the interactions between different institutional actors. More radical observers consider that one needs to examine the "decision-making" process itself, since we are in the presence of actors who are very disparate in terms of their size and the functions that they play in the innovation process. Again, one should stress that the "new" technologies are likely to follow different patterns from the major innovations of the past, although plant breeding will remain central for the foreseeable future in relation to basic food issues.

For our purposes, there are other factors which may also be important. The next major "wave" of innovation will be in the context of substantially falling real prices for major products and a deceleration in production growth in the OECD countries, whereas the earlier innovations were partly stimulated by expansive expectations and expansive policies. Furthermore, the OECD environment in the OECD area for further innovation is beginning to be dominated by "green" issues. The basic food context in many developing countries is in some ways radically different — food self-sufficiency through rapidly rising production of basic foodstuffs is still an important policy target — even though some of the "green" issues are directly relevant.

The pace of future innovation with the "new" technologies and the appropriateness of its products to the basic food requirements of developing countries are of central importance. It should be noted that the "appropriateness" concerns are not new: they have been aired extensively in relation to the Green Revolution. There is room for optimism, however, precisely because of the technical and economic characteristics of the coming technologies and the institutional arrangements that are likely to emerge. The institutional questions are taken up below.

The extent to which bio-chemical processes will imply bulk production of uniform products is of great significance to developing countries. This will affect food security in poor countries. The basis for optimism is that moving down the learning curve with bio-technology will allow a multiplicity of products, designed for particular needs (e.g. soils), in contrast to the process-related economies of scale.

A key question will concern the "costs" of the bio-technology products as the new technology innovations become established. It would be surprising if there were not major "economies of adoption" from moving along the learning curve. These economies will not concern bio-technology itself so much as the "engineering" of conditions for scaling-up bio-technological processes to give acceptable commercial products. They will be economies of scale in the classical sense exemplified by the agro-chemical "process" industries, which supported the Green Revolution[13].

Some of the bio-technology products will be analogous to bulk chemicals, and are likely to transform world markets for some agricultural products. HFCS has already made a major impact on world sugar consumption. The product and the technology were developed in the context of highly protected OECD (essentially US) agriculture. The economies of adoption of HFCS and the discounting of the initial investments nevertheless may have shifted the structure of its production and use to the point where it would retain its competitiveness if agricultural protection were removed. The next generation of bio-technological innovations — however triggered — could transform other international food product markets. Animal feed products based on bio-technologically developed single-cell protein could make a major impact on international cereal feed markets. For example, the USSR (with its current structural inability to raise cereal production) has a massive incentive to find bio-technological, industrially organised alternatives to importing cereal animal feedstuffs.

In Eastern Europe and elsewhere, more sophisticated processing technologies are becoming available for the preparation of flour ingredients, permitting the greater incorporation of local grains. This occurs at a time when the dominant consumption model is moving towards the greater consumption of coarse grains. Thus, the cereals base of the food system, both for direct human consumption and for animal feed, would now seem to be in transition. A shift in dominant food consumption patterns away from the white/wheat model, together with more sophisticated grinding and separation techniques, permit a greater incorporation of local grains into cereals-based foods.

It is important to recognise that there will be major "learning curve" economies with bio-technology, but that they do not point unequivocally in the direction of economies of mass production with limited product variety. They will, however, transform world product markets for some basic foodstuffs.

Institutional issues

Several key issues can be identified:

a) What are the issues about intellectual property?

b) To the extent that innovations occur, how far will they be available to developing countries and to poor farmers in those countries?

c) How far will likely innovations be appropriate to poor countries and to poor people?

d) What are the requirements for poor countries and poor people to obtain new technologies?

As noted above, the dominant strand in the analysis of "institutional" issues is pessimistic about the implications for developing countries and poor people. It points to oligopoly and market power in the present structure of the input and processing industries. National "strategic" objectives may also limit the transfer of new technology innovations to foreign countries, unless these countries accept international property rights in the innovations and pay corresponding royalties. Equally, the costs and risks of new technology innovations may be too high and increasing, and the products of these innovations may be inappropriate to the needs of developing countries and poor people. Finally, the costs of establishing adequate "technological capability" to make use of appropriate innovations within these countries may be prohibitive.

This report is sceptical about all these arguments, and is consequently fairly up-beat about the prospects for "new" technology innovations to improve the lot of poor countries and poor people. More precisely, it is argued that the institutional problems about the successful introduction of these innovations are not primarily problems of technology or technology policy, but rather problems about the political ability of these countries' governments to meet the food security requirements of poor people.

At the heart of the scepticism is a question about how far the "new" technologies are different from previous technology advances in their institutional implications, and, beyond this, how far international technology markets have shifted over the past decade. The latter proposition is most obviously relevant in "information technology". In the field of computers, most of the Third World discussion a decade ago was about IBM's monopoly market power and about how peripheral countries could come to terms with it. In 1990, this is no longer a major issue. While IBM still has market domination in some equipment, any user can buy equipment at prices (in real terms) far below those of 1979, and a Third World country wanting to develop its own hardware industry can find willing and credible foreign collaborators. The central question for the bio-technology innovations is how far the present market power of input and processing firms will persist when the prospective innovations start to come in.

Intellectual property rights are important in seeds, and it is argued that they will become increasingly significant with bio-technology innovations. The problem here is that there is no strong tradition of patenting seeds, while bio-technology is a largely uncharted area for intellectual property protection. In some existing, primarily developed country markets, "plant breeder" rights give a measure of protection, although this is protection of the "finished" product — the seed — rather than of its genetic composition. It is not clear that these "rights" do in practice give much protection or market power to the holders, even in the countries where they are enforceable. The big seed companies effectively acquire their market power from marketing activities involving branding their products. In some cases, they have promoted hybrid seeds (especially maize), which cannot naturally reproduce by open pollination. Simultaneously, effort is being directed towards incorporating pest resistance in seeds which would then not require chemical pesticide application. In this latter case, special properties obviating the need for particular chemical inputs would be "embodied" in the seed, with exciting and potentially environmentally attractive (in terms of reducing pesticide requirements) and cost-reducing implications.

A major issue with future bio-technology developments concerns the extent to which the intellectual property rights will be held by the large "food system" corporations who could have market power. They might have no great commercial interest in developing markets among poor people for their products. There is currently a distinction — admittedly fragile and shifting — between a large number of relatively small bio-tech firms and the small number of "food system" firms. There are observers who assume, on the basis of the little evidence currently available, that small firms (or university teams) will be "recuperated" by the large firms as soon as they make commercially interesting discoveries. It certainly seems to be the case that the small firms have hitherto been unable to mass market their innovations in the field of agricultural bio-technology.

Thus, we are shifting from the question of whether intellectual property rights are relevant to likely new technology innovations in agriculture, to a focus on the fundamental concern of developing country and poor people access. In assessing the prospects for diffusion, the distinction of the preceding paragraph needs to be addressed: to the extent that we shall continue to see a proliferation of small, or, more precisely, independent, bio-tech firms, why would they not want to sell their innovations to Third World users?

It is frequently assumed that whoever makes a marketable innovation will seek intellectual property protection as a way of recovering his R&D costs. This model of R&D may be less applicable to the next generation of innovations. Although bio-technology remains a relatively risky sector, it is likely to become less so when some solid achievements have been made and the industry moves down the learning curve. Other "new" technology developments, especially with information technology software, are clearly much less risky. Furthermore, it is not clear how far risk is relevant. If a client — most obviously a developing country government or international research organisation — would be willing to assume the risks, why would not a bio-technology firm undertake a specific R&D contract? Equally, why would not a large seed firm?

This raises the question about the "appropriateness" of the likely innovations to the food and agricultural needs of poor people and countries. Here, one should distinguish between a major innovation and subsequent adaptations for particular uses. Subsequent adaptations need not be very expensive in R&D terms. As noted above, this depends on the nature and significance of the "learning curve economies".

The issue cannot, however, be confined to R&D. Even if the R&D costs of developing products appropriate for specific developing country uses need not be considerable, the critical link of efficient diffusion of the products, especially to poor farmers, still needs to be forged. Compared to the difficulties associated with the diffusion process, those associated with the technology development appear modest; once again it is developing country policies rather than exogenous forces which are likely to play the decisive role.

Conclusions

Any discussion of future trends implies assumptions (implicit or explicit) about technology developments. Underlying these technology assumptions are beliefs about technology, which can be characterised as on a spectrum between "technology optimism" and "technology pessimism". These beliefs, which typically are not explicit, are nevertheless informed by facts, and, therefore, it is important to assembie and analyse information on what is happening in R&D and on the processes of technology innovation and diffusion. We cannot however divine the future and know now what innovations from "new technologies" will be available and in use in the longer term. We are also increasingly aware of our ignorance concerning the extent of man-made environmental and ecological changes and the process or the pace of their impacts.

Most discussion of the effects of "new" technologies has been fairly pessimistic in its implications for poor countries and poor people. Necessarily, many of the arguments are speculative. Part of the argument concerns shifts between products. This is already evident with the Green Revolution, which shifted cereal production and consumption from "traditional" varieties, which were not made high-yielding, towards high-yielding wheat and rice, and now, perhaps, maize. There is nothing intrinsic in new bio-technologies which means they will continue to benefit primarily the major cereals, although it is, of course, arguable that the commercial seed producers will tend to favour products which can be marketed in the major commercially producing cereal areas.

The discussion above suggests that bio-technology advances will reduce the importance of classical process-related economies of scale in the "food system", and that the actual R&D (as distinct from diffusion) cost of developing new products is already very low by industrial standards and will continue to fall.

Major technology changes coming from new technologies are in the "pipeline". There is no reason to think that they will not affect the basic equations of food security and agricultural production in the same way that the last generation of technology innovations — the Green Revolution — has transformed the agricultural situation since the late 1970s.

There has been considerable hesitation in the mid-1980s, after an initial optimism, about the pace at which the next generation of innovations would become available even in the most promising markets. This hesitation seems to be dissipating. The issues about gestation periods and about who benefits remain relevant, but there is a renewed optimism that the continuing innovations will occur and that they will have massive impacts on agricultural production and the "food system".

The relevant questions for developing countries are about winners and losers, and how to "lock" into the stream of innovations. The provisional conclusion of this study is that this process should not prove impossible for developing countries, and that the rewards are very great.

The central questions concern the extent to which continuing technology innovations will be dominated by "institutional" (essentially, oligopolistic) factors and the related questions about the costs of developing the technologies. The discussion above reviews the evidence about oligopolisation of agricultural technology development, primarily a result of the "privatisation" of agricultural research. The tentative conclusion is that these factors, while important, should not be overemphasized. Entry costs for new technology development are very much lower than for the last generation of technology developments, and there is no reason to expect that there will be collusive restrictions on developing country access.

Moreover, it is important to recognise the separation between the developers and users of much "new" agricultural technology. Put simply, the developers have much less interest than in some past developments in limiting or trying to control access to the technology. For bio-technology developments, it is difficult to understand why poor people's access to new developments will not be much easier than with the "Green Revolution" technologies. Those technologies were essentially "packaged", both for technology and commercial reasons.

Nevertheless, optimism about technology innovations should be tempered by the uncertainties about the implications for demand prospects for individual commodities and for international competitive advantage. New technologies may well have very radical impacts on the pattern of demand for food and other products. While initially, these impacts will be in the OECD countries, they may have implications in developing country markets sooner rather than later, including in the markets for the basic food products of poor people. Given a relative optimism about the cost of new technology developments and the lack of "access" problems, governments should develop policies which make the most of the technology possibilities for small farmers and for food security, particularly for the most vulnerable.

A central concern is the impact of the new technologies on international competitive advantage. Very plausibly, technological advances will weaken the link between "comparative advantage" and "factor endowments" and shift policy attention towards the "food system", although this is not easily captured in traditional analysis of agriculture.

The central policy issue is about how far market forces (including the better price signals that may come from agricultural reform) will produce the innovations that will promote food security and appropriate agricultural development in developing countries. The tentative conclusion is that, in the main, market forces could lead to the appropriate technology innovations and productivity gains, provided that governments are committed to food security and agricultural growth.

However, to the extent that one judges that market forces will not deliver the required changes, the international policy implications need to be considered. Given the relatively small prospective costs involved in new technology developments and the lack of "transfer" problems, in relation to the relatively large social and organisational problems in promoting accelerated agricultural production from small farmers and greater food security, international finance seems to have an important, but relatively modest part to play as does the issue of "intellectual property rights". Far more important is the diffusion of the available existing and future technologies and the establishment of domestic policies and prices conducive to appropriate and effective application.

NOTES

1. This chapter draws on papers prepared for the Development Centre by Carliene Brenner and Burt Sundquist (see "References") and by Wilkinson and Traill (unpublished). It also draws on OECD's study of biotechnology (OECD, 1989b).
2. See e.g. Fisher and Kenney in Maunder and Renborg.
3. See e.g. Dosi and Schumpeter.
4. OECD (1989b).
5. For a recent review of the issues, see OECD (1989b).
6. FAO (1987), p. 46.
7. See e.g. Schliephake (Chapter 11) and Hall and Coombs (Chapter 12) in Antonelli and Quadrio-Curzio.
8. OTA. On the utility of the "Delphi" technique, see e.g. Bell, p. 206.
9. It can be argued that this reflects a "technology optimism" bias in Delphi techniques for technology forecasting. It may also reflect the economic climate for OECD agriculture in the 1980s.
10. OTA.
11. See Goodman *et al.*
12. See e.g. Hayami and Ruttan.
13. See e.g. Brown (Martin), p. 20.

Chapter 6

TRADE AND FOOD SECURITY

Introduction

In this chapter, we focus on the central issue of developments in international trade and the possible implications for food consumption and production in developing countries. The implications of our analysis of production and consumption is that (with or without changes in OECD policies) major shifts in world food product markets will occur over the coming decades. The following paragraphs present and assess the alternative projections, and consider the implications for food policy in developing countries. China's foreign trade policies on basic foods are expected to exercise a pivotal influence on world food markets around year 2000, and, as reflected in the discussion below, are worthy of particular attention.

The projections

The balancing of consumption and production projections for different regions yields surpluses or deficits which, in accounting terms, are met by world trade. None of the major sets of projections develop demand and supply projections entirely independently, and for this reason, the trade projections cannot be regarded as simply a residual. With the exception of those of Zietz and Valdés, the World Bank and IIASA, the projections do not have a formal modelling framework which equates demand and supply through international prices. Typically, the projections use *ad hoc* (but iterative) procedures. For the large low-income countries, the self-sufficiency implications of demand and supply projections and the plausibility of financing deficits exercise constraining influences. The iterative procedures do not however generally include the rural employment and incomes implications of the different scenarios, so that important links between consumption and production are typically not fully taken into account.

World trade in major food products is projected to rise substantially over the period to year 2000. Table 6.1 shows the net trade in cereal products by major geographical regions which emerges from the different consumption and production forecasts. With the exception of IFPRI, the projections show a major increase in the net import requirements of the developing world, from around 60 million tons in 1984 to between 100 million and 200 million in year 2000. On the World Bank projections, developing countries' share of world cereal imports would reach almost 53 per cent, and for food grains (principally wheat and rice) above 70 per cent. The projections show the Eastern European Economies remaining an important deficit region. OECD countries emerge as the major suppliers to world markets, with net exports rising from around 110 million tons in 1984 to 150 million tons (FAO) or even 270 million tons (World Bank) in year 2000.

Gross trade in cereals is, of course, considerably higher than net trade. In fact the gross figures may still understate the level of total trade, as they include considerable regional aggregation. The projections of developing countries' gross trade corresponding to the Table 6.1 net figures are:

	Projected year 2000 (millions of tons)		
	FAO	WB	IWC
Gross imports	98	263	168
Gross exports	37	62	32
Net deficit	61	201	136

There are considerable differences in the projections of total world trade (i.e. including OECD and Eastern European Economy countries). They show trade rising from an average 200 million tons in the 1984-86 period to a corresponding year 2000 level of 215 (IWC), 328 (IIASA) or 417 (World Bank). Part of the divergence is no doubt due to aggregation problems, but nevertheless there is a marked contrast between the IWC study (see Table 6.2), which projects very little growth in total world trade, and the World Bank and IIASA studies, which envisage 70-80 per cent (150-200 million ton) increases from mid-1980 levels.

Much of the argument in the discussion about demand (consumption — Chapter 2) and supply (production — Chapter 3) reflects uncertainties regarding China (see below). Some scenarios including China point to much bigger global trade volumes, perhaps an additional 200 million tons. Clearly, these have important implications for food markets.

In terms of product composition, rice remains relatively unimportant in global cereals trade, even though the more dynamic projections imply relatively rapid growth. Thus, for the World Bank, global rice trade rises 4.5 per cent annually over the 1987-2000 period to reach 22 million tons. Global trade in both wheat and coarse grains each rise by 80-90 million tons over the 1987-2000 period (with annual growth rates of respectively 4.3 per cent and 5.0 per cent), to reach 211 million tons and 184 million tons respectively. The IIASA projections are broadly comparable. To the extent that internationally traded cereals are used for animal feed, there may be increasing substitutability between wheat and coarse grains (essentially maize and sorghum). However, some of the evidence above suggests that much of the growth in "requirements", which could be met by trade, would be for food, not feed grains. This would point to more rapid growth in wheat (but probably not rice) trade. These product issues deserve more consideration, because they affect the competitiveness and export prospects of different suppliers.

The various projections do not show much prospect for developing country cereal exporters to increase their share of world trade. The most expansionist projection, from the World Bank, envisages developing world cereals exports rising from some 30 million tons in 1987 to some 60.2 million tons in 2000, a corresponding increase in share from 12.7 per cent to 14.4 per cent. The most pessimistic, from the IWC, projects no absolute increase at all. It is striking that both the World Bank and FAO imply that Argentina and Thailand will remain the only significant Third World suppliers.

The implications of these projections should be made explicit. World trade in cereals is projected to rise substantially in the period to year 2000, by about 150 million tons (75 per cent) from mid-1980 levels. The demand/supply discussion above suggests the possibility of much greater quantities, perhaps an additional 100-200 million tons, without identifying which regions will benefit from this growth. The discussion above suggests that the large low-income Asian countries (especially China, India, Bangladesh and Pakistan) are unlikely to emerge as significant net exporters: this is also implied in the projections reviewed. However, could other Asian or Latin American countries emerge as major exporters? The projections suggest this is unlikely to be highly significant, primarily because of supply constraints and, more generally, because of pessimism about national economic interactions in these countries and their effects on agriculture. There are also longer-term ecological concerns about the "sustainability" of large scale intensive production of animal feed materials for export (especially, cassava in Thailand) and social concerns about their structural implications (export versus traditional food crops) in some countries.

The implication of the projections is therefore that it will be the OECD countries which will increase their exports, because these are the countries which have the ecological, technological and "structural" capacity to meet rising export demands, with correspondingly buoyant implications for their agricultural sectors. These projections may reflect excessive "technological" and "structural" pessimism about some developing country exporters. However, they do reinforce the conclusions (expressed in Chapter 7) that in the long run OECD agriculture has little to fear from trade reform (for example, as articulated in the GATT negotiations) as their longer-term position is likely to be strengthened, not weakened, by developing country growth.

Future prospects — China

The projections for China exercise a pivotal position in the global projections. China represented some 17 per cent of total world grains consumption in 1984, and future growth rates are anticipated to be strong, even if they represent a deceleration from historic levels. China's share of world consumption could rise to 22 per cent (Table 2.1) or higher by year 2000.

The World Bank year 2000 projections are based on alternative projections by the Chinese authorities[1]. In spite of considerable analytical effort, China food projections remain problematic, for reasons which include: difficulties in interpreting past trends associated with particular policy changes, notably the Cultural Revolution in the 1960s and the economic reforms of the late 1970s; uncertainty about Chinese food and agricultural statistics, due to historic lack of "openness" (after many years of statistics being considered a state secret, official statistics which are revealed should be treated with caution, especially due to the continuance of a partial "command" economy, which very visibly attaches great importance to the ideological "correctness" of certain indicators).

The projections imply considerable increases in imports. The budgetary implications of these implied imports and the effect of the anticipated imports on world food prices and markets have not however been taken into account.

In the main, the expected increase in China's import demand reflects assumptions regarding consumer shifts between products. The FAO/World Food Survey data suggests that calorie availabilities were adequate on average already in the mid-1980s[2]. It seems to be further generally assumed — not least by the Chinese authorities — that, since China has a rather egalitarian, structured society, adequate average availability means that almost everybody eats as much cereals as they want. Given this, any additional income is used on other foods, especially meat (and, of course, on other products), with very low income elasticities for basic food staples (0.2 or less)[3]. However, recent World Food Council estimates suggest that as much as 6 per cent of China's population may be clinically undernourished[4], and it is argued above (Chapter 2) that this is probably an underestimate.

If one makes the optimistic assumption that most Chinese people are adequately fed and that income elasticities for basic foodstuffs are very low, consumption of food grains will be mainly influenced by demographic trends. This has major consequences. UN population projections, as used by the FAO, give a total Chinese population of 1.26 billion in year 2000, with an implied 1985-2000 growth rate of around 1.5 per cent. Recent evidence suggests that these figures are too low: the

Chinese population in year 2000 will probably be at least 1.3 billion. At today's consumption levels, the extra 100 million (plus) people will need an extra 50 million tons (plus) of food grains. This margin of error is almost equal to the total cereal consumption of sub-Saharan Africa in 1985.

The assumed shift away from basic food cereals would lead to a dramatic increase in cereal requirements for animal feeds. The increase in animal feed requirements between 1982 and year 2000 could be almost threefold (more than 120 million tons) to around 185 million tons. This projected **feed** grain annual increase is enormous — considerably more than total annual 1984 cereal consumption of Latin America.

The requirements outlined above assume that income elasticities for Chinese food consumption of cereals are lower than may be realistic, given the general low income level and increasing (admittedly fragmentary and anecdotal) evidence of extreme poverty and deprivation, especially in less "successful" provinces. IFPRI's projections use an (FAO) income elasticity of 0.17 for total basic food staples consumption (in volume terms), which with IFPRI's GNP growth projections would lift per capita food cereals consumption by 0.6 per cent annually over the 1980-2000 period. This income-induced consumption rise would represent some 20 million tons in year 2000.

Thus, the available projections suggest very great uncertainty for year 2000 total cereals consumption. The totals projected for year 2000 range from a low 284 million tons in IIASA's reference scenario to a high 570 million tons in some OECD calculations. Given differing definitions and base years, the projected totals for year 2000 are less comparable than the projected growth rates. These vary from a very low rate in the IIASA reference scenario, of 1.2 per cent over the 1980-2000 period, to a rather high 2.9 per cent, for the 1984-2000 period, in the World Bank projections. The other projected growth rates are around 2.2-2.4 per cent. It is worth noting that each percentage point difference in the growth rate represents about 50 million tons of consumption difference in year 2000.

Some analysts suggest that Chinese agriculture could meet the projected year 2000 food consumption, even if consumption overshoots the projected levels. Most analysts assume that Chinese food and agricultural strategies will aim for continued broad self-sufficiency. However, there is considerable doubt about how successful Chinese agriculture will be in maintaining the implied growth rates. Furthermore, it may be questioned whether self-sufficiency is an appropriate economic or political objective.

These doubts come both from recent developments and from long-term considerations. As Table 3.2 indicates, total grain production peaked in 1984 and in the subsequent four years was never more than 10 per cent higher, although some of these were drought-affected years. The more substantial doubts concern underlying ecological, economic and social processes. On the ecological side, Lester Brown points to severe water constraints in the North China Plain, where competing agricultural, industrial and residential uses are driving down the water table. He also points to serious soil erosion, especially in the Yellow River basin[5].

On the economic side, all the food consumption projections imply a major shift from food to feed crops. Population and income trends suggest a shift in the regional location of animal feed use towards the coastal provinces. Thus, meeting self-sufficiency objectives at the projected high consumption levels would imply either a major use of rice for animal feed or a major shift in land use from rice to coarse grains and oilseeds. There are limits both to the feasibility and economic efficiency of these alternatives. For example, they imply very large increases in internal transport of feed materials, which given the present state of China's rail and road network seem implausible.

The overall conclusion is that the prospect of large imports of animal feed materials (coarse grains and protein feeds) must be taken seriously. This is all the more so because demand for livestock products is rising fastest in the coastal provinces which are easily accessible to international supplies and are developing international trade links. Technology considerations (see Chapter 5) would suggest that China could become a major user (from domestic or imported sources) of bio-technology-based protein animal feeds.

In a study prepared for the Development Centre, Anderson[6] argues that, in national terms, basic food production is losing out to other economic activities. He also argues that China is simply following trends in other South East Asian societies, especially those with large ethnic Chinese populations. In national terms, comparative advantage is shifting away from basic food production towards other economic activities, which include livestock products and their distribution. In fact, official statistics suggest that the total area sown to grain peaked in the mid-1950s then declined significantly, fluctuating with a narrow range from 1965 to 1979, and declined a further 7 per cent between 1979 and 1985. Most of the area shift went to "industrial" crops. On the other hand, the detailed data suggest that China is very far from having exhausted the productivity gains associated with more appropriate cropping patterns, procurement practices, economic incentives and "X efficiency", while China may be relatively successful in using "new" technology innovations. However, in the Chinese case, the competing activities to basic food production are rural, rather than urban, and compete directly for household savings and even for land. At the same time, one needs to relate this analysis of shifts in national competitive advantage to trends in global markets, since the trade implications (discussed below) would clearly make China a major player on world agricultural markets.

From an international trade point of view, the major global projections appear to be conservative, implying basic agricultural self-sufficiency with very small Chinese trade. In terms of total cereals, the year 2000 projections for Chinese net imports range from 1 million tons (FAO), through 7 million tons (IFPRI), and 28 million tons (IWC) to 43.2 million tons (WB), and 49 million tons (IIASA) as against 6 million tons in the 1983/85 period. Even the highest (WB and IIASA) projections would imply more than 90 per cent self-sufficiency. In contrast to the views expressed — either explicitly or implicitly — in the projections, our analysis suggests that at least 100 million tons of imported feed materials can be envisaged, with major consequences for world markets and prices.

The scale of Chinese imports is the most important single issue for the international projections. Could, would or should China contemplate 100 million tons of imported cereals? Most commentators dismiss this possibility, but it is not at all obvious why this should be so. At current prices, an extra 100 million tons of cereal imports would cost around $10 billion. This may be compared with total 1988 merchandise exports of some $41 billion, and a growth in total exports in the 1980s of around $4 billion annually.

Since these would be essentially feed grain imports, it is unlikely that they would be prohibited on the grounds of "food security" or "self-sufficiency" arguments. One study suggests that the annual national economic (deadweight) costs of maintaining self-sufficiency would be more than 2 per cent of GNP[7]. A 50 per cent liberalisation of present trade distortions would yield annual GNP gains by 1995 of around $14 billion (in 1980-82 prices). Importantly, because of the interrelations between agricultural products, net food imports would fall, although there would be large increases in wheat and coarse grain imports.

Future prospects — prices

The World Bank projects a fall in international prices of major food products in real terms in relation to recent or historical levels. Details are shown in Table 6.2. Taking the fifteen years 1970-84 as a base, prices would fall by an average 50-60 per cent over the period to year 2000. The outlook for rice prices, however, is much more uncertain: the projections undertaken for the Development Centre point to a significant rise, as do those of IIASA[8].

The IIASA Reference Scenario projects little change in cereals prices from longer-term levels (Table 6.3), although for wheat and coarse grains this represents modest falls over the projection period 1980-2000. In line with the Development Centre projections, however, and in contrast to the World Bank, IIASA projects a slight rise in rice prices. The uncertainty about rice prices is important for some large low-income countries.

IIASA emphasizes that its Reference Scenario projections are not forecasts[9], but claims, nevertheless, that its projections are plausible. The divergence between the two sets of projections comes partly from using 1980 as a base year, with the implicit assumption that it was typical. In the case of wheat and, especially, rice, 1980 prices were significantly above the average of the preceding twenty years, and for all the main cereals were well above mid-1980s' prices. The divergence in trends between IIASA and the World Bank also comes from the higher income growth rates generated in the IIASA model and different supply and demand elasticities.

The other longer-term projections reviewed here, from FAO, IFPRI and IWC, make no formal price assumptions, although the FAO report has some discussion of the possible implications of trade liberalisation. Most discussion of future trends in agriculture, self-sufficiency, international trade and competitive advantage for developing countries and of food and agricultural policy implications has probably intuitively assumed that future price levels would remain around their present average levels. The policy discussion has focused on the effects on world prices of various packages of trade liberalisation.

The World Bank projections are econometrically derived from the interaction of demand and supply trends and link the different commodities. In the latest projections, the Bank's regular methodology was supplemented by a "spectral" analysis which examined price movements over a very long period. This seems to confirm the longer-term projections. In less formal terms, these longer-term projected trends can be explained in terms of the massive spare developed world agricultural capacity, which especially in the United States is currently being held out of production: this is assumed to come gradually back into production in the late 1990s. It could be argued that these projections do not sufficiently take account of current OECD policy concerns about environmental threats. They are also explained by decelerating demand growth, especially in developing countries. The projections make no other specific policy changes assumptions.

Assuming a substantial fall in world cereal prices, how plausible would be the year 2000 prospects as set out in the different projections? There are no formal methodological problems, since in the World Bank case the falling prices come directly from the model, and in the other cases prices are formally absent. However, on the demand side, falling international prices may be expected to lead to faster consumption growth, most obviously of livestock products and, thus, of feed grains. Lower world food prices could also encourage low-income developing countries to follow food policies to raise nutritional standards. On the supply side, one might expect some further deceleration in developing country food output, partly through the increased budget costs of maintaining producer prices.

These trends would suggest a shift towards greater world trade, mainly involving higher OECD exports to food deficit developing countries and to Eastern European Economies. This raises issues about food self-sufficiency objectives, food security, and the financial ability of importers to import.

Longer-term price trends for other important temperate foodstuffs are also difficult to interpret. Most projections anticipate a substantial rise in sugar and beef prices, but present markets are very narrow and subject to government policies. Moreover, the introduction of bio-technology-based products would tend progressively to depress prices for sugar and animal feed materials and also for livestock products. In the case of sugar, this is important for developing countries' food and agriculture. International livestock prices, however, are probably not as important to developing countries, except to the extent that they influence patterns of demand and supply for feed materials.

Price elasticities of supply and demand

In the context of this price discussion it is worth raising some of the issues about price elasticities of demand and supply. Price elasticities play an important role in some of the projections reviewed here (WB and IIASA), and are central to most analysis of the impacts of policy changes on demand, supply, trade and international prices discussed in the next chapter. Tables 6.3 and 6.4 introduce four sets of elasticities, from FAO and the USDA (estimates used in OECD's own policy analysis), and from IIASA (generated within the IIASA research). They are medium- to long-term elasticities of quantity shifts in relation to international prices.

Wide divergence exists between the different estimates. These are due to methodological differences in their compilation and, more important, in their use, although these are not always made explicit in their presentation. Results also vary greatly between countries. Some of these differences can be explained intuitively in terms of national levels and patterns of consumption and production of the staple foodstuffs. These factors inform the characterisation of different groups of countries (e.g. low-income, middle-income exporters or importers) as having relatively "high" or "low" price elasticities.

While the use of elasticities in the different models is often sophisticated and "own" price elasticities are accompanied by cross price elasticities, a worrying question concerns how far we should use such historically derived elasticities (mainly calculated in the 1970s from historical time series) for projections to the year 2000 (e.g. IIASA) or for medium-term policy analysis (e.g. OECD's MTM analysis). An examination of future trends suggests that there may be "qualitative" shifts under way, which would not necessarily be captured in price elasticities based on the 1970s experience. Perhaps, most obviously, there may be asymmetries of response, for example, as producers learn to use new techniques when prices are high, but do not necessarily abandon them when prices fall, or as consumers' tastes shift but then do not shift back. Similarly, the discussion of supply trends in Chapter 3 suggests that, in large parts of the developing world, the scope for arable area increases is becoming increasingly physically constrained. It is important, also, that some of the projected price falls are relatively large, which may suggest that econometrically derived year-to-year supply and demand elasticities will not adequately capture their effects.

From the point of view of nutrition and food security, it is important to consider the price responsiveness of poor people. In his analysis of the fragmentary data available from 15 studies based on consumer surveys, Alderman concludes (cautiously) that poor people have much higher consumption responses than average and rich people[10]. He suggests, for example, that the price elasticity (of expenditure) for rice of the poorest 10 per cent of a population will be 80 per cent higher than the mean value for the whole population, and that similar differences would apply for livestock products, wheat and coarse grains.

This would reinforce the importance of cost-reducing technology innovations in basic food production. The wider implications for food security and for aggregate trends are less certain. Alderman's analysis suggests that the average consumption price elasticities built into most of the models reviewed here are too low, and that the aggregate effects of the projected price falls may be considerably greater than is implied in the projections. It also suggests that, with different cost-reducing prospects for different products, there may be greater price-induced consumption shifts between major products than is reflected in the projections. Linking this to the supply and technology discussion of Chapters 3 and 5, this could suggest greater shifts (than projected) towards livestock products and some basic foodstuffs (wheat and maize) at the expense of more traditional crops (such as rice, tubers and minor coarse grains). And, since livestock products are involved, there would be secondary, reinforcing effects on the major animal feed materials, especially maize. It could also raise doubts about the beneficial welfare effects of reform in OECD agricultural policies (reviewed in Chapter 7), which would tend to raise world prices for major food products.

Food security and international trade

According to the World Food Council: "as it has evolved in the 1980s, the concept of food security has generally come to mean all people at all times having access to enough food for an active and healthy life"[11]. Although this seems straightforward, the implications are very complex and give rise to considerable technical and political disagreement. It is relevant to link the discussion to the central presentation here of longer-term trends, and to assess the policy implications. For that purpose, it is convenient to adopt two of the classifications that are used in the discussion: the distinctions between global, national and individual food security, and between chronic and temporary insecurity.

The discussion suggests a paradox. The world is producing enough calories to feed itself now, and the overall projections are relatively optimistic (real prices seem likely to fall substantially, and the available price elasticities of supply suggest that world production would increase sharply if prices failed to fall). Yet the nutrition projections reviewed in Chapter 2 suggest that the absolute number of hungry people will continue to rise, perhaps by five million clinically at risk in the period to year 2000.

The analysis of income elasticities of demand for basic foodstuffs suggests that most projections may tend to adopt rather low elasticities. The concept is a difficult one, reflecting national average behaviour and, therefore, assumptions both about income distribution and about the food consumption patterns of different groups within the country. Redistributing income does not straightforwardly raise cereal consumption, because livestock products are increasingly cereal-intensive. Nevertheless, the analysis suggests that raising the assumed average elasticity for the developing world to 0.5 — at the upper limit of most observers' assumptions of what is plausible — would raise year 2000 world cereal consumption by 350 million tons, roughly 15.5 per cent. Similarly, raising per capita GDP growth in developing countries by 1.0 percentage point, an optimistic development scenario for the 1990s, would raise world cereal consumption by very roughly 100 million tons, somewhat less than 5 per cent.

Some analysts, particularly in Europe, emphasize the manipulative aspects of trading firms, organisations and governments in world food product markets[12]. This line of argument is separate from the issues about OECD farm and trade policies, although some observers justify the maintenance of these policies as a response to market manipulation. Although the data are fragmentary, FAO considers that some 85-90 per cent of developing countries' cereal imports involves six major international trading companies, five of which are not "public" companies[13]. However, in spite of this massive degree of market concentration, most observers do not see these six major firms as significantly threatening the interests of developing countries, either as importers or exporters of cereals. Market collusion does not seem to be a problem, and, importantly, these firms are overwhelmingly "traders" not "producers".

So, globally, there is probably no chronic food security problem. This conclusion is in marked contrast to the pessimism of the mid-1970s. There are some doubts about the ecological implications of longer-term trends (see Chapter 3), but on balance the assessment in Chapters 3 and 4 is that continuing technology change can take care of any likely growth in basic food demand, and in particular of the nutritional needs of hungry people. The hunger problem needs therefore to be conceived differently.

This is a strong conclusion. The prospective food security issues, which will remain dramatic, are about **national** policies and about **international trade**. The projections seem to imply a further paradox about **national** developments. Very broadly, most developing countries will have enough calories available in year 2000 from domestic production and imports to feed adequately all their population. Yet, the projections suggest that they will not do so, while at the same time they will become less "self-sufficient" in basic foodstuffs.

Most of the discussion about food security at the national level has been in terms of "self-sufficiency" ratios. The projections made for the Development Centre suggest a considerable decline in developing country self-sufficiency for major foodstuffs (which are internationally traded), for all important developing regions. Trade liberalisation would not significantly affect these ratios (see Chapter 7 below and Table 7.7). FAO's projections are less radical, but are not substantially different. The Centre projections are most dramatic for sub-Saharan Africa, whose self-sufficiency ratio in cereals would fall from 84 per cent in the 1981-83 period to around 55 per cent in year 2000 (and slightly lower with trade liberalisation). In volume terms, however, as discussed above, sub-Saharan African imports would not represent more than one quarter of total developing country imports.

The World Food Council and FAO argue, more or less explicitly, that national food self-sufficiency is fundamental to food security. The presentations have nuances, because some developing countries obviously have a revealed comparative advantage in exporting non-food products and in importing basic foodstuffs (e.g. Middle East petroleum exporters). However, the assumption is that most developing countries should aim for self-sufficiency in basic foodstuffs, just as the European Community countries were aiming in the 1960s and 1970s and the Eastern European Economies still are. On this view, national governments, especially in developing countries, should insulate themselves from world markets. The discussion then becomes one about what "reference" prices to chose for national food and agricultural policies. The discussion above and in Chapter 7 suggests that with or without policy changes, most reference prices will be falling substantially.

Self-sufficiency is not a panacea for poverty and nutritional concerns within most developing countries. It may be that there is no plausible international price for major cereal products at which a country like Ethiopia has a comparative advantage in growing its traditional staple cereals. As shown in the Development Centre's case study on Ethiopia, such a situation might strain economists' notions of international comparative advantage[14].

The major cereal importers are middle-income countries and a good part of imports are for feed. Because countries which can afford to import are often the better-off countries, discussion concerning the impact of changed world market scenarios, for example, arising from OECD trade liberalisation, cannot simply be translated into implications for the food consumption of the world's poorest people.

One important school of thought argues that one should not consider food imports by developing countries in terms of meeting self-sufficiency shortfalls or, indeed, as competing with national production[15]. These analysts argue that food imports, at least for rapidly developing countries, are positively correlated with local food production. Various correlations indicate that the more rapidly a country develops its basic food production, the higher will be its food imports. The argument involves the assumption that a successful food-based agricultural development will have multiplier effects that raise basic food demand even beyond the initial stimulus coming from additional incomes in basic food production. This would correspond to a certain "take-off" phase, during which food (and presumably animal feed) requirements rise very fast. The positive correlations primarily concern today's middle-income developing countries. However, they could concern tomorrow's China.

This thesis implies the comforting message that there need be no conflict between agricultural-based development strategies for developing countries and relatively expansionist agricultural policies in OECD countries. The main problem, for the sceptics, is to understand how — if applied to low-income countries, and especially to China — the food imports would be financed. Probably, it is implied that these rapidly (and appropriately) developing economies would be finding international competitive advantage outside basic foodstuffs. However, in the case of the very large low-income countries of Asia, it is not clear where this international competitive advantage would be. This discussion is most important for China.

With substantially falling prices, the rate of increase in the cost of imports would be much less than that in import volumes. The projections made for the Centre imply an increase in the real cost of developing countries' imports of cereals, between 1981-83 and year 2000, of 174 per cent, with corresponding increases of: Asia — 29 per cent, North Africa/Middle East — 143 per cent, sub-Saharan Africa — 350 per cent, Latin America — 293 per cent. A rough calculation for China suggests that projected cereal imports for year 2000 would represent no more than 4 per cent of total average mid-1980s imports: even doubling this level would not seem a crippling burden. The shares would not be very different for the other major Asian countries, with the possible exception of Bangladesh. The situation for some sub-Saharan African countries would be very different, particularly in view of their modest economic growth prospects.

As suggested above, food security can also be considered in "individual" or "local" terms. Much of the discussion in earlier chapters, on global trends, income distribution, nutrition, environmental concerns, bio-technology and price elasticities suggests that this is an important dimension. At the same time, the discussion suggests that individual or local food security is strongly linked to national interactions and global trends, although the links are very complex. There is now a very considerable literature around "food entitlements" in relation to food security[16]. Much of this is about the incomes of vulnerable groups and the food prices they face:

this links directly to the national interactions and international trends, although there are very few data to sustain a quantitative discussion. Some of it is about "institutions". The discussion above suggests that much of it should be about technology (Chapters 3 and 5) and about prices (in Chapter 6)

Underlying the discussion are potentially conflicting attitudes to national and international interactions and to international markets. On the one hand are assumptions that macroeconomic measures (e.g. income distribution) and international trends (e.g. falling prices) can directly influence the "entitlements" of poor people. On the other hand is a concern about institutional arrangements and technological possibilities in relation to specific groups of people, and political attitudes to them — more generally problems of "governance"[17]. This report, which is primarily concerned with aggregate trends, cannot clarify these conflicts, but it should not be assumed that they are irrelevant to the aggregate trends.

There is a largely unexplored issue about the role of women in the determination of trends in supply of and demand for food. It is clear that, in developing countries, women are very important both in the production of food and in the preparation of its consumption. It is also clear that they are nutritionally disadvantaged at present[18]. Increased consciousness of women's importance may shift the supply/demand parameters. There could be effects on both production and consumption, although the primary effect would be on the consumption side, in terms of choice of products. For the present, we have no evidence on what these effects might be in aggregative terms, and especially in relation to future projections. This, however, does not mean that they will not be important.

On balance, it seems desirable that the focus of the food security discussion should shift from global or national preoccupations to the concerns of particular groups at risk, even though the overall numbers are enormous (and heavily concentrated in Asia). This is ultimately because global (and, in most cases, national) food availabilities do not seem to be the problem. This does not mean that international market trends or national macroeconomic interactions are irrelevant. However, this conflicts with much of the present "food security" discourse, which has been conducted in national terms.

Conclusions

The longer-term projections suggest continuing rapid growth in world trade in basic foodstuffs, especially wheat and coarse grains. This would essentially be OECD countries exporting to a wide range of developing countries, but in volume terms primarily to Asia (and especially China). Precisely because of the geographical pattern, there must be great uncertainty about the volumes, not so much because the countries will be unable to finance the imports, but because they may continue with self-sufficiency policies.

Despite all the uncertainties, the projections have a convergent pessimism about the prospects for developing country exporters of temperate foodstuffs, and (to anticipate Chapter 7) this does not depend on protectionist policies. Rather, it reflects analysis which suggests that OECD agriculture is better placed to take advantage of rapidly expanding markets.

The major uncertainty concerns China. Official statistics and the available projections probably understate population growth rates and the extent of undernourishment. On the other hand, much of the projected increase in cereal consumption and imports concerns feed grains for livestock production. Differing assumptions regarding these variables change the anticipated cereal imports by as much as 100 million tons.

International prices for basic foodstuffs over the long term will follow a downward trend, falling substantially in real terms in relation to recent average levels. In Chapter 7, we indicate that these falls are likely to swamp any short run effects of changes in agricultural policies. Possible exceptions would be rice, sugar and some livestock products. Thus, the projected growth in the financing requirements for food imports is much lower than the growth in volume terms.

Food security will not be a question of global availability of calories. Nor, if the trade projections are realised, should it be a question of national availabilities.

The conclusions on nutrition (Chapter 2) and food security suggest, first, that staggering numbers of the world's people are severely undernourished. Second, while the different projections of longer-term demand and supply trends show considerable divergencies, none of them seems to imply that the number of undernourished people will decline. The FAO projections explicitly imply that they will increase. Third, all the projections to the year 2000 imply that the world will have enough food to feed itself.

There are normative questions about food security and the policy implications, especially for the OECD countries. The political and economic consequences of over 350 million hungry people will have to be faced. The projections imply that these people will represent more than 20 per cent of sub-Saharan Africa's population, but a much lower proportion of the low-income Asian countries. It is far from certain that the large low-income Asian countries will continue to "manage" their poverty problems without significant effects on food and agricultural policies.

The responses of developing country governments and their policies provide the key. Given all the other (and generally more immediate) policy concerns, they may not however respond effectively and in a timely manner to the longer-term nutrition or food security issues.

The focus of this report is on future trends, and the global market interactions are particularly important. Here the projections show large increases in sub-Saharan African food imports, although the **uncertainties** about Asian imports are much bigger than any likely absolute level of African imports. In general, the projections for Asian countries (and especially China and India) are biased towards food self-sufficiency, but around nutritional and "entitlement" patterns that are likely to leave hundreds of millions of people hungry. It is worth considering the extent to which greater food trade could contribute to a different longer-term nutritional outcome, either based on food-aid or a self-financing contribution to a different "entitlements-based" development strategy.

Food security is frequently seen as implying national strategies for food self-sufficiency. Inevitably, the projected large rise in developing country food imports implies substantial falls in self-sufficiency ratios. Sub-Saharan Africa, as a region, might be little more than 50 per cent self-sufficient in cereals. However, in general, it can be argued that rising food imports are desirable for low-income developing countries, even in the context of an appropriate agriculturally led development strategy.

Another aspect of food security concerns the instability of international food product markets. To the extent that this has been due to their "narrowness", instability is likely to decline irrespective of changes in protectionist policies, as trade increases faster than production[19]. To some extent, observers have seen a trade-off between national and international stability. For national governments and individual producers and consumers, greater stability is an important goal, both because it allows for more effective government planning and because it reduces risk, which in turn facilitates food security and promotes investment and technological innovation.

In the context of considerably increased trade in basic foodstuffs, substantially reduced national food self-sufficiency ratios and continuing rising global hunger, greatly increased levels of food aid must be a serious policy option. The well-known objections to food aid, as other than disaster relief, lose some of their validity.

NOTES

1. See Chapter 2 and Tables 2.8 and 2.9.
2. Alexandratos, Chapter 2.
3. The GLS model (see Yang and Tyers) assumes that the rice elasticity will fall from 0.1 in the mid-1980s to 0 in the late 1990s.
4. WFC (1989).
5. Anderson (1990).
6. Anderson (1990).
7. Yang and Tyers.
8. See Zietz and Valdés, and Parikh (1988a).
9. Parikh *et al.*
10. Alderman.
11. WFC (1989).
12. See Susanna Davies in Butler, Chapter 6, and Charvet.
13. FAO (1987b).
14. Pickett.
15. Mellor (1988a), (1988b) and (1988c).
16. See e.g. Sen (1981, 1986 and 1989). See also Streeten.
17. See e.g. Pickett (1989 and 1991), and Anderson (1988).
18. Behrman *et al.*
19. For further discussion of the evidence, see Goldin and Knudsen, especially Chapter 17.

Chapter 7

AGRICULTURAL POLICIES AND STRATEGIES

Introduction

Earlier chapters have focused on underlying trends in demand, supply and trade for basic foodstuffs, and have emphasized the role of technology trends and the off-farm "food system". In this chapter we discuss how agricultural policies and their analysis relate to these underlying trends[1].

The Development Centre, in the context of its 1987-89 work programme, commissioned a series of country case studies with a focus on agricultural policy as well as a quantitative analysis of the effects of agricultural policy reform. This latter study, conducted by Zietz and Valdés, examined important temperate zone food products in both OECD and developing countries, taking explicit account of underlying longer-term trends[2]. The results are presented in terms of year 2000 outcomes which compare various policy reform scenarios with a base case.

The present report focuses centrally on basic food products, and the Zietz/Valdés analysis is limited to such products. Nevertheless, issues about other agricultural products are relevant. These products represent the major share of the agricultural exports of some developing countries, and, therefore, of total foreign exchange earnings.

From a policy analysis point of view, developing country agricultural exports may be broadly defined as falling into three categories:

a) **Standard temperate products** (or tropical substitutes). These compete directly with OECD production, and international trade is dominated by OECD countries' agricultural policies. At present, developing country exports of these products involve only a rather small number of (primarily middle-income) developing countries, but longer-term market prospects suggest a major expansion in developing and Eastern European countries' imports (which would be unaffected by OECD agricultural policies).

b) **Tropical beverages and raw materials** (coffee, cocoa, tea, natural fibres and spices). These products represent the major part of total developing country agricultural exports. They have little directly to do with OECD agricultural policies and have rather modest prospects in terms of longer-term price or volume trends. Such prospects as they have essentially concern the policies of the Eastern European Economies and, perhaps eventually, of middle-income developing countries[3] .

c) **"New" products**. Developing country exports of these products have been rising rapidly, but in statistical terms are not well reported. They include various vegetables, fruits and processed products with relatively buoyant market prospects. However, while these market prospects are much influenced by (OECD and developing country) import and production policies, the policy impacts are very complex and not well captured in broad measures of agricultural support.

Much of the available policy analysis concerns the standard temperate zone products. This results from, on the one hand, a concern about nutrition and food security, and, on the other, from the fact that these products represent the major part of the agricultural product **imports** of developing countries. However, the limitations of such analysis are important. The "temperate" products are probably the most promising in the longer term as developing world exports.

Existing analysis has had only modest success in relating export growth to macro and microeconomic processes in the exporting countries. The role of policies in restraining (or promoting) trade in the importing countries similarly remains incomplete. Many of the issues extend beyond the immediate focus of agricultural policies, and the policy interventions are not well captured in general composite measures of net protection.

A corollary of this recognition is that analysis should be concerned with the diversity of developing countries. Even more important from a food security point of view, it should be concerned with different groups of people within developing countries, and particularly the least favoured. International agricultural policy changes which on balance are positive for world trade and for developing countries will not have uniform beneficial effects on developing countries and on all groups within individual developing countries. There will be losers as well as winners. The process of adjustment requires that they be identified and that the losses be minimised and gains maximised, allowing substantial opportunities for the compensation of the losers from the gainers and overall aggregate improvements.

The analysis of agricultural policies[4]

Over the past decade there have been major shifts in thinking about the role of policies in relation to agriculture, especially within the OECD countries. These shifts have included:

- — a greater recognition that domestic policies within one country, and not simply foreign trade policies, affect economic development within other countries;
- — a greater recognition of the interactions within a particular country between the food and agriculture sectors and the rest of the national economy;
- — a growing recognition that developing countries' interest in world trade in food products is primarily as importers rather than exporters.

Individual countries' policies have consequences for the economic situation and the welfare of other countries. The earlier belief that only border measures, i.e. import controls and export interventions in the form of either export assistance or export taxation, had an impact on the interests of the trading partners no longer holds true. It is now generally recognised that all forms of public intervention in the agricultural sector have external effects. Policies like research or tax concessions to farmers, for example, affect the competitive position of a country's agricultural sector and therefore are not neutral for third countries.

Until recently, the effects of agricultural policies were thought to be circumscribed to the food and agricultural economy, affecting primarily the volume and composition of output, volume and composition of consumption, prices at national and international level, volume and flows of trade, farm incomes and farm employment. Clearly, however, the effects of agricultural policies go beyond the food and agricultural system: these policies have economy-wide effects through the intersectoral allocation of resources and through the factor awards. Agricultural policies exercise an influence on overall growth, on efficiency in the utilisation of a country's resources, on savings and investments and even on the value of the national currency. And, just as agricultural policies affect macroeconomic performance, macroeconomic policies affect the performances of the agricultural sector. These interactions vary from country to country according to the role of agriculture in the national economy, and the extent and nature of the "distortions" coming from different policy interventions.

A growing awareness of the diversity of interactions has fortunately gone hand in hand with expanding analytical capabilities. With the advance in computer modelling techniques, there has been a proliferation of attempts to model the policy implications of the interactions. For analysis within particular countries, general equilibrium frameworks have proved apposite: for example, the Development Centre has obtained interesting insights in its country case study on Thailand[5], through the application of a computable general equilibrium model. The Development Centre in its 1990-92 work programme is engaged in a major global general equilibrium modelling exercise. This Rural-Urban-North-South (RUNS) model will allow simulation of trade liberalisation as well as other policy shocks.

While the general equilibrium approach is well suited to the examination of international macroeconomic interactions and inter-sectoral relations, the inevitable sector aggregations do imply the sacrifice of interpretative power with respect to certain sector-specific policy questions. In parallel to the general equilibrium work which the Centre has sponsored, it has also, notably in the context of its international interactions analysis, sponsored a partial equilibrium approach, which nevertheless incorporates a substantial non-agricultural sector with exogenous income growth.

The quantitative projections presented below are derived from the Zietz and Valdés study commissioned by the Centre and are illustrative of expected trends. Inevitably, they involve strong simplifying assumptions in the representation of the data and of policies. They nevertheless point to areas where tensions or potential tensions may arise among the various groups of countries. The focus of the analysis is the interaction between the policies of the developed market economy countries, taken as a group, and the policies of the developing countries, taken also as a group. However, as neither of these groups of countries is homogeneous, the discussion often takes place in terms of sub-groups.

Quantitative analysis of the effects of policy changes is crucially dependent on two types of parameter, on the one hand the elasticities of response of consumers and producers to changes in prices and incomes, and, on the other hand, some quantitative assessment of the net effects of present policies.

For the assessment of the effects of present policies, there has been convergence in the various studies over the past decade towards composite measures of "net protection", involving Producer Subsidy Equivalents (PSEs) and Consumer Subsidy Equivalents (CSEs). Essentially, these involve assessing the net effects of all the policy influences which cause prices received by farmers (PSEs) or paid by consumers (CSEs) to diverge from the corresponding international prices at the country border. As undertaken by OECD for its Member countries, in the context of its MTM modelling studies, this involves the computation of the financial value of all the detailed government interventions which affect food prices.

It is broadly assumed that the economies are in general equilibrium, and in particular that published nominal exchange rates are appropriate. Clearly, for many developing countries, neither of these assumptions can easily be made, and, given this, it could be problematic for many of them to make detailed calculations of the net effect of the many administrative interventions. A variety of expedients have thus been used to obtain broad indicators, some of which are no more than estimates of the gap between border prices and producer or consumer prices, converted at what is judged to be an equilibrium exchange rate. The estimates used in the projections established for the Centre, and presented below, come from a variety of sources: in general, for the OECD countries they use OECD's own estimates, and for other countries they use the estimates compiled in a study conducted by Krueger, Schiff and Valdés for the World Bank[6].

The composite measures cannot adequately capture all the dynamics of food and agriculture policies. This in part is due to the underlying methodology which calls for an aggregation and compilation of different indicators. Thus a given percentage reduction in "net protection" can be translated into practical policies in a very large number of different ways, which may — across the response elasticities — produce quite different results. The OECD Secretariat has within its own MTM model and for its Member countries considered how far the range of outcomes might vary for different formulations of a same broadly defined change in protection (e.g. a 10 per cent reduction). On the whole, the results suggest that different policy formulations of the same "net" protection reduction would have significantly different results.

Most of the quantitative studies have been primarily static and primarily normative: they establish that, in the absence of other longer-term trends, almost all countries are better off from a reduction in net protection. They in general do not address the question of how the reduction may come about and assume that over the longer period lobbies and opposition political forces are neutralised. However, farmers and other interest groups with substantial vested interests in the food system have proved influential in diverting policy changes from their expressed intention. Here, it is worthwhile considering the further complication that most farmers have relatively important "off-farm" incomes, while most people in rural areas are not classified as farmers or farm-workers, although they may be partially involved in agriculture.

The different PSE/CSE-type composite measures of net protection do not diverge as much as one might have expected and are relatively convergent between the different studies, at least as far as the basic food products are concerned. The estimates of PSEs and CSEs used in this analysis are presented in Table 7.1 below. They show that:

- there is fairly consistent discrimination against basic food production in food deficit developing countries, except (interestingly) in some middle-income countries;
- basic food exporting developing countries have reduced their export competitiveness by discriminating against export agriculture.

Agricultural policies in OECD countries

Developments in the food and agricultural sector of all OECD countries are primarily the consequence of economic and technological forces observed throughout their economies. Thus, the rapid decline in agricultural population is more the consequence of the pulling effect of other sectors rather than the pushing effect from within agriculture. In turn, the increasing capital intensity of agriculture comes from the economy-wide decline in costs of capital in relation to labour. The rapid technological development in agriculture can in part be attributed to agricultural research, but the real force behind it is the rising technological level throughout the economy. Agricultural policies have had the effect of accelerating or decelerating at the margin the rate and extent of these underlying forces. When support and protection reach and exceed levels of more than 40 per cent, the effects of the policies cannot be minimised.

At the same time, agricultural policies embody, explicitly or implicitly, a range of "not straightforwardly economic" objectives. These are, in general, about sustaining rural communities (through income support, on-farm and off-farm employment generation, provision of physical and service infrastructure), and, increasingly, about environmental and ecological concerns. There are also still some ill-articulated objectives about self-sufficiency, food security and stability[7].

The consequences of the existing OECD trade and economic policies fall outside the scope of this discussion. It is sufficient here to say that part of the support and protection granted to the agricultural sector in several countries was intended to offset the effects of practices implemented in other countries. Thus the total cost of support and protection in the OECD countries (some $270 billion in 1988) is the consequence of the policies initiated by each country to reach stated domestic objectives (usually in terms of income levels for farmers) and/or to offset negative effects of the policies of their trading partners (for example, through competitive export subsidisation).

In respect of the rest of the world, the major effects of past policies in the OECD countries have been felt in the following areas: restrictive import policies, ample export supplies at declining prices, important price fluctuations internationally, the provision of food aid, and smaller than otherwise rates of overall economic activity.

To make many of the domestic policies operative, the OECD countries have had recourse to import restrictions of one sort or another: tariffs, levies, minimum import prices, quantitative restrictions, voluntary restraints, state trading, etc. These restrictions were intended to give a preference to national production in domestic markets and also to maintain a certain pre-determined level of prices in these markets. These practices have not generally discriminated between developed and developing exporters.

Several developing countries have the ability of supplying the international market with sizeable quantities of such products as cereals, sugar, meats, oilseeds, fruit and vegetables including wine. The increasing food self-sufficiency in OECD countries, reflected in the implementation of import controls, has resulted in the gradual dislocation of traditional trade flows. For example, the EEC has moved from being the major world importer of beef and dairy products to become the major exporter, Japan has long since ceased to be an importer of rice, and the sugar economy in the United States has been so profoundly transformed by the development of isoglucose out of maize (made possible by the high level of guaranteed price for sugar) that imports of sugar have dramatically declined.

Relaxation of these support policies would eventually give rise to larger imports, and the beneficiaries would be both OECD and developing exporting countries. For example, in the case of sugar, despite the commodity being a typical product grown in developing countries, one of the most efficient and low cost producers is Australia. Many developing countries also would have been better off if OECD countries had recourse to less restrictive import policies. This concerns not only the traditional products but also some products which, due to modern advances in production and in utilisation, can be produced and marketed on a large scale. Cassava is an example, but also is an example of the effects of less restrictive import policies: the large increases in imports of cereal substitutes in Western Europe have had a significant effect on the economies of the exporting countries like Thailand.

Several studies have tried to measure the impact of trade liberalisation by OECD countries on developing country exports. World Bank studies suggest that the benefits to developing countries of total OECD liberalisation could be of the order of $6 billion per year[8]. The benefits would be concentrated in developing countries which have the potential to take advantage of these increased trade possibilities and would represent about 8 per cent of total developing country agricultural exports in 1987.

Support to agriculture in OECD countries has cost far more in terms of household incomes than the size of the annual development assistance provided by these countries. The large distortions in the use of national resources and the trade distortions caused by the agricultural policies applied in the last quarter of a century have convinced governments and public opinion that these policies need to be reformed. Governments have in particular tried to avoid the production of surpluses with the aim of cutting the budgetary expenditures required to dispose of these surpluses. This reduction in surpluses has been attempted both by exercising pressure on producer prices and by implementing administrative methods of supply control.

Agricultural policies which through the price mechanism aim to secure adequate farm incomes to the large number of relatively small producers requires extensive budgetary support. The idea of providing direct income payments dissociated from the level of production is being widely discussed as a more efficient means of support for small farmers. Such direct support systems may soon be implemented by a number of countries. To the extent that these schemes fulfil a social objective with practically no influence on the level of output, their effects on developing countries would be neutral.

Parallel with the discussion of alternative policies, governments are actively engaged in the Uruguay Round of multilateral trade negotiations which aims to result in more open and freer trade in agricultural products. This is to be achieved through a reduction in present levels of support and protection, and through measures securing better access to import markets and less distorting recourse to export measures.

The consequences for developing countries of trade liberalisation have been reviewed by Goldin and Knudsen. They point to increases in international prices (the actual trend in world prices is downward but trade liberalisation could offset part of this secular decline). This would benefit developing country exporters but place an additional burden on the importing developing countries. The negotiations in GATT are contemplating the provision of some sort of assistance to offset these effects in the short run.

The world prices resulting from a better balance between supply and demand could provide a better indication of the real costs of production, against which each country could compare its own situation. Countries could encourage their domestic production through appropriate policies for the purpose of meeting a larger share of their food requirements; and in several cases countries might find it economic to start new lines of production which they would not have started given the prevailing international market conditions. These new lines of production would be destined to meet both national and international demand. This argument is partly psychological: the developing country players have a right to a "level playing field with fixed goal posts".

The different models of agricultural trade liberalisation produce broadly similar results, and almost without exception point to higher cereal prices. The projections made for the Centre, shown in Table 7.2, suggest that the effects of OECD agricultural liberalisation for major temperate commodities would be modest price increases for wheat and rice, somewhat stronger price increases for beef and sugar, and price falls for coarse grains and soya. Moreover, apart from beef and sugar, the projected price changes from OECD policy reform would be small in relation to projected underlying longer-term price trends.

Some other modelling studies, whose results are also summarised in Table 7.2, suggest more dramatic price shifts. However, the various results are highly sensitive to the choice of base period and resulting PSE parameters. With the exception of the

OECD's MTM model, the simulations tend to assume total agricultural policy liberalisation (elimination of PSEs) and thus represent a maximum of what could be obtained through instantaneous and full liberalisation.

The subsequent tables (Tables 7.3 to 7.8) indicate how projected year 2000 quantities would shift for the main temperate food products under various liberalisation scenarios. For the present, the interest is in the shifts that result from OECD ("IC") liberalisation (assumed to be total elimination of PSEs and CSEs). The individual results are somewhat surprising. In the case of animal feeds (coarse grains and soy products) they are counterintuitive: developing country net exports fall when OECD countries eliminate protection. However, overall, the results are very modest (Table 7.4): developing country net cereal exports would be little more than 1 million tons higher with OECD liberalisation than the approximation of 200 million tons trade projected for year 2000. Projected gross developing country cereal imports would change somewhat more significantly (Table 7.5), but the net volumes involved (around 1 million tons) are negligible in relation to the projected totals and to the projected increase from 1981-83 (125 million tons). Tables 7.6 and 7.7 show shifts in self-sufficiency ratios: these are further discussed below.

The results reflect the direct effects of agricultural policy changes, although they capture some of the underlying longer-term trends and some of the less direct effects through agricultural income growth. However, there is currently great interest in the wider economic effects of agricultural policies. The OECD has undertaken a review of available studies[9], and developed its own set of general equilibrium models for important regions within the OECD[10].

With existing agricultural policies, net transfers to agriculture within the OECD countries are massive and have risen sharply. The OECD Secretariat's own estimate is that they represented some $270 billion in 1988, as against some $155 billion in the 1979/81 period[11]. Similarly, the weighted average of PSEs for major OECD countries rose from 32 per cent in 1979/81 to 50 per cent in 1986 and 1987. There can be no doubt that the elimination of net support to OECD agriculture would have important effects on the OECD economy in aggregate. Within the OECD agricultural and food processing sectors, there would be major shifts as protected OECD production was replaced by imports. Recent OECD calculations suggest that with complete OECD agricultural liberalisation, OECD imports would fall in volume terms by almost 5 per cent for crude agricultural products, but rise by almost 270 per cent for processed products and beverages, from their 1980/81 benchmark year. Non-OECD countries' exports to OECD would rise by about 5 per cent for crude agricultural products and by more than 130 per cent for processed products[12].

Complete elimination of OECD agricultural protection would lead to a 2.7 per cent increase in non-OECD import volume, associated with a 0.8 per cent improvement in non-OECD countries' terms of trade. Behind this lies an almost 1.0 per cent net increase in OECD real income associated with the elimination of agricultural support. This concept, the so-called "dead-weight" gain, is a trade-off between gains to consumers and the rest of the macroeconomy and losses to agricultural producers. Other estimates of dead-weight gains from policy reform[13] tend to yield lower estimates: the results are, inevitably, very sensitive to the net protection estimates (which have been rising rapidly during the 1980s).

A dead-weight gain associated with total elimination of OECD agricultural policies of the order of 1.0 per cent of OECD's GDP is of great significance to OECD's own macroeconomic policy concerns. For developing countries, however, the implications of even massive OECD policy reform are much less clear. Goldin and Knudsen emphasize that the available analysis suggests that there would be losers as well as winners. The OECD's analysis implies that the greater efficiency associated with reduced agricultural protection coupled with an improvement in OECD's net terms of trade (and the assumed requirement to balance OECD's foreign accounts with non-OECD countries) would lead to a more than 10 per cent increase in OECD's non-agricultural exports to non-OECD countries and to a more than 5 per cent fall in the volume of OECD's non-agricultural imports. Thus, while the world as a whole may be better off if OECD eliminates its agricultural protection, the greater overall OECD economic efficiency implies that there will be some non-OECD losers (whether sectors or countries).

There could, of course, be "dynamic" effects which are not captured even in such general equilibrium models, although they explicitly attempt to analyse medium-term effects. These "dynamic" effects would feed through food product markets and thus to developing countries. They would impact on supply elasticities and be associated with greater transparency, predictability and especially stability in the global markets. Where they imply higher prices, they should mean greater dynamism and technology innovation for the products concerned, although these positive effects will in part be offset by the slowing of dynamism in those markets where agriculture and agricultural research have been supported through net protection.

One major uncertainty concerns the extent to which the economic parameters — essentially the supply elasticities — currently capture the reactions of OECD farmers. Perhaps the major consequence of OECD agricultural policies has been to shift resources towards land values and, probably, to shift capital out of agriculture. On the other hand, it is increasingly evident that a large part of OECD's small farmers, especially in Western Europe and Japan, are only partially employed in agriculture and have non-farm incomes. These factors mean that agricultural production responses and returns to land may not respond in expected ways to across-the-board reduction in support.

In the Australian studies of EEC policies[14], agriculture is sub-divided into large and small farm operations with different assumed behavioural responses — essentially large farmers respond to market price signals, while small farmers may not: since large farmers represent the major part of EEC production, aggregate production is price-responsive. This may deal with the part-time farmer problem, but, with returns to land representing such a large share of agricultural turnover, the market assumptions for large farmers require further examination.

There is some agreement that reduction in OECD policies would lead to more stable, predictable global food product markets. Two aspects should be distinguished. First, the increasing volume of world trade would reduce the narrowness of some global markets, although, as noted above, in most major food product markets, the increase in trade associated with OECD policy changes is likely to be very small in relation to the expected underlying growth in these markets. Second, OECD policies have been used, more or less deliberately, to stabilize domestic markets, thereby transferring short-term fluctuations onto world markets. In this sense, a reduction in OECD support policies should improve the transparency and stability of world markets. This greater stability would have significant effects on developing country food and agriculture.

Policies of Eastern European Economies

The policies of the Eastern European Economies are of great importance for the international food economy and for the developing countries. The significance of the reforms currently under way in Eastern Europe for world agricultural markets has yet to be determined, but already it is clear that it will lead to significant changes. Since the USSR is potentially the biggest Eastern European Economy player on world food markets, the reform of its economy is particularly pivotal.

Eastern European Economy consumption of citrus, bananas and other tropical products is very low. It seems that this is due to non-availability rather than to lack of consumer demand. This in turn is due to the restrictive import policy carried out in this respect by the trading agencies. As demand in the developed market economies is already saturated, the prospects for the developing countries which are producers and exporters of tropical foods depend to a large extent upon the policies to be followed by the Eastern European Economies, and, perhaps, by middle-income developing countries.

The situation is more complex for temperate zone products. The emergence of the Soviet Union since the early 1970s as a significant importer of grains has had a profound impact on the cereals sector internationally. The quantities purchased in recent years are large in relation to total world trade, although they are marginal in relation to the domestic requirements of these countries. Except for the difficulties experienced at the beginning of the 1970s in satisfying this import demand (the tripling of world wheat prices in that period is an indication of the consequences incurred), the international agricultural economy, and notably the grain economy of the OECD countries and of countries like Argentina, was able to adjust quickly and to satisfy this new import demand. The initial difficulties were due to the unexpected character of the purchases rather than the serious adjustment problems which they created in other countries.

Notwithstanding the ability of the world grains economy to cope with these purchases, the 1970s episode demonstrated the precarious nature of the situation of the food importing developing countries. In the brief 1970s period of short supplies internationally, some developing countries were priced out of the market. In the subsequent period, when price subsided, prices, though declining, were kept at levels higher than those which would have prevailed in the absence of these purchases.

The size of the Soviet Union, in particular, and therefore of its likely purchases, the practice of state trading with the ensuing lack of predictability and transparency, and the fact that more of these transactions take place in the context of bilateral agreements can in the short run (and in some cases in the longer run too) be detrimental to the food importing developing countries. The degree of the negative effect is difficult to assess, as it can only be evaluated relative to what would have been the level of grains production in the OECD area and in Argentina in the absence of the Eastern European Economies' purchases. Similarly for meat and dairy products. It is true that the purchases of these products, notably by the Soviet Union, took place because exporters were offering bargain prices: the fact remains that prices internationally would have been even lower in the absence of these purchases.

For the future, different hypotheses can be formulated. One would be that the Soviet Union maintains and even increases its purchases. This is the scenario presented in the projections above. Should the Soviet Union become self-sufficient, the international grain economy would experience lower prices. This means that the success of the Soviet Union (and of China) in solving its agricultural problems would have a downward effect on world prices. Such a decrease in prices would reflect the actual market situation and not, as at present, the effect of subsidised exports of surplus production by OECD countries.

Developing countries' policies

Contrary to what happens in developed countries where the agricultural sector is now a small proportion of the national economy and where, with few exceptions, agricultural policies are not a decisive component of overall economic policies, in most developing countries agriculture still accounts for a large share of total economic activity, and agricultural and macroeconomic policies are closely linked. This means that a variation in the agricultural economy has economy-wide effects which are far greater than is usual in the developed countries. This means too that macroeconomic policies, in particular monetary, fiscal, taxation and exchange rate policies, can have a far greater impact on agriculture in these countries than agricultural policies proper.

A major study, sponsored by the World Bank[15], of the effects of developing country policies on agriculture (covering 18 developing countries) shows decisively that "indirect" (economy-wide) policies are much more important than "direct" (agriculture-specific) measures. Even where the net "direct" effects are positive to agriculture (which tends to depend on whether agriculture is export-oriented), they are normally swamped by negative indirect effects, representing on average a 27 per cent tax on agriculture.

Earlier chapters have discussed the policy implications of underlying trends in food consumption, production and trade, together with issues about technology and the food system. The overview of developing country food consumption trends in Chapter 2 suggested that population growth will be the most important determinant of total consumption growth in the longer term. Growth in average income per head will probably be more important than income distribution in determining total consumption growth. In terms of policy analysis, this suggests a framework which can capture the factors determining aggregate macroeconomic growth, although it also points to the importance of analysing the effects of macroeconomic policy changes on different groups of food consumers.

The analysis of production trends stressed the role of investment in physical and human infrastructure, and of technology developments. Given that agriculture represents a large share in national output, this again points to the relevance of a quantitative macroeconomic framework which captures capital accumulation and technical progress. At the same time, agricultural production is significantly responsive to price influences even over the longer term.

These underlying trends suggest the importance in policy analysis, for both demand and supply, of a macroeconomic framework and a general equilibrium framework. However, the importance of structural and institutional factors (including issues about technology and food system) suggest that it will be difficult to capture their specificities in any manageable quantitative framework. At the same time, there is plenty of empirical evidence to suggest the need for considerable agricultural commodity disaggregation to capture the specificities of inter-commodity interactions, even over the longer term.

In these circumstances, it seems important to situate the present discussion of developing country agricultural policies in the context of a quantitative framework that: (i) captures longer-term trends — a year 2000 framework; (ii) has considerable product specificity for basic foodstuffs; (iii) has some aggregative economic features; (iv) relates to the discussion of trade and international comparative advantage; and (v) is capable of efficient continuing use. The quantitative projections from Zietz and Valdés presented below reflect these concerns.

Agricultural policies are represented — as with the OECD countries — in terms of the central trade-related concepts of PSEs and CSEs. The analysis, thus, links the projections to considerable other recent empirical research[16]. These measures capture, to the extent that the data allow, many of the particular policies which influence developing country food and agriculture in the longer term, including price policies, exchange rate policies and quantitative restrictions on imports and exports.

The resulting projections are striking. Policies relating to agriculture in developing countries seem to have had more important (negative) effects on developing country production and world trade for major basic foodstuffs than the policies of OECD countries. World markets would be considerably disturbed by developing country policy reform, but developing countries' own situations would be considerably improved. Whereas elimination of OECD agricultural policies would have rather little effect on international prices for major food products (except sugar), elimination of developing country (negative) policies would drive them strongly downwards. Table 7.3 shows the results for individual products for the total elimination of PSEs and CSEs for both developing and OECD countries. Year 2000 prices, which were projected to fall substantially without policy changes (for wheat and coarse grains) and to remain substantially unchanged for other products (except sugar), are driven down substantially by developing country agricultural liberalisation. Simultaneous liberalisation by both developing and OECD countries changes the results very little.

The results suggest important conclusions for development policy discussion. Much of the discussion about international markets and developing country food and agricultural policies has been about how to deal with international price distortions introduced by OECD countries. The present conclusions suggest that these concerns focus on only part of the problem: the major global market distortions which require further attention are those introduced by developing countries' own food and agricultural policies.

Policies within developing countries are shifting towards agricultural liberalisation for reasons of national self-interest, as well as because of pressure from the World Bank, IMF and other external agencies. It is these policy changes which are likely to have the major influence on world markets over the longer-term period, and it is clear that they are likely to drive world food prices downwards in relation to the already downwards trend.

In aggregate, however, elimination of developing country policy distortions (as measured by PSEs and CSEs) has relatively modest effects on world trade by comparison with the overall projections for world trade growth. Various indicators are shown in Table 7.5. Changes are significant for coarse grains [net developing country imports are 16 million tons (almost 20 per cent) lower], for beef (net imports rise by more than 70 per cent) and for soybeans (net exports rise by more than 40 per cent).

Developing country liberalisation drives down the year 2000 cereal import needs of developing countries (Table 7.8), and this is no doubt the source of the major differences between OECD and developing country liberalisation. In aggregate, the fall occurs primarily in Asia (by 20 million tons), and, to a much smaller extent, in the North Africa/Middle East region. Sub-Saharan and Latin American cereal import needs actually rise marginally in volume terms (by 6 million tons). However, in terms of financial costs, even in the sub-Saharan case, the total import bill is reduced by trade liberalisation, and, for Asia and the North Africa/Middle East region, it is dramatically reduced. Essentially, this is the result of falling cereal product prices. These value falls are in real terms.

Developing country export prospects

The trade projections under different policy scenarios may seem somewhat pessimistic about the longer-term export prospects for developing countries. Essentially, the "pessimism" — which is discussed in Chapter 6 — comes from the supply side. Most of the available projections reviewed in Chapter 6 imply that increased trade in major food products — with or without trade liberalisation — will not lead to greatly increased developing country export volumes. It may be that the projections and the projection methodology (essentially, the supply elasticities) are too modest because they incorporate assumptions that effective agricultural reforms will not happen. It is also the case that developing country domestic markets rise more rapidly with agricultural policy reforms. Agricultural policy reform may also lead to shifts in the product composition of both agricultural production and exports. For example, in the Centre's Thai case study, some of the agricultural policy reform scenarios, although raising overall agricultural output and productivity, push down the projected net agricultural exports[17].

Developing country supply elasticities used in the available projections of world trade may be too low. It may also be that quantitative analysis does not adequately take account of the extent to which "protectionism" (in both OECD, Eastern European and developing country markets) is reflected in qualitative restraints on imports from particular sources. Thus, the quantitative projections could understate the real export prospects for some developing exporters.

Conclusions

Our focus of analysis is on the relationship between policy-induced changes and the underlying trends. The conclusion is that agricultural policy reform in OECD countries is an important factor affecting longer-term developing country food and agricultural issues, but that policy reforms within the developing countries themselves are of even greater importance. This does not imply that present OECD efforts towards reform are mistaken: on the contrary, important benefits would accrue, but these would be primarily within the OECD countries themselves. Indirectly, there would be benefits also to the world economy, and to the world trading system, and thus to developing countries and developing country food production and the food security of poor people. The results presented also suggest that the most significant effects of agricultural policy reform would be outside the basic food sector — in livestock or processed products.

The discussion is primarily focused on temperate foodstuffs (including sugar), both because these are most relevant to developing countries' food concerns and because they are central to OECD agricultural policies. However, they only account for around one third of developing countries' agricultural exports. This leads to two rather surprising conclusions about reform of **OECD** agricultural policies. First, in spite of the massive protection and cost of the policies, their total elimination would have a modest effect on developing countries. This is, of course, a "net" result: there would be winners and losers. The biggest winners would be the OECD countries themselves, and the losers those countries which are dependent on temperate food imports. Food security concerns cannot therefore be ignored, for although liberalisation will provide overall gains, the very real threat to poor people, particularly urban consumers in food importing countries, needs to be addressed.

Of course, other OECD policies relating to non-temperate agricultural products and to processed products could lift the export earnings of developing countries and the range of countries involved might ensure that food security was favourably affected. Those policies and products are largely outside the scope of this study. Similarly, there would be indirect positive macroeconomic effects on the world economy, although it would be hazardous to predict the extent to which this would improve food security.

On the other hand, the usual hypotheses about OECD agricultural reform's effects, via international prices, on developing countries' food producers and consumers also seem to be of less importance than is sometimes stressed. The projections show that, with the important exception of sugar, any price effects would in the medium and long term be offset by the underlying downward trend in world prices.

Policies and developments in the **Eastern European Economies** could have a considerable influence on world markets for our products, both because they are potentially large "swing" traders (Chapter 6 suggests that they will remain considerable net importers) and because their trading activities have not always been predictable or transparent.

By contrast, **developing countries**' agricultural policy changes could have relatively large effects on world markets for these temperate products. More neutral policies towards agriculture (reducing negative protection) would push down world prices. Food self-sufficiency levels would generally rise, and the import cereal bill would generally fall, including for sub-Saharan Africa.

NOTES

1. The Development Centre organised jointly with the World Bank in October 1989 a seminar to review the state of economic modelling of agricultural trade policy reform. See Goldin and Knudsen.
2. Zietz and Valdés (1989).
3. An exception concerns certain (primarily European) imports of animal feedstuffs (primarily cassava from Thailand). These are heavily influenced by OECD agricultural policies.
4. This section draws heavily on notes prepared by Albert Simantov.
5. See Siamwalla *et al.*
6. For an overview of this study's results, see Krueger, Schiff and Valdés.
7. For a review of the various objectives of policies, see Winters (1988).
8. These are summarised in the World Bank's *World Development Report* for 1986.
9. Winters (1987).
10. Burniaux *et al.*; OECD (1990); and Goldin and Knudsen.
11. OECD (1989a).
12. Burniaux *et al.* in Chapter 10 of Goldin and Knudsen.
13. Winters (1987).
14. Centre for International Economics.
15. Krueger, Schiff and Valdés.
16. See e.g. Krueger *et al.*, Anderson, Vollrath.
17. See Siamwalla *et al.*

Chapter 8

INTERNATIONAL COMPARATIVE ADVANTAGE AND PRODUCTION COSTS[1]

Introduction

This chapter aims to examine the available theory and evidence concerning comparative advantage in the context of the longer-term trends in basic food and agriculture. The theory of comparative advantage attempts to explain why countries trade, how far they should trade in particular commodities and what resulting trade patterns will emerge. It investigates the extent to which we may apply notions of comparative advantage to the analysis of future prospects in agricultural production and trade in OECD and developing countries. It examines the theory and the measurement of comparative advantage with a view to understanding trends in production and trade in agriculture. However, most of the empirical research is "static", in that it compares costs of production or establishes production functions at a certain point in time.

The following discussion has three sections. First, the theoretical considerations are briefly introduced so far as they relate to agriculture. Second, some of the empirical research is introduced. Third, some of the important issues are taken up, particularly insofar as they relate to the other themes of this report.

The theory of comparative advantage

The theory of comparative advantage attempts to explain why countries trade, how far they should trade in particular commodities and what we expect to happen. Here, we consider how far the theory can help us with normative and policy issues, on the one hand, and with future projections, on the other hand. Most discussion has been in the framework of neo-classical theory, but there have been conflicting trends. It has proved difficult to validate the theoretical propositions in terms of international trade statistics, even with considerable refinement and sophistication of the theory. This has led in recent years to "new" trade theories, which incorporate hypotheses that do not come directly from neo-classical theory.

The notion of "comparative advantage" as a determinant of international trade comes from Ricardo. Subsequently, the principle of comparative advantage has come to be accepted as an almost universal law of economics. Essentially, there have been two conflicting strands in the development of comparative advantage theory, which can be labelled as "Ricardo" and "Heckscher-Ohlin", and the conflict between them is especially relevant to agriculture. In Ricardian comparative advantage, trade is driven by technology. Countries use different production techniques to produce the same commodity, and this shows up in different levels of factor productivity.

In the Heckscher-Ohlin development of "comparative advantage", by contrast, trade results from different initial factor endowments. Countries import goods which require relatively large amounts of factors which are in relatively short supply and thus expensive. They export goods whose production requires relatively large amounts of factors with which they are relatively well-endowed. There is little emphasis on variations in technology.

While Ricardo placed emphasis on physical and natural influences over competitiveness, technological and human factors were given weight by later economists.

The negative results of tests of the factor-proportions theory have left international economists searching for alternative explanations of trade patterns. The studies in the comparative statics of growth and trade were followed by the Oniki-Uzawa dynamic model in which the capital-labour ratios of the countries became the endogenous variables, whose ultimate values are derived from technology, the savings functions and population growth. These models facilitated the comparison between short-run comparative advantage, determined by the capital-labour ratio, and long-run comparative advantage, determined by the propensity to save and population growth.

Inevitably, a general problem with the development of the theory is that, as it moves away from its original simplicity, it becomes increasingly difficult to verify empirically, or to be used for policy analysis and projections. In particular, for most practical purposes, commodity and country disaggregation are required. Thus, most of the empirical work — especially for policy purposes — is only loosely based on theoretical assumptions, although it retains the language, the concepts and the analytical insights of comparative advantage theory.

More recently, the underlying assumptions of international trade have been challenged, with the focus on the institutional, technological and other historical factors accounting for the imperfectly competitive nature of international trade. The "New Trade Theory" developed by Krugman and others does not negate comparative advantage, but it does emphasize that factor endowments are themselves inadequate explanations of international trade. [See Goldin (1990c) for a discussion of the different theories and a comprehensive bibliography.]

The theory and agriculture

Clearly, these differences in emphasis are relevant to the discussion of agricultural trade. As one recent review puts it: "On the one hand, a resource-based theory which emphasizes differing land, rural labour and capital endowments seems important in distinguishing agricultural development possibilities among nations. A land rich nation with abundant agricultural capital should be expected to be a significant agricultural producer. On the other hand, technologies upon which agricultural production is based surely differ across countries. What is needed is a synthesis of the two approaches"[2].

The original Ricardian concern with agriculture appears to have been of peripheral interest in the subsequent literature on comparative advantage, which, almost without exception, focuses on industry in the developed world. The recent interest in comparative advantage has tended to renew the emphasis on technological explanations of trade in manufactures. To the extent that developing countries have been included in the analysis, the concern has been with industrial competitiveness and not with developing country agriculture.

To the extent that economists have applied the theory of comparative advantage to agriculture and to developing countries they may be broadly categorised as falling within one of two schools. On the one hand there are those who appear keen to defend the guiding classical principle of comparative advantage, according to which growth is promoted by specialisation. The neo-classicists draw their inspiration from Ricardo, Mill and Marshall, while their critics are inspired by Schumpeter, Williams and others who have argued that comparative advantage is essentially a static concept that ignores a variety of dynamic elements. They have shown that the modern version of the comparative cost doctrine is essentially a simplified version of static general equilibrium theory. The optimum pattern of production and trade for a country is determined from a comparison of the opportunity cost of producing a given commodity with the price at which the commodity can be imported or exported[3] .

In recent years, Abbott, Thompson and Haley have specifically addressed the question of comparative advantage in agriculture (see e.g. Haley and Abbott). They draw on the Ricardo-Viner modelling tradition in the development of a three-factor (including land) model of agricultural trade. Emphasis is placed on the role of the short-run rigidity of sector-specific capital stocks, the role of qualitative differences in land endowments, and on non-homothetic preferences. The model is comparative static, in that long-run, full equilibrium adjustment is considered, and not the path of that adjustment.

The question of the adjustment path is the focus of a recent investigation by Haley and Abbott into the determinants of comparative advantage in agriculture. Their study indicates that nations dependent on agricultural trade tend to have capital-intensive agricultural systems and that demand factors (population and income growth) differentiate net agricultural exporters from importers. Also important is their finding that on the margin, natural resource conditions alone do not serve to differentiate nations on the basis of production or trade. For natural resources to have an impact on production, there must be investment; agricultural capital complements rather than substitutes for land or other natural resources endowments.

The role of investment, as well as natural resource endowment, in determining comparative advantage is clearly revealed in the recent work of Abbott and others. Their model cannot however be used to operationalise the analysis of changing comparative advantage. This is particularly the case for developing countries, where analysis of comparative advantage needs to include a recognition of the possibility of structural disequilibrium in factor markets; the inclusion of indirect (market and non-market) effects of expanding a given type of production; simultaneous determination of levels of consumption, imports and variations in the demand for exports.

Such a framework has not yet been constructed. Neither are we able to assume, as is the case in the literature cited above, that trade is a proxy for comparative advantage. Due to distortions, it need not reflect factor endowments or costs. It is to a consideration of these elements — and competitive, rather than comparative, advantage — that we now turn.

Different empirical approaches

Costs and prices

The estimation of factor costs poses serious difficulties, if the results are to be used as the basis for international comparisons. In order to bypass the problems posed by production costs estimates, international comparisons may be based simply on production data. For example, it is possible to compare yields, labour productivity, energy use or other production parameters without reference to input costs or prices.

For those interested in comparative advantage, these data are of vital importance. Technical data do not however provide an adequate account of the allocation of resources. Some measure of the efficiency of production and the allocation of scarce resources within a country is required in order to assess comparative advantage. To the extent that costs present the best guide to the demand and supply for resources, they are an essential element in an analysis of comparative advantage.

Numerous problems arise when attempting to derive production cost comparisons. Leaving aside the problem of finding comparable cost data, initial difficulties include the question of whether to use shadow or nominal prices. Almost inevitably, difficulties also are encountered in the determination of exchange rates and the valuation of capital, land and labour. Various attempts have been made to evade some of these obstacles. One approach is simply to say that costs are revealed in final product prices. High product prices reflect high costs and low domestic costs reflect low production costs.

The equivalence of prices with costs is attractive because prices are generally more transparent than costs. However, this equivalence neglects the distortions arising from market power as well as from subsidies, quotas, taxes, tariffs and other institutional interventions in the market.

Land, labour and capital

Any comparative cost analysis faces problems about the valuation of land, labour and capital. These are taken up further below and explored in Goldin's study on comparative advantage.

Joint products

The question of joint production and joint products poses serious problems in the estimation of agricultural production costs. A high proportion of the total production costs for many agricultural commodities is not directly attributable to a single enterprise. Many fixed costs as well as variable costs for the use of land, machinery, labour and management are often not easily divisible by product. The identification of the product itself may cause difficulties, and one agricultural crop may be identifiable with different sub-products, for example sugar cane with raw sugar, molasses and bagasse. In addition, many crops are grown in rotation, which raises questions not only about the allocation of land, labour and capital values but also regarding the allocation of costs of soil enrichment or the erosion reducing impact of the rotational crops.

The fact that factors of production generally have many uses means that changes in the value of one application impact throughout the system, although to differing degrees. For this reason changes in the value of one crop affect the costs of production of other crops. Furthermore, this interdependency extends well beyond the agricultural sector, so that changes within the manufacturing or services sector lead to changes in factor costs in the agricultural sector.

The diversity of production cost studies is evident from the sample of studies reviewed by Goldin (1990c). The range of methodologies and countries and crops offered undermines attempts to piece together the jigsaw of changing comparative advantage. The problem is aggravated further by the apparent absence of time series data of sufficient quality and length to enable an analysis of global or even national trends. The existing studies tend to be associated with no more than a dozen institutions. Among the most widely known are those of the USDA and notably its annual "Costs of Production" studies of the US farm sector.

In addition to its national studies, the USDA has been associated with international cost comparisons. Such studies include the 1986 examination of the international competitiveness of US wheat and the comparative study undertaken by Cornell University, on production costs for cereals in the European Community and the United States. The question of agricultural competitiveness is also the direct concern of the US International Trade Commission (ITC). The ITC has to date conducted studies which include comparative analysis of countries exporting oilseeds, citrus, meat, flowers and certain vegetables to the United States, and these studies may well yield much of value to those interested in factor costs. In this context, it is also worth considering the work of the US Office of Technology Assessment (OTA) which in 1986 engaged in a major review of US competitiveness in agricultural trade. The OTA study provides particularly valuable perspectives on technology influences on agricultural competitiveness.

The FAO's "Economic Accounts for Agriculture" between 1961 and 1977 provided a useful data source for comparisons of production costs. It would appear that the FAO no longer publishes a detailed analysis of production costs outside of its annual fertilizer yearbook, which measures the application and cost of the principal chemical fertilizers.

The Farm Accountancy Data Network (FADN) has been established under EEC sponsorship to provide annual data on farm income, expenses and returns in each of the member states. The majority of EEC countries have not yet systematised their national cost data on an annual basis. National estimates tend to under-represent small producers and therefore underestimate the average production costs. Furthermore, national averages tend to mask regional differences as well as intra-regional differences, so that the national average may not provide an accurate reflection of the situation facing farmers either in particular regions or even nationally.

While farm cost data in OECD countries is far from complete, it compares very favourably with that of developing countries. Available data suggests that a comparison of costs in OECD countries is a feasible undertaking. International comparisons of production costs which include developing countries are much more problematic.

The comparative depth of the national data in Western Europe and the United States has facilitated comparisons such as that carried out by Prof. Stanton of Cornell University. His study compares production costs for cereals in the European

Community with the United States for the period 1977 to 1984. Using similar farm accounting data, it may also be possible to compare costs in other commodities and perhaps even to extend the coverage to other data-rich regions of the world, such as Canada, Australia and Japan. International comparisons of production costs which include developing countries are much more problematic.

Engineering cost approach

Among the groups currently examining the question of international comparisons of factor costs are two who share in common a methodological bias in favour of the engineering cost approach and a concern to compare developed and developing countries using a commodity specific approach. The engineering cost approach provides the framework for the international studies of production costs being undertaken at the Mediterranean Agronomic Institute (IAMM) in Montpellier and at Landell Mills Commodities Studies (LMCS) in Oxford.

IAMM, in the context of its convention with the French Ministry of Agriculture and the Planning Commission, has used engineering cost components to build a linear programming model designed to analyse international differences in production costs (Flichman). In its simplest form, the model examines one product and assumes all prices are given. The model shows the efficiency of different technologies and provides perspectives on the choice of minimum cost technology. Rent is a residual within the model and is not itself included as a factor cost input. This is not a shortcoming of the model but reflects the fact that the model aims to examine international comparisons of efficiency.

An interesting feature of the Montpellier model is its use of the Erosion Productivity Impact Calculator (EPIC), devised by Texas A&M University in association with the USDA. EPIC provides a framework for associating different inputs and the intensity of their application with the output. Plant growth and biomass formation are specified according to genetic criteria which then interact with climatical, soil and other significant input factors. The model was devised to examine erosion and is being adapted by the Mediterranean Agronomic Institute to provide the coefficients required in a comprehensive engineering cost approach to comparing technological efficiency in production. To date, comparisons of the efficiency of production of maize, wheat, sunflower and soybean production have been made between different regions of France, Argentina and the United States.

The extent to which the EPIC model could be adapted to analyse factor costs and comparative advantage requires further investigation. Among the factors which need to be introduced are land values and shadow prices and differential exchange rates. The exclusion of land costs and of taxes and subsidies from the analysis means that the IAMM studies provide an incomplete examination of competitiveness, although they do provide an indication of relative economic efficiency.

The engineering cost model developed by Landell Mills Commodities Studies of Oxford is not based on the genetically specific coefficients provided by the EPIC framework, although the LMCS cost analysis is also based on a system of "technical blueprints". To date, LMCS has developed comprehensive international comparisons of production costs for sugar, rubber, oilseeds, cocoa and coffee. For each crop, the production process is divided into a number of distinct sub-processes. For each such sub-process, various options or technologies are distinguished.

The accuracy of the production cost estimates derived from engineering cost models reflects the underlying cost data and technology assumptions. An advantage of the engineering cost approach is that, in general, costs assembled for the analysis of one crop are applicable to other applications, so that the extension of the analysis to additional crops requires the estimation of new technological coefficients and an extension, but not laborious redetermination, of the cost data. A further advantage of the engineering cost approach is that it lends itself to sensitivity and time series analysis. A further advantage of the engineering cost approaches is that they lend themselves to linear programming and therefore could be used to determine optimum patterns of technological transformation. For example, the application of the engineering cost data to linear programming could determine the least cost technology. Such information has many uses, including the analysis of investment opportunities.

However, the failure of the engineering cost approaches adequately to deal with issues associated with the valuation of land, labour and capital, and, especially for developing countries, the choice of exchange rate, erodes the credibility of these international cost comparisons. Comparisons of costs, including those using engineering cost methodologies, require extensive comparable cost data. In the final analysis, it is the absence of these and the practically prohibitive data collection and measurement problems involved, which preclude a comprehensive analysis of relative costs embracing developing countries.

Revealed comparative advantage

Balassa and others have suggested that in the absence of sufficient data on factor costs it may be possible to indicate revealed comparative advantage by examining the trade performance of individual countries. This is defined as the share of a product group in one country's exports divided by that product group's share of world trade. The assumption is that the commodity pattern of trade reflects relative costs as well as differences in non-price factors and that comparative advantage can be expected to determine the structure of exports. The higher the net exports within a particular commodity group, the greater the revealed comparative advantage. Balassa, however, restricted his analysis to manufactured goods on the grounds that distortions in primary product trade meant that this trade would not reflect comparative advantage. To what extent, it may be asked, may models of agricultural trade liberalisation, which examine the implications of the removal of distortions, provide insights into comparative advantage?

Several such models have been introduced in preceding chapters in relation to the projections and to the analysis of agricultural policy (Goldin and Knudsen). It is worth considering whether these trade liberalisation studies offer a means to identify revealed trends in costs and comparative advantage.

In the FAO projections (Alexandratos), no production functions which embrace costs and technology are specified. The question therefore arises whether it is possible to identify trends in comparative advantage through the projections. In part this depends on how one defines comparative advantage; if comparative advantage reflects costs (rather than costs plus government and other support) the projections may not be able to help us, for they implicitly assume the continuation of current support levels. In addition, the assumption that there will be a tendency towards self-sufficiency among the major developing country deficit countries may bias the FAO projections against trade based on comparative advantage.

The IIASA study (Parikh) applies a general equilibrium approach to an examination of the removal of distortions between trade (border) prices and domestic prices. For the purposes of examining revealed comparative advantage, the scenario in which all market economies liberalise is most relevant. The IIASA study notes that when more countries remove distortions, the scope for exploiting comparative advantage increases, and global gains in efficiency should result. The model assumes that agricultural trade is fully liberalised in 1986 so that between that year and the year 2000 domestic prices in a country equal its trade prices. The broad pattern is that when agricultural prices increase with trade liberalisation countries put more factors into agricultural production. However, global production levels have to be consistent with global demand, and because the changes in demand for agricultural products due to liberalisation are small, changes in total global production levels are modest. These changes provide an indication of revealed comparative advantage. However, the IIASA model, like all the other trade liberalisation models, is based on elasticity estimates derived from historical production and consumption trends. It does not reveal factor costs and provides only a schematic consideration of production functions (production functions are derived for land, labour and capital using shadow prices) and no endogenous technical change.

In addition to providing important insights into comparative advantage, the modelling of agricultural liberalisation emphasizes the relationship between international and domestic interventions. The global general equilibrium models, and a number of the partial models, such as that of Valdés and Zietz (Zietz and Valdés 1986 and 1989), review the implications of different macroeconomic policies on production and trade. They highlight the extent to which macroeconomic policy influences relative costs and national, as well as international, resource allocation.

Prior to the development in the 1980s of trade liberalisation models, and in particular, prior to the application of general equilibrium analysis to the examination of resource allocation, a number of research institutes sponsored the development of measures of revealed comparative advantage.

One obvious hypothesis is that revealed comparative advantage for poor countries is linked to economic growth. This has been illustrated for three East Asian countries by Anderson, in his study for the Development Centre. More generally, he has demonstrated a strong negative correlation between, on the one hand, income per head, and, on the other hand, agriculture's share of gross domestic product, employment and exports in a cross-sectional regression analysis of 70 countries with populations in excess of one million (based on World Bank data for 1981). In the case of the agricultural share in exports, there was also a significant negative correlation with population density per unit of agricultural land. For the three East Asian countries, agriculture's share of GDP, employment and exports has declined steadily over the past three decades, with the share in exports falling, for Korea, from 89 per cent in 1956 to 5 per cent in 1987, and for Taiwan, from 92 per cent in 1953 to 6 per cent in 1987 (see Table 8.1).

These results support theoretical considerations which suggest "that a poor country opening up to international trade will have large shares of production and employment in the primary sectors, particularly agriculture, but that these will decline with economic growth. Initially the country's trade will tend to specialise in the export of primary products, though less so the more densely populated the country. The proportion of those primary exports that is agricultural will be larger, the greater this country's endowment of agricultural land relative to minerals compared with that ratio globally. If the country's domestic incomes and capita to labour ratio grow more rapidly than the rest of the world's, its export specialisation will gradually switch away from primary products (in raw or lightly processed form) to manufactures in the absence of distortionary policies."[4]

The dynamic comparative advantage model developed by Haley and Abbott yields interesting insights for international comparative advantage in agriculture.

The model has identified key components to a cross-sectional study of agricultural trade. They are resource availability and allocation (which includes the level of capital accumulation), relative agricultural prices, income and savings behavior. It has emphasized that initial conditions on factor allocations are important in accounting for the flow of trade. This stems from the fact that factor mobility in and out of agriculture is imperfect. Moreover, the existing levels of land and sector-specific labour and capital, as well as implemented techniques, affect the marginal productivities upon which reallocation of resources is based[5].

The changes in the trade mix over time are attributed to changes in production and consumption behaviour. For the former the important determinants are the changes in primary factors and in the sector-specific capital stock. The formulation stresses that initial conditions can have a substantial impact on the direction and magnitude of the change. Differing initial conditions among countries are hypothesised to be important explainers of differing production responses. For consumption, changes in per capita income, population and savings behaviours account for changes in demand for agricultural goods. Production and consumption changes simultaneously considered can help explain the changes in agricultural trade patterns over time[6].

The data involved in the regressions, primarily from the World Bank, involved 98 countries for the years 1960, 1965, 1970 and 1977. Countries were grouped geographically and according to the classification: net exporter, self-sufficient and net importer. Indicators (ratios) were developed. The ratios have certain implications for differentiating nations on the basis of agricultural trade status. For export countries, land is an abundant resource, and demand pressures from large populations are low. The productivity of rural labour exceeds that of the self-sufficient but not that of the import countries. This is not true, however, for the industrialised countries where labour productivity for the export countries is highest. For import countries, land is more scarce and demand pressures from large populations relative to agricultural potential are high. For the self-sufficient countries, land is a scarce resource, and demand pressures relative to agricultural potential are moderate. Use of capital in agriculture is least for these self-sufficient countries[7].

The conclusions from the regression analysis have more validity and some suggest very interesting conclusions. First, the availability of "raw" land was hardly significant, while "improved" land is important in explaining trade status. Second, countries more dependent on agricultural trade tend to have more capital-intensive agriculture. Third, labour and capital are relatively substitutable, while land tends to complement both labour and capital. Fourth, the results confirm the importance of "demand" factors — per capita income, population, savings and declining share of agricultural goods in consumption — in explaining trade status. Fifth, "trade resistance factors" — especially undervalued exchange rates and domestic price distortions — were found, surprisingly, to be unimportant.

Whereas Johnson and Balassa focused on manufacturing, Krueger and Anderson have extended the analysis to primary products. This modification separates out natural resources from the definition of capital. The analysis is thus of an economy with two tradable sectors, producing primary products and manufactures, and three factors of production: natural resources, which are specific to the primary sector, capital which is specific to the manufacturing sector, and labour which is used in both sectors and is mobile[8]. Comparative advantage between manufacturers and primary products is determined by the relative endowments of man-made capital and natural resources. Accordingly, as Anderson has empirically verified, with capital accumulation, a country gradually changes from being predominantly a primary producer to a producer of manufacturers. As Anderson has shown, the theory suggests that a poor country opening up to international trade will have large shares of production and employment in the primary sectors, particularly agriculture, but that these will decline with economic growth. Furthermore, the fact that capital is required in addition to natural resources and labour in primary production strengthens the conclusion that natural-resource-poor, densely populated countries will begin manufacturing at an earlier stage of capital availability per worker than resource-rich countries.

Revealed comparative advantage: the rice example

International comparisons of factor costs in rice production within Asia have been greatly facilitated by studies undertaken by the Food Research Institute, Resources for the Future and the Asian Development Bank.

The study undertaken under the auspices of the Food Research Institute (FRI) includes two major rice exporters, Thailand and the United States, and two importers nearing self-sufficiency, Philippines and Taiwan. The project measures comparative advantage in rice production, first, among regions, seasons or techniques within single countries and, second, across several countries.

The FRI analysis builds on the formula that a country has a comparative advantage in rice production if the social opportunity costs of producing an incremental unit of rice are less than the border price of rice. The analysis is based on the measurement of net social opportunity costs and hence on the distinction between social and private profitability. Relative comparative advantage across countries is measured by ranking each countries' ratio of the domestic resource costs (DRC) per unit of foreign exchange earned or saved to the shadow price of foreign exchange.

Within countries, the DRC approach allows a comparison of the relative efficiencies of region of production or of alternative technologies. International comparisons of efficiency are derived from the ranking of the regions or techniques with the lowest DRC coefficients in each country. After allowing for price differentials due to quality differentials, the study concludes that Thailand appears to have a substantial advantage for both first and second crop production over the other countries studied.

Although the DRC does not capture the effects of technical change, technological change influences the patterns of comparative advantage (and DRC coefficients) in the future. The study consequently is able to conclude that, except for Thailand, the technologies surveyed were inefficient at prevailing prices, implying that subsidisation and/or the introduction of new technologies would be necessary to maintain existing production levels in the United States, Taiwan and the Philippines.

The study also concluded that labour costs in the four countries surveyed were of similar importance in determining comparative advantage. This tends to support the contention that increases in per unit labour costs and decreases in labour usage have been largely offsetting throughout the process of technological change in the production of rice.

The FRI conclusions are derived from a comparative static analysis and a full consideration is not given to trends in labour use and labour cost. By contrast, the Resources for the Future (RFF) examination of the Asian rice economy explicitly examines trends in labour use and productivity. The difficulties associated with measuring labour costs or returns to labour, and notably the difficulty of measuring the family labour input, are highlighted in the Resources for the Future study. The study concludes that although labour productivity has been steadily increasing throughout the Asian rice growing world this has only been associated with a sustained growth in real wages in East Asia (excluding China). The Resources for the Future study does not however attempt to conduct a comparative analysis of wages or other costs; the concern is simply with assessing trends within each country.

The Asian Development Bank (ADB) in recent years has conducted case studies on the rice economy in Korea, Malaysia, Bangladesh, India and Indonesia. The Indonesian case study is explicitly concerned with the question of comparative advantage. The other studies focus on the question of rice market intervention policies, although indications of revealed comparative advantage may be gleaned from the data concerning the differences between domestic and border prices in those countries. An interesting conclusion of the Indonesian case study is that although Indonesia's remarkable success in increasing rice production has been achieved through deliberate government intervention, its comparative advantage is now being reduced through the promotion by the government of inefficient paddy production.

The ADB study of Indonesia, in common with the studies conducted by FRI, measures comparative advantage in terms of the domestic resource cost (DRC) of foreign exchange earned/saved from rice production. The DRC is viewed as the economic value of domestic resources (primary non-traded factors of production) in domestic currency units necessary for earning or saving a unit of foreign exchange. If the DRC for rice is less than the appropriate price of foreign exchange or the shadow exchange rate (SER), then comparative advantage exists in rice production.

The DRC technique used in the ADB and FRI studies compares prevailing technologies within and across countries at a given point in time. The assumptions of constant cost technologies and zero elasticities of input substitution (fixed production coefficients) mean that the determination of comparative advantage is static. The DRC analysis provides useful insights in the understanding of existing differences in production patterns and technologies, but cannot capture the effects of technical change, and can only be used in a dynamic sense if production technologies and growth patterns do not alter input mixes and factor costs. This seriously undermines the use of DRCs to determine trends in comparative advantage.

The DRC approach to the measurement of revealed comparative advantage is conducted with reference to border or traded prices which in themselves may not reflect international competitive equilibrium prices. For example, in the case of rice, less than 5 per cent of world production is traded and any major shift in production seriously impacts on the world price. The partial and static nature of the DRC technique limits its usefulness as an indicator of long-term comparative advantage. In many applications it may provide a useful proxy for a factor costs analysis of comparative advantage, but in others offers no short cut to the exploration of comparative advantage. It would appear therefore, that international comparisons of factor costs remain a vital element in the understanding of changing comparative advantage in agriculture.

Issues and conclusions

Probably the most difficult problems about the analysis of comparative advantage in agriculture concern the related issues of the valuation of labour, land and capital employed. In some crude sense, these items correspond to "value added" in agriculture. Their share in the total cost of food to the consumer is surprisingly low and falling, and so far as export crops are concerned, the same argument probably also applies. However, this is primarily due to the influence of "downstream" off-farm activities. If the analysis is made at the level of farm-gate prices, the share of purchased inputs is frequently very small.

A major part of the problem comes from the supposition that none of these three factors (labour, land or capital) is very mobile in the short run. Thus, their opportunity cost is difficult to assess from the available statistics. Moreover, there are typically "institutional" constraints. So, it is frequently very difficult to judge how far agricultural incomes would have to fall before farm labour, especially with self-employed labour, moved out of agriculture.

A central problem with the assessment of land and labour costs is that much of the notional returns are really returns to management or to capital investment. It is difficult to identify or isolate these elements, and still more to assess their importance for international comparisons of comparative advantage. Microeconomic studies suggest that there can be very large differences in "returns" to plots of land with the same agronomic conditions and producing the same products.

Land, of course, can shift between crops and livestock activities or be taken out of agriculture altogether. However, the market for land is frequently "narrow" and fragmented, with institutional constraints. Moreover, if the focus of the analysis is on fairly radical counterfactual assumptions about agricultural prospects (coming from technology or policy changes), existing land market prices may not give much guidance to farmer responses. More generally, in economic research (e.g. Flichman) and the "real" world of (very narrow) land markets, returns to land (and therefore, land prices) are greatly influenced by institutional considerations (most obviously, fiscal regimes and land tenure legislation, but also credit facilities etc.).

As noted above, land needs to be considered together with capital. "Raw" land has very little value in most circumstances, and comparative advantage comes from the application of capital investment in various ways. One must admit, of course, that there are "inherent" natural advantages: the Montpellier studies (Flichman) come close to concluding that Argentine wheat production must be more efficient than French production, on any plausible price assumptions for inputs and outputs (in spite of the much greater application of capital to the most efficient French wheat lands). In agronomic terms, the Argentinean Pampas wheatlands are simply more productive than the French wheatlands (in the Beauce region).

Nevertheless, most of the discussion of agricultural comparative advantage is about "improved" land and, therefore, about capital investment. There are two broad problems here. The first is that much on-farm capital investment takes the form of family labour inputs, and is, therefore, very difficult to quantify. The second is that off-farm investment in physical and human infrastructure seems very important: again this is difficult to assess or quantify.

An emphasis on capital accumulation as a decisive determinant of comparative advantage takes one into the area of macroeconomic policies and the interactions between food agriculture, other agriculture and the rest of the national economy. Such an analysis has been undertaken for the Development Centre by Mundlak, Cavallo and Domenech.

To the extent that we are especially interested in the comparative advantage of poor farmers, the analysis needs further elaboration. It is plausible that most of the on-farm investment of these farmers takes the form of labour inputs in land improvement. It is also plausible that these farmers are very dependent on the services coming from public investment in physical and human infrastructure. However, the available statistics do not reveal how far poor farmers benefit from public infrastructure investment, but most evidence does suggest that they are disfavoured in relation to larger farmers.

The role of demand in the discussion of international comparative advantage in basic food products should be stressed. Most developing countries and most poor people are not producing food for export markets. There is a big "wedge" between export and import border prices for basic food products, which gives a substantial natural protection to local producers. Much of the discussion (as in Mellor or Anderson) is about the relative rates of growth of national food consumption and production and the consequential effects on comparative advantage, and about the macroeconomic implications of financing basic food imports if consumption is rising faster than production. One implication of this is that analysis of comparative advantage needs to be examined within a general equilibrium framework.

A central concern of this study has been with the effects of agricultural and macroeconomic policies on world trade in food products (and, thus, on developing country food consumption). This is related to the discussion of international comparative advantage. On the whole, the results of available analysis, reviewed below, suggest that fairly small shifts would occur from changes in OECD policies, and somewhat larger shifts from changes in developing countries' own policies. Of course, this type of analysis is driven by supply and demand elasticities which reflect, but do not make explicit, assumptions about comparative advantage. Nevertheless, the results from the Haley/Abbott study reviewed above suggest that trade policy distortions cannot explain much about trade in agricultural products.

A major issue in the discussion of international comparative advantage is the present "narrowness" of international markets in food products. For most of the empirical analysis above it is important to take international prices as a point of reference for the comparative advantage discussion. Yet, with international trade representing a fairly small proportion of world production or consumption of major food products, and with very large fluctuations in international product prices, one could doubt the relevance of international prices to international comparative advantage analysis. However, as noted above, policy shifts may have relatively limited direct effects on world markets, although they may either increase or decrease their instability.

It has been argued that there are problems about the "small country" assumptions in most comparative advantage discussions. Essentially, the assumption is that no country can influence international prices, either as an importer or an exporter. There is a related problem for international policy advice, which has been termed the "fallacy of composition" or "adding-up" problem. Even if each small country is a "price taker", if they are all encouraged (most obviously, by the World Bank/IMF) to simultaneously follow their "international comparative advantage", as dictated by international prices, the outcome may be shifts in supply, demand and world prices, which would leave at least some of them worse off. Given the "narrowness" of most basic food products, it is obvious that one must expect that some countries (most obviously, China) will be able to influence world markets and world prices through their own purchases or sales and that groups of small countries may have similar effects.

Conclusion

A key problem is that the notion of comparative advantage is essentially static and refers to the optimisation of resource allocation at a given time. It aims to identify the configuration of products that a country can produce given existing factor endowments and technologies and assuming free trade. The emphasis on national resource allocation may mean that a country can lose its competitiveness in some product relative to another country, and yet the production of that product may still be in accordance with the country's comparative advantage.

Among the strengths of the neo-classical relation between factor costs and trade is its logical coherence. In a neo-classical world production will tend to be determined on a basis of costs. In such a world, costs and prices are synonymous and trade is determined by comparative advantage. However, it is generally agreed that costs of labour, land and capital, especially in developing countries, do not reflect their opportunity costs with any accuracy because of market imperfections, although there is wide disagreement as to the extent of the typical discrepancies and how these may change over time.

The diversity of production cost studies is evident from the sample of studies covered in this review. The range of methodologies and countries and crops offered undermines attempts to piece together the jigsaw of changing comparative advantage. The problem is aggravated further by the apparent absence of time series data of sufficient quality and length to enable an analysis of global or even national trends.

The attempt to identify patterns of trade with factor costs is, however, as we have illustrated above, fraught with difficulties. Indeed, we have shown that factor costs are not directly revealed in trade and that there is no simple theoretical or empirical identification of trends in factor costs with trends in trade.

In order to second-guess comparative advantage, reference may be made to relative costs and competitive advantage. The discussion above has however shown that in practice the definition and measurement of factor costs is as difficult as that of factor endowments. Our review of some of the literature on the subject of factor costs reveals a number of clues regarding the difficulties and the potential insights offered by an analysis of factor costs. Clearly, theoretical, methodological and empirical obstacles remain in the way of an analysis of trends in factor costs. Further difficulties exist if we are to relate these trends in costs to comparative advantage. Various attempts, such as those evident in evaluations of "revealed comparative advantage", attempt to circumvent these difficulties. These are severely compromised by the fact that trade, particularly in agriculture, is severely distorted by non-market interventions.

Government and other interventions limit the extent to which comparative advantage is allowed to dictate patterns of international agricultural trade. To the extent that the 1990s will be associated with international trade liberalisation and that this will be accompanied by domestic liberalisation and structural adjustment, comparative advantage will play a greater role in production and trade. Trade liberalisation and the reduction of government support for agriculture may be expected to increase the significance of factor endowments and comparative advantage in an understanding of future trends in agricultural production and trade.

Developing countries are increasingly unable to afford distortions and appear most likely to engage in structural adjustments. For them, efficiency and cost can be expected to become more important. An awareness of the importance of comparative advantage is thus likely to become more important to both actual and potential developing country participants in agricultural trade, even if the meaning and estimation of this concept remain elusive.

NOTES

1. This chapter is based on a study prepared for the Centre by Ian Goldin (see Goldin, 1990c). However, the analysis here seeks to present the discussion of that paper in relation to the other themes of this report, and so the interpretation and conclusion are somewhat different.
2. See Haley and Abbott.
3. See Goldin (1990c); and Goldin and Knudsen.
4. See Anderson (1990), p. 22.
5. Haley and Abbott, pp. 2-3.
6. *Ibid.*
7. *Ibid.*
8. This analysis draws on Anderson (1990), pp. 17-31.

Chapter 9

CONCLUSIONS

Introduction

The study brings together research material on the relevance of international trends to developments in basic food and agriculture in developing countries. It is based on both research conducted by the Development Centre and an overview of other recent research. The starting point for this synthesis report is the hypothesis that the policy discussion of issues should be situated in the context of a medium- or longer-term quantitative framework of projections of demand, supply, trade and prices. This framework is presented in Chapters 2, 3 and 6 and is summarised in the next section. The hypothesis appears to be justified: the important shifts in the projected quantities of basic foodstuffs (essentially cereals) consumed, produced and, especially, traded and the expected price trends transform much of the policy discussion and the research agenda.

The overall conclusion of trying to locate the policy discussion into a longer-term quantitative framework is, inevitably, that we face huge uncertainties. This has, of course, research implications, but it also has some tentative policy implications. It is possible to conclude, as below, that agricultural policy and trade policy reform in OECD countries will prove more relevant to the OECD countries themselves than to poor country food and agriculture. The burden of development is largely on the developing countries themselves. Hence the capacity of these countries to "manage" agricultural development and food security is at the heart of the debate, which simultaneously has to embrace the uncertainties about technology and the environment.

This report is complementary to the other outputs of the Development Centre's research on "Changing Comparative Advantage in Food and Agriculture", especially the major volume on trade policy analysis[1] and the overview of current international policy concerns[2].

This study has addressed broad policy concerns, offering perspectives on:

i) What are the prospects for global markets in food products?

ii) How well is the world feeding its people?

iii) To what extent will technology trends continue to promote global food production and change the pattern of products demanded by consumers?

iv) How far will ecological trends and public perceptions about them affect production trends in developing and, still more, OECD countries?

v) How far will the growing industrialisation of the "food system" change the prospects for basic food consumption and production?

vi) What is the role of policies, in both developed and developing countries?

vii) How far are production costs and comparative advantage relevant to the likely outcomes and policy choices of developing countries?

The detailed conclusions on these different questions are presented at the end of the substantive chapters and are taken up below.

Behind these broad policy issues one can identify concerns which benefit from being discussed, but to which there are no easy answers. The most basic preoccupation concerns "governance". In the OECD countries, it is accepted that agricultural policies are driven by "lobbies", which reflect a complicated range of economic and social interests. More generally, the changing perception of social and political priorities, especially in relation to environmental concerns and the implications of developments in Eastern Europe, will have implications for food and agriculture; these perceptions will be mediated through "lobbies" and political processes, which are very difficult to capture in quantitative analysis. In the Eastern European countries and, still more, the poor developing countries, the problems of "governance" are pervasive and dominating. Most of the present analysis of agricultural trends and policies assumes that national governments can implement macroeconomic and food and agricultural policies, and even "strategies": to many observers, this is an optimistic assumption.

The "governance" issue is particularly important in the discussion of "food security" and, more generally, of "sustainable development", reviewed in Chapters 3 and 6, and taken up below. To the extent that national governments are incapable or unwilling to provide for their nutritionally deprived people or to combat environmental degradation, there are normative international policy implications and positive implications for longer-term prospects. These may include an increased reliance on self-help, local food self-sufficiency and local solutions to food security and ecological problems, but a central conclusion of this study is that international market trends will become more important and increasingly will interact with the food and agricultural situation of poor people[3].

Perceptions and judgments about technology and the "environment" reflect attitudes which are ultimately in the area of "beliefs" not facts. It is important to narrow the area of factual uncertainty, and this report seeks to promote this process by situating the discussion in a quantified framework and more or less known trends in technology and the environment. Ultimately, however, there remain "perceptions", "attitudes" or "beliefs" about "technology" and "ecology", which colour substantially assessments of likely developments, even for the medium term. These are probably more important than the analogous, and much more familiar, problems about "attitudes" to the role of market mechanisms.

A much more practical, but nevertheless central preoccupation concerns the shifting place of basic food in the structure of national economies, which even threatens the traditional notion of "subsistence" agriculture. The discussion in Chapters 3 and 4, reviewed below, suggests both that the share of off-farm inputs and downstream processing is increasing and that — even on optimistic assumptions — most employment opportunities generated by agriculturally based development strategies will not be in basic food production.

The following sections review in more detail the conclusions of the individual substantive chapters, starting with a presentation of the medium-term quantitative framework as a basis for the policy discussion. The final section pulls together conclusions, especially for research and policy priorities.

At this very general level of preoccupation, there are further, heterogeneous concerns which are of great importance, but which cannot easily be integrated into a coherent discussion of food and agriculture, largely because they are not reflected in the available statistical data or economic analysis, although they are obviously relevant to food and agriculture. These currently include: political and military conflicts, agriculture-based narcotics, smuggling, the AIDS epidemic (especially in Africa)[4], the role of women in food and agriculture, and, more generally, religious and cultural traditions. How far should these be taken into longer-term assessments of demand, supply, and trade, and into the associated policy discussion? Most food and agricultural analysis proceeds as though these problems cannot be explicitly taken into account. It would be convenient to assume that their impact on medium/longer-term outcomes will be random, and that, therefore, they should be ignored. This hardly seems plausible. At the least, some of these issues (political conflicts, narcotics and smuggling) already imply that the available statistical data may be subject to very large errors and biases. We would argue, however, that these do not invalidate the broad conclusions which emerge about demand trends (and especially nutrition), supply trends and perspectives for world trade.

At the policy level, recognition of the importance of these topics, and their "governance" implications, could reinforce scepticism about the role of national governments to manage basic food and agricultural policies, and point to a greater reliance on local solutions. However, the projected international market trends are likely to prevail, unless there is catastrophic political conflict.

An overview of the year 2000 projections

Since the central purpose of this research has been to situate the policy discussion in the context of longer trends, it is worth summarising the principal conclusions from the detailed discussions of consumption, production and trade prospects for major foodstuffs (Chapters 2, 3 and 6).

Taking cereals as a proxy for consumption of basic foodstuffs, consumption trends (annual average growth rates in volume terms) seem to be broadly as follows:

	World	OECD	Developing
1970-84	2.5	1.2	3.6
1984-2000	2.2	1.6	2.6

These results are a broad synthesis of the different projections reviewed in Chapter 2. An important deceleration is in prospect, especially in the developing countries. However, the greatest uncertainty concerns market growth in the OECD countries, in spite of the much lower growth rates already established in this region, and this reflects essentially uncertainties about livestock sector developments.

Taking FAO data and projections as an indicator of overall "agricultural demand", the deceleration is more modest. Average annual rates of growth decelerate between 1961-85 and 1984-2000 as follows: developing countries, from 3.5 per cent to 3.1 per cent; OECD countries, from 1.5 per cent to 0.8 per cent. This suggests that — apart from any statistical or projection differences — demand for non-basic foodstuffs will be more buoyant than for basic foodstuffs (including livestock products, represented as a proxy by feed grains).

The most striking feature of the production projections (Chapter 3) is that the medium-term deceleration is expected to occur primarily in developing countries. Thus, while total world cereals production growth would decelerate from 2.8 per cent in the 1970-84 period to 2.0 per cent in the 1984-2000 period, the corresponding decelerations would be from 2.8 per cent to 2.1 per cent for the OECD countries, and from 3.4 per cent to 2.0 per cent for the developing countries.

All the projections show a major sustained rise in world trade in basic foodstuffs, following the massive increases of the 1970s, even within the present protectionist world trading system. Net world trade in cereals could rise from some 60 million tons in 1984 to between 100 and 200 million tons in year 2000, and even the upper figure does not directly take account of the scope for policy reforms or a radical attack on food security issues. Developing countries' share of global imports would rise above 50 per cent and, perhaps, much higher. OECD countries would be the major source of world exports, with net exports perhaps doubling to above 200 million tons. It is difficult to overstate the importance of these conclusions for the discussion of agricultural policies and world trade.

World prices for major foodstuffs are projected to fall massively from their average levels in the past decade, for cereals by perhaps more than 50 per cent. With the exception of sugar and some livestock products, no plausible policy changes would be significant in relation to the underlying downwards drift.

The discussion of issues and the review of available projections clearly point to very large increases in international food trade over the period to year 2000 and beyond. Global food markets have traditionally been very "narrow", with major fluctuations in quantities traded and (especially) prices. Recently, much of the analysis and discussion has been about the effects on global markets of OECD country food and agricultural policies, and, more recently about the corresponding effects of developing country and Eastern European policies. Undoubtedly, the policies are currently dominating the global markets, with very obvious effects on prices.

However, if the global supply/demand projections point to greatly increased world trade, especially involving greatly increased developing world imports, these short-term policy concerns may be less important than seems at present. All the major food projections reviewed in Chapter 6 point to large increases in world trade in basic food products and, still more, to a massive shift in the direction of trade towards developing countries as food importers. However, the presentation above suggests that all these projections may be conservative in the sense that they assume that the developing countries aim primarily (and relatively successfully) for broad food self-sufficiency. The discussion above suggests that these broad aims may not be realised, because consumption could and should rise faster than projected and because production may not rise as fast. This suggests that much bigger volumes of trade in food products are plausible.

The most expansionist of the trade projections reviewed in Chapter 6 (from the World Bank) suggests that total gross world trade in cereals might rise to 417 million tons in year 2000, with developing country imports at 263 million tons. However, the discussion of Chinese trends suggests that China will need up to 100 million tons of cereals more than is currently projected, while the discussion of food trends in other low-income countries could also point to very large additional world cereal consumption, if governments were committed (or forced to commit themselves) to meeting food entitlements. Thus, it would be realistic to add another 200 million tons to world cereal "requirements" in year 2000, and this should be added to world trade. The impact on world cereal markets and their organisation would be large.

Much of the discussion about increased developing country food imports has concerned middle-income countries. These countries have been increasing their food imports in line with population growth, while at least some of them, especially in the North Africa/Middle East region, face relatively strong constraints on raising basic food production. The projected rates of growth of food consumption are rather high, reflecting primarily high-income growth assumptions and shifts in consumption patterns. There may now be doubts about these consumption growth prospects, given the deceleration in world economic growth (by comparison with earlier projections) and the massive decline in petroleum prices. There could also be questions about the prospects for national agricultural production. Nevertheless, the available projections for middle-income countries should probably be accepted as minima, implying that these middle-income countries may be importing at least 80 million tons in the year 2000.

Clearly, there is considerable uncertainty regarding the food import trends of developing countries. There is a persuasive case[5] for arguing that sustained development and successful economic transformation for most of the middle-income countries will need to be agriculturally based, as was the development experience of the now industrialised OECD countries, South Korea and Taiwan. The first uncertainty comes from the recognition that this is not the implicit view of most of the governments concerned. However, supposing that these governments did become committed to the need for agriculturally based development, what would be the implications for global markets? Here, the uncertainty is much larger. There would be shifts in both demand and supply for food products, as different incomes were generated with different demand responses for food while, at the same time, the levels and (more especially) the product composition of food production shifted.

Food security

The conclusions on nutrition and food security are depressing and puzzling. First, the calculations (reviewed in Chapter 2) suggest that staggering numbers of the world's people are severely undernourished. Second, while the different projections of longer-term demand and supply trends show considerable divergence, none of them seems to imply that the number of undernourished people would decline. The FAO projections explicitly imply that they will increase. Third, however, all the year 2000 projections imply that the world will have enough food to feed itself.

There are normative questions about food security and the policy implications, especially for the OECD countries. However, one should initially consider the puzzling questions about what is actually likely to happen. What do we expect the more than 300 million hungry people to do politically and economically over the decade of the 1990s? The projections imply that these people will represent more than 20 per cent of sub-Saharan Africa's population, but a much lower proportion of the low-income Asian countries. Perhaps the large low-income Asian countries will continue to "manage" their poverty problems without significant effects on food and agricultural policies: this is far from sure. What would be the implications for the projections, and for the associated economic analysis, of taking the hunger problem more seriously?

A large part of the puzzle concerns the assumptions made about developing country governments and their policies. Given all the other (and generally more immediate) policy concerns, how far do developing country governments really care about longer-term nutrition or food security issues? Even so, more detached analysts may wonder how far over the longer term these policies will be obliged to adapt to the expected extent of hunger, and, perhaps more important, poor people's perceptions of their deprivation. What would be the implications for global food markets and for economic analysis of longer-term trends? How far should the projections and the associated economic analysis be more directly concerned with "food entitlement" mechanisms, with the direct links between agricultural production, rural incomes and food consumption and with the impacts of food prices on poor people's food consumption? How far are the present, very evident, problems of urban food entitlements really short-term (adjustment) problems, which will not affect longer-term trends?

For this report, the most puzzling aspect of these problems concerns the global market implications. This is probably, primarily, an issue about Asian countries. While the projections show large increases in sub-Saharan African food imports, the **uncertainties** about Asian imports are much bigger than any likely absolute level of African imports. In general, the projections for Asian countries (and especially China and India) are biased towards food self-sufficiency, but around nutritional and "entitlement" patterns that are likely to leave hundreds of millions of people hungry. How far will or could greater food trade contribute to a different longer-term nutritional outcome? How far would this greater trade need to be considered in humanitarian, food aid terms? Alternatively, how far could it credibly be considered as a self-financing contribution to a different, "entitlements-based" development strategy?

Technology

It is now accepted that technology innovations, especially involving the use of information technology and bio-technology, will transform world agriculture, producing a new "revolution" even more radical than the agro-chemical revolution of the 1960s and 1970s. The precise nature and timetable of this prospective revolution is nevertheless unknown.

The effects of information technology advances are already widespread, especially in the OECD countries. Analysis of the effects and possibilities is however constrained by the dearth of analysis, which hitherto has concentrated on micro studies. The potential impacts of bio-technology are more straightforward, but it is nevertheless very difficult to judge the effects on world agriculture. In the 1990s, there will certainly be some significant effects on livestock product markets. There should also be significant impacts in plant protection, including for cereals. The next decade should also see developing cereal varieties better adapted to "more hostile" geographical and climatic environments. However, there is great uncertainty about the most important break-through in plant genetics — nitrogen-fixing in basic cereals. Lastly, there could be developments in industrial use of agricultural raw materials, for energy or chemicals, which would significantly affect global markets for basic foodstuffs.

It is clear that none of the available projections reviewed above, nor much of the historical analysis, pays much direct attention to technology or to ecological shifts, although they incorporate assumptions about various technical indicators of productivity growth. It is unlikely that together or individually they capture adequately the effects of the "new" technologies. These effects are unlikely to be captured in "trend" increases in productivity; nor are (for comparable reasons) the possible effects of man-made ecological changes.

There is an important contrast between the developments in prospect and the agro-chemical-based "green" revolution of the past two decades. That revolution was dominated by the R&D and industrial characteristics of bulk chemical "process" industries. It led to standard products not always adapted to the needs of particular, nutritionally vulnerable groups of people. Applications of the next generation of technology innovations will seem more various and "diffuse" than earlier ones. "Start-up" costs, especially for R&D but also for some manufacture, will be less dominating and "access" to technology will not be as important a constraint as in earlier decades.

The relative optimism regarding technology is an important and encouraging conclusion for developing countries and their poor people. Discussion of "technology for developing countries" in the 1990s need not be dominated by "oligopoly" and TNCs, as has happened over the past two decades. On the one hand, the developers of technology innovations will increasingly recover their costs without seeking to involve themselves in the use of the innovations. On the other hand, potential users will be able to afford to commission products adapted to their needs. This would include governments of even the most destitute sub-Saharan countries or even non-governmental organisations or local government agencies.

There nevertheless are threats to developing countries and to their poor people. While technology developments need not marginalise the products and production of poor people, they will tend to reinforce the tendencies already present for international trade to increase around a few cereals (especially, maize) with substantially falling real prices.

The market implications of accepting that new technology developments will be less dominated by oligopoly point to getting domestic agricultural prices in line with international prices and encouraging international trade in technology innovation products. "Intellectual property" is certainly an issue, but is unlikely to prove a major stumbling block to technological diffusion. On the other hand, some developing countries will have interest in promoting technology developments tailored to their specific geographical and climatic conditions. The specific developments will take place in a context of shifts in international product markets. They will also take place in the context of liberalisation and structural adjustment. This implies changes in the public/private balance of research and extension, as well as changes in the patterns of investment and incentives affecting the choice of inputs and outputs.

Environmental and ecological issues

It is now clear that, within the OECD countries, the 1990s (and beyond) will be dominated by environmental and ecological concerns. These concerns will have implications for developing countries, both directly in international discussions of global environmental issues, and through changes in international food and input product markets.

The available global projections of demand, supply and trade for basic food products make some implicit assumptions about these issues. On the developing country side, they make assumptions about the scope for increasing yields on environmentally threatened, but intensively cultivated, land, especially in South and East Asia, but also in sub-Saharan Africa. On the OECD country side, they make assumptions which correspond to the effects of current environmental concern on the "carrying-capacity" of arable (and pasture) land.

One cannot identify binding physical constraints (except in a few specific cases) on increased basic foodstuff production, unless one assumes that there will be no further yield-increasing innovations in technology — a very pessimistic assumption in the light of current bio-technology developments.

Given the projections of greatly increased world trade in cereals, the biggest uncertainties concern OECD production. On balance, the conclusion is that market and institutional forces within the OECD countries will ensure that they do produce (or over-produce) the basic foods (cereals) "needed" in the 1990s.

Nevertheless, there are longer-term concerns, essentially about "global warming", which could affect the economics of production of basic foodstuffs (especially maize and wheat) for global markets in the 1990s and beyond. For the present, there is no way of knowing what those effects will be. The global research community should certainly devote research resources to exploring the likely effects, but it is not clear that "threatened" countries could, or should, take individual action. "Individual action" would essentially be concerned with taking out insurance against exceptional climatic occurrences.

The food system

"Off-farm" activities are increasingly dominating food production and consumption, even for poor people in developing countries. The most important developments are likely to be "downstream", in the processing of basic foods, while technology developments seem likely ultimately to reduce agriculture's dependence on agro-chemical (and, perhaps, mechanical) inputs.

While most of the "off-farm" activities in developing countries are "informal" and "unorganised", an increasing share is in the modern sector, especially in Latin America. These trends should develop in Africa and Asia during the 1990s, in spite of their continuing lower degree of urbanisation.

The modern sector is increasingly structured by international firms. Again, this trend should continue in the 1990s, especially in developing countries. However, as noted above, with the technology developments in prospect, continued concentration in organisation will depend less on economies of manufacturing scale in process industries.

Policies

The analysis of food and agricultural policies suggests that changes in OECD support policies would clearly have short-term influences on world food product markets. However, these effects would not be as dramatic as is often supposed, and some of them would be counterintuitive (essentially because of the complexities of the poultry/livestock sector). Developing countries would not be clear winners. The OECD countries would be the clear winners: for developing countries, the outcome would be much less certain. A few exporters would clearly gain, although the projections are pessimistic about their domestic ability to capture their potential gains.

The long-term real price trend is downward. Reductions in OECD subsidies would in the short term lead to higher prices for basic foodstuffs, hurting food importers. World domestic product would rise marginally, but the terms of trade of the OECD region would also improve marginally. However, to the extent that the OECD policies were gradually adjusted, the likely effects on prices and volumes of world trade will probably be lost in the underlying shifts in these markets.

The most important conclusion from the policy analysis concerns the implications of changing developing country policies, which are much more important than those of OECD countries. While this may be politically uncomfortable, it is perhaps not surprising, given that levels of anti-agriculture "distortion" (e.g. through trade, exchange rate and pricing policies) are greater in general in developing countries and that their share of world imports is projected to rise substantially.

Comparative advantage

The analysis of comparative advantage highlighted the difficulties of translating the theory into policy and practice. Existing major global food markets are very narrow and cannot tell us much about international competitiveness. This is all the more so because they are very visibly dominated by the agricultural policies of OECD countries. There is now plenty of analytical evidence that world markets would look quite different if policies were changed. However, the analysis presented here suggests that, even without these "desirable" policy changes, global markets will look dramatically different in the longer term. This presentation tries to outline what some of those shifts might be. There is however an uncertainty about how significant international trade — essentially developing country imports — could or should be. International prices for major cereals will fall substantially, and this must affect any assessment of international competitive advantage.

The analysis of comparative advantage in agriculture concerns the related issues of the valuation of labour, land and capital employed. Since none of these three factors (labour, land or capital) is very mobile in the short run, their opportunity cost is difficult to assess. Moreover, there are typically "institutional" constraints. It is frequently very difficult to judge how far agricultural incomes would need to fall before farm labour, especially with self-employed farm families, moved out of staple crop or livestock activities. Similarly, much of the returns to "land" are in fact returns to capital investment in the "improvement" of land. To a considerable extent these investments are product-specific and not mobile in the short term. Ultimately, however, they may increase the adaptability of land to different crop requirements. Nevertheless, if the concern is with the extent to which falling domestic or international prices will reduce production, the importance of land values, "rents", signals the need for caution. In particular, there are no adequate elasticities indicating the response of OECD farmers to the general fall in farm incomes that could be associated with OECD agricultural policy reform.

Beyond this, one is left with a disturbing paradox. The whole body of thought on "comparative advantage" originated with the effects of factor endowments, including natural resources. So, one should be interested in endowments of labour and land. On the other hand, much thinking within the OECD countries has been about how policies can make activities viable which would have no "natural" comparative advantage. The evidence is that these policies have been massively successful, and the projections suggest that this success will continue. Importantly, this continuing success does not depend on continued agricultural protection. The evidence could be construed as suggesting that comparative advantage theory is not working in agriculture.

One should not exaggerate this scepticism about comparative advantage. Genuine reduction in agricultural protection within the OECD countries would lead to some production (and consumption) shifts, especially in Europe and Japan. The "net" effects would be clearly positive. However, to a considerable extent, these countries have "acquired" comparative advantage, and this has now little to do with location-specific geographical or climatic characteristics or with the cost of unskilled labour. It has much to do with the development of the (primarily downstream) "food system", although not necessarily much to do with physical proximity to markets. The national economic costs have undoubtedly been considerable.

Conclusion

The evidence from our examination of the theory and practice of comparative advantage, and from the series of country studies undertaken by the Development Centre, points unequivocally to the key role of human capital and technology in enhancing competitiveness. Education and infrastructure provide the backbone for development. This principle applies to agriculture as it does to industry.

Our analysis points to the extent of the challenge facing the OECD and developing countries. It suggests that the OECD countries will continue to account for much of agricultural growth. Reforms in agricultural policies in OECD countries will enhance their and developing country prospects. OECD policies regarding developing country debt and concerning the sharing of technological developments and responsibilities are however likely to prove more important. Developing countries meanwhile will continue to carry the burden of development. Their future depends critically on the extent to which they are to apply appropriate macroeconomic and sectoral policies. For the many millions faced by chronic poverty and malnutrition, this inevitably implies a redoubling of the commitment to growth with redistribution.

NOTES

1. See Goldin and Knudsen, especially the conclusion.
2. See Aziz.
3. For an attempt to handle systematically some of these issues, see Anderson (1988).
4. See e.g. Wahren. WHO estimates that 6 to 8 million are infected by HIV worldwide and that the cumulative world total may be as high as 20 million in the year 2000, of which over 75 per cent are expected to be in developing countries. Sub-Saharan Africa is already worst affected; at least 4 million people are assumed to be infected; of which a half are thought to be women — almost 80 per cent of the global female total. In certain countries, such as Uganda and Rwanda, over 5 per cent of the population is already infected.

Table 2.1
Total Grains Consumption

	million tons						share in total (%)					growth rate (% p.a.)		
	69-71	79-81	84	86	87	2000	69-71	79-81	84	86	2000	70-84	80-84	84-2000
World	1 135.6	1 453.0	1 595.2	1 655.7	1 667.4	2 260.6	100.0	100.0	100.0	100.0	100.0	2.5	2.4	2.2
Developing Countries	496.4	704.7	812.7	831.7	831.3	1 233.3	43.7	48.5	50.9	50.2	54.6	3.6	3.6	2.6
Asia	374.8	529.5	626.0	630.0	628.0	954.2	33.0	36.4	39.2	38.1	42.2	3.7	4.3	2.7
China	169.6	254.3	311.0	308.5	319.7	493.1	14.9	17.5	19.5	18.6	21.8	4.4	5.2	2.9
India	92.1	116.2	133.1	130.5	119.4	181.2	8.1	8.0	8.3	7.9	8.0	2.7	3.5	1.9
Pakistan	9.9	13.4	14.8	15.7	15.3	24.5	0.9	0.9	0.9	0.9	1.1	2.9	2.5	3.2
Africa	59.5	83.0	91.3	98.3	100.7	137.4	5.2	5.7	5.7	5.9	6.1	3.1	2.4	2.6
America	62.1	92.2	95.4	103.4	102.6	141.7	5.5	6.3	6.0	6.2	6.3	3.1	0.9	2.5
Brazil	22.0	35.3	33.7	37.4	42.4	55.5	1.9	2.4	2.1	2.3	2.5	3.1	-1.2	3.2
E. Europe & USSR	240.9	303.0	309.4	325.3	332.5	412.9	21.2	20.9	19.4	19.6	19.9	1.8	0.5	1.8
OECD	398.3	445.3	473.1	498.7	503.6	614.4	35.1	30.6	29.7	30.1	27.2	1.2	1.5	1.6
N.America	190.7	201.9	223.6	246.2	248.4	302.2	16.8	13.9	14.0	16.8	13.4	1.1	2.6	1.9
W.Europe	173.5	200.7	204.6	204.8	206.7	253.5	15.3	13.8	12.8	15.3	11.2	1.2	0.5	1.3
EC-10	126.0	136.9	136.1	134.2	134.6	160.2	11.1	9.4	8.5	11.1	7.1	0.6	-0.1	1.0
S.Europe	35.4	47.6	52.3	53.9	55.1	71.9	3.1	3.3	3.3	3.1	3.2	2.8	2.4	2.0
Other	12.1	16.2	16.2	16.7	17.0	21.4	1.1	1.1	1.0	1.1	0.9	2.1	0.0	1.8
Japan	27.9	35.6	37.8	40.3	40.9	49.6	2.5	2.5	2.4	2.5	2.2	2.2	1.5	1.7
Oceania	6.2	7.1	7.1	7.4	7.6	9.1	0.5	0.5	0.4	0.5	0.4	1.0	0.0	1.6

Source: World Bank, 1989a. Development Centre estimates.

Table 2.2
Wheat Consumption

	million tons						share in total (%)					growth rate (% p.a.)		
	69-71	79-81	84	86	87	2000	69-71	79-81	84	86	2000	70-84	80-84	84-2000
World	334.6	440.9	500.3	513.7	521.8	732.9	100.0	100.0	100.0	100.0	100.0	2.9	3.2	2.4
Developing Countries	113.0	192.5	236.4	251.5	259.8	420.6	33.8	43.7	47.3	49.0	57.4	5.4	5.3	3.7
Asia	82.6	146.6	184.3	195.3	201.3	335.6	24.7	33.3	36.8	38.0	45.8	5.9	5.9	3.8
China	33.6	71.1	95.2	101.5	105.7	178.7	10.0	16.1	19.0	19.8	24.4	7.7	7.6	4.0
India	22.4	35.6	43.0	44.2	47.6	74.8	6.7	8.1	8.6	8.6	10.2	4.8	4.8	3.5
Pakistan	7.8	11.1	12.4	13.3	13.3	22.5	2.3	2.5	2.5	2.6	3.1	3.4	2.8	3.8
Africa	14.3	23.7	28.0	29.7	31.2	48.4	4.3	5.4	5.6	5.8	6.6	4.9	4.3	3.5
America	16.1	22.2	24.1	26.5	27.3	36.6	4.8	5.0	4.8	5.2	5.0	2.9	2.1	2.6
Brazil	3.6	6.7	6.5	8.7	9.2	13.4	1.1	1.5	1.3	1.7	1.8	4.3	-0.8	4.6
E. Europe & USSR	121.7	140.1	132.8	137.9	138.4	151.7	36.4	31.8	26.5	26.8	26.5	0.6	-1.3	0.8
OECD	99.9	108.3	131.1	124.3	123.6	160.6	29.9	24.6	26.2	24.2	21.9	2.0	4.9	1.3
N.America	26.4	27.1	37.8	38.7	35.9	52.6	7.9	6.1	7.6	7.5	7.2	2.6	8.7	2.1
W.Europe	65.2	71.6	83.4	75.8	77.7	96.0	19.5	16.2	16.7	14.8	13.1	1.8	3.9	0.9
EC-10	45.5	46.8	55.1	47.2	48.5	60.3	13.6	10.6	11.0	9.2	8.2	1.4	4.2	0.6
S.Europe	16.6	21.6	24.7	25.0	25.6	32.3	5.0	4.9	4.9	4.9	4.4	2.9	3.4	1.7
Other	3.1	3.2	3.6	3.6	3.6	3.4	0.9	0.7	0.7	0.7	0.5	1.1	3.0	-0.4
Japan	5.3	6.1	6.4	6.6	6.7	7.7	1.6	1.4	1.3	1.3	1.1	1.4	1.2	1.2
Oceania	3.0	3.5	3.5	3.2	3.3	4.3	0.9	0.8	0.7	0.6	0.6	1.1	0.0	1.3

Source: See Table 2.1.

Table 2.3
Rice Consumption

	million tons						share in total (%)					growth rate (% p.a.)		
	69-71	79-81	84	86	87	2000	69-71	79-81	84	86	2000	70-84	80-84	84-2000
World	210.7	271.6	314.9	315.7	304.7	449.1	100.0	100.0	100.0	100.0	100.0	2.9	3.8	2.2
Developing Countries	194.3	254.3	297.9	298.8	287.8	433.6	92.2	93.6	94.6	94.6	96.5	3.1	4.0	2.4
Asia	182.7	235.8	278.3	279.6	268.3	404.4	86.7	86.8	88.4	88.6	90.0	3.1	4.2	2.4
China	73.4	99.2	123.9	120.4	121.6	202.9	34.8	36.5	39.3	38.1	45.2	3.8	5.7	3.1
India	42.1	51.1	58.5	59.9	48.5	71.1	20.0	18.8	18.6	19.0	15.8	2.4	3.4	1.2
Pakistan	2.1	2.3	2.4	2.4	2.0	2.0	1.0	0.8	0.8	0.8	0.4	1.0	1.1	-1.1
Africa	5.0	7.9	8.8	8.5	8.6	13.0	2.4	2.9	2.8	2.7	2.9	4.1	2.7	2.5
America	6.6	10.6	10.8	10.7	10.9	16.2	3.1	3.9	3.4	3.4	3.6	3.6	0.5	2.6
Brazil	4.0	6.3	6.0	6.4	6.6	10.8	1.9	2.3	1.9	2.0	2.4	2.9	-1.2	3.7
E. Europe & USSR	1.4	2.9	2.6	2.8	2.9	4.0	0.7	1.1	0.8	0.9	1.0	4.5	-2.7	2.7
OECD	15.0	14.4	14.4	14.1	14.0	11.5	7.1	5.3	4.6	4.5	2.6	-0.3	0.0	-1.4
N.America	1.3	2.2	2.0	2.2	2.3	3.0	0.6	0.8	0.6	0.7	0.7	3.1	-2.4	2.6
W.Europe	2.1	1.8	2.1	2.0	2.0	2.2	1.0	0.7	0.7	0.6	0.5	0.0	3.9	0.3
EC-10	1.0	1.1	1.2	1.2	1.2	1.4	0.5	0.4	0.4	0.4	0.3	1.3	2.2	1.0
Japan	11.5	10.3	10.2	9.8	9.6	6.2	5.5	3.8	3.2	3.1	1.4	-0.9	-0.2	-3.1
Oceania	0.1	0.1	0.1	0.1	0.1	0.1	0.0	0.0	0.0	0.0	0.0	0.0	0.0	0.0

Source: See Table 2.1.

Table 2.4
Coarse Grain Consumption

	million tons						share in total (%)					growth rate (% p.a.)		
	69-71	79-81	84	86	87	2000	69-71	79-81	84	86	2000	70-84	80-84	84-2000
World	590.3	740.5	780.0	826.3	840.9	1 078.6	100.0	100.0	100.0	100.0	100.0	2.0	1.3	2.0
Developing Countries	189.1	257.9	278.4	281.4	283.7	379.1	32.0	34.8	35.7	34.1	35.1	2.8	1.9	1.9
Asia	109.5	147.1	163.4	155.1	158.4	214.2	18.5	19.9	20.9	18.8	19.9	2.9	2.7	1.7
China	62.6	84.0	91.9	86.6	92.4	111.5	10.6	11.3	11.8	10.5	10.3	2.8	2.3	1.2
India	27.6	29.5	31.6	26.4	23.3	35.3	4.7	4.0	4.1	3.2	3.3	1.0	1.7	0.7
Pakistan														
Africa	40.2	51.4	54.5	60.1	60.9	76.0	6.8	6.9	7.0	7.3	7.0	2.2	1.5	2.1
America	39.4	59.4	60.5	66.2	64.4	88.9	6.7	8.0	7.8	8.0	8.2	3.1	0.5	2.4
Brazil	14.4	22.3	21.2	22.3	26.6	31.3	2.4	3.0	2.7	2.7	2.9	2.8	-1.3	2.5
E. Europe & USSR	117.8	160.0	174.0	184.6	191.2	257.2	20.0	21.6	22.3	22.3	22.7	2.8	2.1	2.5
OECD	283.4	322.6	327.6	360.3	366.0	442.3	48.0	43.6	42.0	43.6	41.0	1.0	0.4	1.9
N.America	163.0	172.6	183.8	205.3	210.2	246.6	27.6	23.3	23.6	24.8	22.9	0.9	1.6	1.9
W.Europe	106.2	127.3	119.1	127.0	127.0	155.3	18.0	17.2	15.3	15.4	14.4	0.8	-1.7	1.7
EC-10	79.5	89.0	79.8	85.8	84.9	98.5	13.5	12.0	10.2	10.4	9.1	0.0	-2.7	1.3
S.Europe	17.8	25.4	26.8	28.2	28.8	38.9	3.0	3.4	3.4	3.4	3.6	3.0	1.4	2.4
Other	8.9	12.9	12.5	13.0	13.3	17.9	1.5	1.7	1.6	1.6	1.7	2.5	-0.8	2.3
Japan	11.1	19.2	21.2	23.9	24.6	35.7	1.9	2.6	2.7	2.9	3.3	4.7	2.5	3.3
Oceania	3.1	3.5	3.5	4.1	4.2	4.7	0.5	0.5	0.4	0.5	0.4	0.9	0.0	1.9

Source: See Table 2.1

Table 2.5

Population and Food Consumption Projections to Year 2000
(quantities — annual average growth rate in per cent)

	Population	Food Consumption						
		FAO[a][b]		IFPRI[c]	World Bank[d]	IWC[e]	IIASA[f]	Z&V[g]
World	1.6	n.a.	n.a.	n.a.	2.0	1.5	1.8	2.40
Developing countries								
Total	1.9	3.1	2.7	2.7	2.6	2.5	2.5	n.a.
(Excluding China)	2.2	2.9	n.a.	3.0	n.a.	n.a.	3.2	2.9
Asia	1.5	3.1	2.4	2.3	2.7	2.5	n.a.	n.a.
(Excluding China)	1.8	2.8	2.5	2.4	n.a.	n.a.	n.a.	n.a.
North Africa/ Middle East	2.5	3.1	3.0	3.8	n.a.	2.5	n.a.	n.a.
Sub-Saharan Africa	3.3	3.5	3.9	3.6	n.a.	3.4	n.a.	n.a.
Africa (Total)	n.a.	n.a.	n.a.	n.a.	2.6	3.1	n.a.	n.a.
Latin America	2.0	2.7	2.9	3.2	2.5	2.5	n.a.	n.a.
Industrialised countries	0.6	n.a.	n.a.	n.a.	1.7	0.0	n.a.	n.a.
OECD	0.6	0.8	n.a.	n.a.	1.6	n.a.	1.7	1.9
E. Europe & USSR	0.7	1.2	n.a.	n.a.	1.8	n.a.	0.6	n.a.

a. Total food and agricultural products, 1983/85-2000.
b. Cereals.
c. Major food staples, 1980-2000.
d. Total cereals, 1984-2000.
e. Total grains, 1985-2000.
f. Total cereals, 1980-2000.
g. Total cereals, 1982-2000 (excludes China, E. Europe and USSR).

Source: See text. The different published sources use different country groupings, principally concerned with the inclusion/exclusion of industrialised countries and China, and the groupings of Africa and Middle East countries. This explains the gaps in this table.

Table 2.6

Developing Country Commodity Balances for Cereals[a]
(million tons)

	Food	Feed	Other Use	Domestic Disappearance	Exports	Imports	Net Trade	Production	SSR[b]
Wheat									
1961/63	65.5	2.2	14.2	81.8	2.5	21.4	-18.9	64.3	78.6
1969/71	97.7	3.9	18.6	120.2	2.4	26.5	-24.0	96.5	80.3
1979/81	171.2	7.4	26.9	205.5	5.3	52.3	-47.0	157.3	76.5
1983/85	209.7	9.6	30.6	249.8	10.5	58.6	-48.1	200.6	80.3
2000	296.1	25.9	44.4	366.4	n.a.	n.a.	-63.8	302.5	82.6
Rice (paddy)									
1961/63	182.0	1.4	23.7	207.2	8.3	7.0	1.3	205.5	99.2
1969/71	245.4	2.8	30.0	278.2	8.0	8.5	-0.5	283.3	101.8
1979/81	330.6	4.9	37.3	372.9	11.2	12.7	-1.5	367.6	98.6
1983/85	379.0	7.4	41.4	427.8	11.7	11.4	0.3	436.1	102.0
2000	515.6	20.9	55.5	592.0	n.a.	n.a.	-2.7	589.3	99.5
Maize									
1961/63	42.0	16.1	8.3	66.4	4.0	1.8	2.2	69.5	104.6
1969/71	51.2	32.2	11.0	94.4	9.2	2.3	6.9	102.5	108.6
1979/81	72.9	67.0	16.2	156.1	9.1	16.8	-7.7	149.0	95.4
1983/85	78.4	76.6	18.5	173.5	12.8	18.1	-5.3	168.4	97.1
2000	96.0	188.2	31.9	316.1	n.a.	n.a.	-16.3	299.8	94.8
Other coarse grains									
1961/63	56.8	10.5	12.4	79.7	1.8	2.1	-0.3	80.9	101.6
1969/71	63.2	15.8	12.1	91.0	3.1	2.4	0.7	92.3	101.4
1979/81	63.9	27.9	11.8	103.6	5.1	8.9	-3.9	100.1	96.7
1983/85	63.7	35.2	12.7	111.6	6.1	13.7	-7.6	102.3	91.7
2000	84.6	69.0	18.7	182.3	n.a.	n.a.	-13.2	159.0	92.3
Total cereals (rice included in milled form)									
1961/63	285.7	29.7	50.6	366.1	13.9	30.0	-16.1	351.8	96.1
1969/71	375.7	53.8	61.6	491.1	20.0	36.9	-16.8	480.3	97.8
1979/81	528.6	105.6	79.8	713.9	26.9	86.5	-59.5	651.6	91.3
1983/85	604.5	126.3	89.4	820.3	37.2	98.0	-60.8	762.2	92.9
2000	820.6	297.1	132.0	1249.6	n.a.	n.a.	-95.2	1154.4	92.4

a. Aggregates for 94 countries.
b. Self sufficiency ratio — per cent.

Source: Alexandratos, Table 6.

Table 2.7
Developing Country Food Consumption
(Kg per head per year)[a]

	Cereals[b]	Tubers[c]	Vegetable[d] oilseeds	Sugar[e]	Meat[f]	Milk[g]
94 Developing countries						
1983/85	173	63	7	18	14	34
2000	174	60	9	22	18	41
93 Developing countries (excluding China)						
1983/85	154	63	8	23	12	46
2000	162	67	10	26	15	51
SSA						
1983/85	113	192	8	9	10	27
2000	121	196	8	11	11	27
Middle East/N. Africa						
1983/85	212	28	12	33	21	72
2000	204	28	14	37	24	77
Asia						
1983/85	184	44	6	14	10	21
2000	187	32	9	18	15	28
Asia (excl. China)						
1983/85	159	30	7	19	5	34
2000	173	28	9	23	7	39
Latin America						
1983/85	136	73	9	44	37	94
2000	143	71	11	49	41	107
Low-income countries						
1983/85	179	57	6	13	10	24
2000	179	50	8	16	15	30
Low-income countries (excl. China)						
1983/85	149	51	7	17	5	40
2000	161	57	8	20	6	42
Low-income countries (excl. China & India)						
1983/85	145	89	6	11	9	32
2000	154	96	7	14	11	34
Middle-income countries						
1983/85	160	78	10	30	22	54
2000	163	78	12	35	25	62

a. Direct human consumption only.
b. Rice is included in milled form.
c. Including roots and plantains.
d. Oil equivalent.
e. Raw equivalent.
f. Carcass weight, excluding offals.
g. Milk & dairy products.
Source: Alexandratos, Table 3.3.

Table 2.8

Determinants of Future Cereal Consumption

	1980 pop (bn)	Growth rate in: Pop	GDP/head	2000 % rise gdp/h	Income elasticity	2000 % rise cons./head	Growth rate of food/head % per annum	Total food	pop. share in growth %	food cons (mn tons) 1980	2000
World	4.4	1.6	2.0	0.5	0.2	0.1	0.5	2.1	77.5	1 453.0	2 221.2
Developing countries											
Total	3.3	1.9	2.3	0.6	0.2	0.1	0.6	2.6	74.7	704.7	1 167.5
(excluding China)	2.2	2.1	1.9	0.5	0.3	0.1	0.6	2.7	77.9	n.a.	n.a.
Asia	2.3	1.6	2.9	0.8	0.2	0.2	0.7	2.4	68.7	529.5	843.7
(excluding China)	1.2	1.9	2.9	0.8	0.3	0.2	0.9	2.8	68.1	n.a.	n.a.
China	1.1	1.3	3.0	0.8	0.2	0.2	0.8	2.1	63.4	254.3	382.3
S. Asia	0.9	2.0	2.7	0.7	0.3	0.2	1.0	3.0	67.5	183.0	329.3
N. Africa/Middle East	0.2	2.6	2.7	0.7	0.1	0.1	0.3	2.9	88.4	84.0	150.2
SSA	0.4	3.1	-0.6	-0.1	0.5	-0.1	-0.3	2.8	110.4	58.0	100.8
Latin America	0.4	1.8	0.9	0.2	0.3	0.1	0.3	2.1	86.3	92.2	139.5
Industrialised Countries											
Total	0.7	0.4	2.1	0.5	0.1	0.1	0.3	0.7	61.4	748.3	858.4
OECD	0.7	0.4	2.2	0.5	0.1	0.1	0.3	0.7	60.0	445.3	508.7
N. America	0.3	0.6	1.9	0.5	0.1	0.0	0.2	0.8	72.8	201.9	238.0
W. Europe	0.4	0.2	2.3	0.6	0.1	0.1	0.3	0.5	41.6	200.7	220.9
Japan	0.1	0.4	2.6	0.7	0.1	0.1	0.3	0.7	55.2	35.6	41.2
E. Europe & USSR	0.0	0.5	1.9	0.5	0.1	0.0	0.2	0.7	69.1	303.0	350.1

Source: Development Centre Estimates. See Text for Discussion of Sources of Estimates

Table 2.9

Projected Income Elasticities of Demand for Basic Food Staples (averages — 1980-2000)

Direct Food Consumption				
Less than 0.0	0.0 — 0.1	0.1 — 0.2	0.2 — 0.3	0.3
Argentina	Afghanistan	Benin	Colombia	Angola
Chile	Algeria	Bolivia	Costa Rica	Burkina Faso
Cuba	Bangladesh	Burundi	Dominican Rep.	Chad
Hong Kong	Brazil	China	Ecuador	Ethiopia
Indonesia	Burma	Congo	El Salvador	Haiti
Iran	Cameroon	Gabon	Fiji	Kampuchia
Ivory Coast	Egypt	Ghana	Guinea	Lesotho
Jamaica	Gambia	Guyana	India	Liberia
N. Korea	Guatemala	Honduras	Laos	Mauritania
Kuwait	Iraq	Jordan	Madagascar	Somalia
Lebanon	S. Korea	Kenya	Mali	Sudan
Libya	Mauritius	Mongolia	Mozambique	
Malawi	Niger	Nepal	Senegal	
Malaysia	Nigeria	Nicaragua	Sierra Leone	
Mexico	Pakistan	Paraguay	Uganda	
Morocco	PNG	Peru	Viet Nam	
Panama	Tanzania	Philippines	YAR	
S. Arabia	Trinidad	Rwanda	YPR	
Singapore	Uruguay	Sri Lanka		
Syria		Surinam		
Thailand		Togo		
Tunisia		Venezuela		
Turkey		Zaire		
Zimbabwe		Zambia		

Table 2.9 (cont)

Projected Income Elasticities of Demand for Basic Food Staples (averages — 1980-2000)

		Feed Use			
0.2 — 0.4	0.4 — 0.5	0.6 — 0.8	0.8 — 1.0	1.0 — 1.2	More than 1.2
Argentina	Brazil	El Salvador	Angola	Afghanistan	Burkina Faso
Gabon	Chile	Guatemala	Bolivia	Algeria	Guinea
Hong Kong	Colombia	Honduras	Cameroon	Bangladesh	Indonesia
Jamaica	Costa Rica	Lebanon	Chad	Benin	Jordan
Kuwait	Cuba	Libya	China	Burma	Kampuchea
Mongolia	Fiji	Malaysia	Congo	Burundi	Nepal
Paraguay	Iran	Peru	Dominica	Ghana	Sri Lanka
S. Arabia	Mexico	Philippines	Ecuador	Guyana	Viet Nam
Singapore	Nicaragua	Sudan	Egypt	Haiti	
Uruguay	Panama	Surinam	Ethiopia	India	
	PNG	Syria	Gambia	N. Korea	
	S. Korea	Zambia	Iraq	Lesotho	
	Thailand		Ivory Coast	Liberia	
	Trinidad		Kenya	Malawi	
	Venezuela		Laos	Mauritius	
			Madagascar	Morocco	
			Mali	Mozambique	
			Mauritania	Niger	
			Pakistan	Nigeria	
			Senegal	Rwanda	
			Somalia	Sierra Leone	
			Tunisia	Tanzania	
			Turkey	Togo	
			YAR	Uganda	
			YDR		
			Zaire		
			Zimbabwe		

Note: Countries are omitted for which no FAO data are available.
Source: Paulino, p. 72. Based on FAO data.

Table 2.10

Income Elasticities of Demand

	Wheat	Coarse grains	Rice	Beef	Sugar	Soybeans
Argentina	-0.11	0.30	0.3	0.03	0.21	0.14
Brazil	0.4	0.18	0.1	0.5	0.2	0.0
India	0.3	0.3	0.1	1.2	0.46	0.1
Rest of Asia	0.5	0.17	0.3	0.42	0.63	0.66
SSA	0.5	-0.18	1.0	0.25	0.71	0.43
Latin America	0.3	0.25	0.5	0.1	0.25	0.00
China	0.5	0.17	0.82	0.42	0.63	0.66

Note: Caution should be exercised in the interpretation of some of these elasticities, as they are derived from a very narrow data base (e.g. rice in SSA) or historical records which fail to take account of recent trends (e.g. soybeans in Latin America).

Source: Zietz and Valdés, 1989.

Table 2.11

Food Availabilities for Direct Human Consumption (calories per capita per day)

	1983-85
World	2 660
Developing Countries	
94 Developing countries	2 420
93 Developing countries	
(excluding China)	2 360
SSA	2 050
N. East/N. Africa	2 980
Asia	2 380
Asia (excluding China)	2 250
Latin America	2 700
Low-income countries	2 310
Low-income countries (excluding China)	2 130
Low-income countries (excluding China and India)	2 090
Middle-income countries	2 660
Developed countries	3 370
North America	3 630
Western Europe	3 380
Other developed market economies	2 890
E. Europe & USSR	3 410

Source: Alexandratos, Table 2.1.

Table 2.12

Distribution of Developing Countries by Calories per Capita

	1961/63	1969/71	1979/81	1983/85
Under 1 900 calories p.c.				
No. of countries	23	7	8	9
Population (million)	985	65	173	196
Population excl. China	311	65	173	196
Population excl. China and India	311	65	173	196
1 900-2 500 calories p.c.				
No. of countries	66	74	54	50
Population (million)	1 036	2 331	2 467	1 446
Population excl. China	1 036	1 516	1 489	1 446
Population excl. China and India	573	961	800	702
Over 2 500 calories p.c.				
No. of countries	5	13	32	35
Population (million)	100	184	590	1 859
Population excl. China	100	184	590	831
Population excl. China and India	100	184	590	831

Source: Alexandratos, Table 2.2.

Table 2.13
Estimates of Undernutrition: 89 Developing Countries

	1969/71	1979/81	1983/85	2000
I. **Below 1.2 BMR**		% of Population		
89 Countries	18.6	14.7	14.6	10.5
Africa (sub-Saharan)	23.5	21.9	26.0	20.3
N. East/N. Africa	15.7	6.7	5.6	4.6
Asia	19.5	15.6	14.3	8.7
Latin America	12.7	9.8	9.5	8.0
		No. of Persons (million)		
89 Countries	316	320	348	353
Africa (sub-Saharan)	63	78	105	137
N. East/N. Africa	28	16	15	18
Asia	190	191	191	155
Latin America	35	35	37	43
II. **Below 1.4 BMR**		% of Population		
89 Countries	27.0	21.8	21.5	15.6
Africa (sub-Saharan)	32.6	30.6	35.2	28.7
N. East/N. Africa	22.9	10.8	9.1	7.6
Asia	28.7	23.5	21.8	13.9
Latin America	18.5	14.6	14.2	11.6
		No. of Persons (million)		
89 Countries	460	475	512	523
Africa (sub-Saharan)	86	110	142	194
N. East/N. Africa	41	25	24	29
Asia	281	288	291	246
Latin America	51	52	55	62

Source: Alexandratos, Table 3.4. For explanation of concepts and methodology, see Alexandratos.

Table 3.1

Growth of Gross Agricultural Production and Self-Sufficiency Ratios(1) 94 Developing Countries

		Growth Rates				SIR (1)			
		61-70	70-80	80-85	61-85	61/63	69/71	79/81	83/85
		Per cent per year				Per cent			
94	Developing countries	3.5	3.0	3.9	3.2	106.4	105.7	100.3	101.1
93	Developing countries (excluding China)	2.7	3.0	3.0	2.9	109.8	107.5	101.2	101.4
	Africa (sub-Saharan)	2.8	1.5	2.0	2.0	119.8	117.0	102.9	100.8
	Near East/N. Africa	3.0	3.1	2.4	2.9	100.9	97.4	80.1	75.6
	Asia	3.8	3.2	4.9	3.5	100.9	101.9	99.5	102.0
	Asia (excluding China)	2.5	3.1	4.0	3.0	103.7	102.8	100.8	103.5
	Latin America	3.0	3.3	2.3	3.0	119.9	115.7	113.0	113.9
	Low-income countries	3.7	2.7	4.8	3.2	101.0	102.0	98.2	100.1
	Low-income countries (excluding China)	2.3	2.2	3.7	2.4	103.9	103.0	98.4	100.1
	Low-income countries (excluding China and India)	2.7	1.9	3.0	2.3	111.0	106.0	100.8	99.9
	Middle-income countries	3.1	3.5	2.6	3.2	114.9	111.1	103.2	102.3
Developed Countries		2.7	1.9	1.6	2.0	96.7	96.7	100.0	99.9
Market economies		2.2	2.1	1.4	2.0	95.7	95.7	103.8	102.6
	North America	2.1	2.3	1.2	2.0	105.5	105.2	120.1	113.5
	Western Europe	2.0	1.9	1.5	1.8	86.6	87.4	92.8	95.7
	Others	3.3	2.1	1.8	2.2	102.5	98.4	97.3	95.5
E. Europe & USSR		3.7	1.5	2.1	2.0	98.9	98.7	92.8	94.0

1. *Self-Sufficiency Ratios (SSR)* - $\frac{\textit{Production}}{\textit{Domestic use excluding stock changes}}$ *per cent*

Source: Alexandratos, Table 2.6

Table 3.2

Total Grains Production

	million tons					share in total (%)				growth rate (% p.a.)		
	69-71	79-81	84	87	2000	69-71	79-81	84	2000	70-84	80-84	84-2000
World	1 215.0	1 585.0	1 796.0	1 741.0	2 477.0	100	100	100	100	2.8	3.2	2.0
Developing Countries	560.2	766.3	899.1	872.2	1 244.0	46.12	48.34	50.06	50.21	3.4	4.1	2.0
Asia	442.2	601.3	729.6	697.0	1 009.0	36.4	37.93	40.62	40.72	3.6	0.5	2.0
China	199.1	286.6	366.0	357.3	538.7	16.39	18.08	20.38	21.75	4.4	6.3	2.4
India	111.2	138.4	164.4	140.0	205.4	9.155	8.73	9.153	8.293	2.8	4.4	1.4
Africa	51.0	72.7	63.4	75.4	86.6	4.199	4.586	3.53	3.497	1.6	-0.3	2.0
America	67.0	92.3	106.1	99.8	148.5	5.516	5.822	5.907	5.996	3.3	3.5	2.1
E. Europe & USSR	229.9	248.7	264.2	287.4	344.7	18.93	15.69	14.71	16.5	0.1	1.5	1.7
USSR	167.9	170.2	157.4	199.4	226.0	13.82	10.74	8.763	9.125	0.0	-0.2	2.3
E.Europe	61.8	78.8	98.5	87.8	118.5	5.088	4.971	5.484	4.785	3.4	5.7	1.2
OECD	428.6	570.3	632.8	581.5	888.4	35.28	35.97	35.23	35.87	2.8	2.6	2.1
N.America	244.2	343.7	357.2	331.2	545.3	20.1	21.68	19.89	22.02	2.8	0.1	2.7
US	209.8	301.0	314.0	278.9	468.1	17.27	18.99	17.48	18.9	2.9	1.1	2.5
Canada	34.4	42.7	43.1	52.2	77.1	2.832	2.693	2.4	3.113	1.6	0.2	3.7
W.Europe	152.9	190.2	230.3	214.7	288.9	12.59	12.0	12.82	11.66	0.3	4.9	1.4
EC-10	106.5	132.6	164.4	147.6	203.2	8.768	8.364	9.153	8.204	3.1	5.5	1.3
S.Europe	33.8	42.3	46.7	48.8	62.0	2.783	2.668	2.6	2.503	2.3	2.5	1.8
Other	12.6	15.3	19.2	18.3	23.7	1.037	0.965	1.069	0.957	3.1	5.8	1.3
Japan	16.4	14.3	16.0	14.3	12.5	1.35	0.902	0.891	0.505	0.0	2.8	-0.2
Oceania	15.1	22.1	28.8	20.7	41.0	1.243	1.394	1.603	1.655	4.7	6.8	2.2

Note: Rice is on paddy basis.
Source: World Bank, 1989a. Development Centre estimates.

Table 3.3
Wheat Production

	million tons					share in total (%)				growth rate (% p.a.)		
	69-71	79-81	84	87	2000	69-71	79-81	84	2000	70-84	80-84	84-2000
World	317.1	439.6	516.1	503.1	738.3	100	100	100	100	3.5	4.1	2.3
Developing countries	78.2	143.2	190.3	196.9	289.4	24.66	32.58	36.87	39.2	6.6	7.4	2.7
Asia	66.6	119.2	159.7	163.5	239.9	21.0	27.12	30.94	32.49	6.4	7.6	2.6
China	29.7	59.2	87.8	89.7	141.0	9.366	13.47	17.01	19.1	0.8	10.4	0.3
India	20.9	34.6	45.5	45.6	62.5	6.591	7.871	8.816	8.465	5.7	7.1	0.2
Africa	a	9.0	9.5	12.0	12.5	a	2.047	1.841	1.693	a	1.4	1.7
America	11.6	15.0	21.1	21.4	37.0	3.658	3.412	4.088	5.012	4.4	8.9	3.6
Eastern Europe & USSR	114.3	115.8	108.7	113.6	128.5	36.05	26.34	21.06	24.8	0.0	-0.2	1.1
USSR	92.8	89.8	68.6	80.5	90.8	29.27	20.43	13.29	12.3	-0.2	-0.7	1.8
E.Europe	21.5	26.5	36.5	33.1	37.7	6.78	6.028	7.072	5.106	3.9	8.3	0.2
OECD	124.6	180.6	217.1	192.6	320.4	39.29	41.08	42.07	43.4	0.4	4.7	2.5
N.America	53.9	86.6	91.8	83.5	165.1	17.0	19.7	17.79	22.36	3.9	1.5	3.7
US	40.0	66.2	70.6	57.2	125.4	12.61	15.06	13.68	16.98	4.1	1.6	3.7
Canada	13.9	20.4	21.2	26.3	39.6	4.383	4.641	4.108	5.364	3.1	0.1	0.4
W.Europe	61.4	78.6	105.6	96.1	126.6	19.36	17.88	20.46	17.15	3.9	7.7	1.1
EC-10	41.4	54.6	78.3	67.7	94.5	13.06	12.42	15.17	12.8	4.7	9.4	1.2
S.Europe	16.8	20.9	23.2	24.7	29.3	5.298	4.754	4.495	3.969	2.3	2.6	1.5
Other	3.2	3.1	4.1	3.7	2.8	1.009	0.705	0.794	0.379	1.8	7.2	-0.2
Japan		0.6	0.7	0.9	0.9	0.0	0.136	0.136	0.122		3.9	1.6
Oceania	9.3	14.8	19.0	12.1	27.8	2.933	3.367	3.681	3.765	5.2	6.4	2.4

a. Included in coarse grains — see Table 3.5.

Source: See Table 3.2.

Table 3.4
Rice Production

	million tons					share in total (%)				growth rate (% p.a.)		
	69-71	79-81	84	87	2000	69-71	79-81	84	2000	70-84	80-84	84-2000
World	308.5	395.9	467.0	447.4	656.7	100	100	100	100	0.3	4.2	2.2
Developing Countries	285.6	370.7	440.3	422.7	627.9	92.58	93.63	94.28	95.61	3.1	4.4	2.2
Asia	268.3	346.5	414.2	395.3	594.8	86.97	87.52	88.69	90.57	3.2	4.6	2.3
China	106.8	145.7	181.2	174	291.2	34.62	36.8	38.8	44.34	3.8	5.6	0.3
India	62.9	74.7	87.6	71.5	107.1	20.39	18.87	18.76	16.31	2.4	4.1	1.3
Africa	7.3	8.7	9.1	9.8	9.8	2.366	2.198	1.949	1.492	1.6	1.1	0.5
America	10.0	15.5	17.0	17.6	23.3	3.241	3.915	3.64	3.548	3.9	2.3	2.0
E. Europe & USSR	1.5	2.7	2.9	3.1	4.5	0.486	0.682	0.621	0.7	4.8	1.8	2.8
of which USSR	1.3	2.5	2.8	2.9	4.3	0.421	0.631	0.6	0.655	5.6	2.9	2.7
OECD	21.4	22.5	23.8	21.6	24.3	6.937	5.683	5.096	3.7	0.8	1.4	0.1
N.America	4.0	7.0	6.3	5.8	9.7	1.297	1.768	1.349	1.477	3.3	-0.3	2.7
US	4.0	7.0	6.3	5.8	9.7	1.297	1.768	1.349	1.477	3.3	-0.3	2.7
W.Europe	1.4	1.5	2.0	2.0	2.4	0.454	0.379	0.428	0.365	2.6	7.5	1.1
Japan	15.7	13.3	14.9	13.0	11.2	5.089	3.359	3.191	1.705	0.0	2.9	-2.0
Oceania	0.3	0.7	0.6	0.8	1.0	0.097	0.177	0.128	0.152	5.1	-0.4	3.2

Note: Rice is on paddy basis.
Source: See Table 3.2: World Bank Price Prospects.

Table 3.5
Coarse Grains Production

	million tons					share in total (%)				growth rate (% p.a.)		
	69-71	79-81	84	87	2000	69-71	79-81	84	2000	70-84	80-84	84-2000
World	593.1	749.8	813.0	790.6	1 082.0	100	100	100	100	2.3	2.0	1.8
Developing Countries	196.4	252.4	268.5	252.6	326.3	33.11	33.66	33.03	30.17	2.3	1.6	1.2
Asia	107.3	135.6	155.7	138.2	173.8	18.09	18.08	19.15	16.07	2.7	3.5	0.7
China	62.6	81.7	97.0	93.6	106.5	10.55	10.9	11.93	9.846	3.2	4.4	0.6
India	27.4	29.1	31.3	22.9	35.8	4.62	3.881	3.85	3.31	1.0	1.8	0.8
Africa	43.7	55.0	44.8	53.6	64.3	7.368	7.335	5.51	5.944	0.2	-5.0	2.3
America	45.4	61.8	68.0	60.8	88.2	7.655	8.242	8.364	8.154	2.9	2.4	1.6
E. Europe & USSR	114.1	130.2	152.6	170.7	211.7	19.24	17.36	18.77	20	2.1	4.0	2.1
USSR	73.8	77.9	86.0	116.0	130.9	12.44	10.39	10.58	12.1	1.1	2.5	2.7
E.Europe	40.3	52.3	62.0	54.7	80.8	6.795	6.975	7.626	7.47	3.1	4.3	1.7
OECD	282.6	367.2	391.9	367.3	543.7	47.65	48.97	48.2	50.26	2.4	1.6	2.1
N.America	186.3	250.1	259.1	241.9	370.5	31.41	33.36	31.87	34.25	2.4	0.9	2.3
US	165.8	227.8	237.1	215.9	333.0	27.95	30.38	29.16	30.78	2.6	1.0	2.1
Canada	20.5	22.3	21.9	25.9	37.5	3.456	2.974	2.694	3.467	0.5	0.0	3.4
W.Europe	90.1	110.1	123.2	117.2	160.6	15.19	14.68	15.15	14.85	2.3	2.9	1.7
EC-10	63.7	76.5	84.6	78.5	107.0	10.74	10.2	10.41	9.892	2.0	2.5	1.5
S.Europe	17.0	21.4	23.5	24.1	32.7	2.866	2.854	2.891	3.023	2.3	2.4	2.1
Other	9.4	12.2	15.1	14.6	20.9	1.585	1.627	1.857	1.932	3.4	5.5	2.1
Japan	0.7	0.4	0.4	0.4	0.4	0.118	0.053	0.049	0.037	-4.0	0.0	0.0
Oceania	5.5	6.6	9.2	7.8	12.2	0.927	0.88	1.132	1.128	3.7	8.7	1.8

Source: See Table 3.2.

Table 3.6
Cereal Production Projections
(quantities [a] — annual average growth rate — per cent — 1984-2000)

	FAO	IFPRI	World Bank	IWC	IIASA
Base year for projections	1983-85	1980	1984	1985	1980
World	n.a.	n.a.	2.0	1.3	1.5
Developing countries					
Total	2.6	2.9	2.0	2.3	1.0
(excluding China)	n.a.	2.9	1.7	n.a.	n.a.
Asia	2.4	2.9	2.0	2.3	n.a.
(excluding China)	2.2	3.0	1.6	n.a.	n.a.
North Africa/Middle East	2.7	2.9	n.a.	2.9	n.a.
Sub-Saharan Africa	3.3	2.1	n.a.	2.6	n.a.
Total Africa	n.a.	n.a.	1.9	2.7	n.a.
Latin America	3.3	3.0	2.1	2.4	n.a.
Developed countries	n.a.	n.a.	n.a.	0.1	n.a.
OECD	0.9	n.a.	2.1	n.a.	1.8
E. Europe & USSR	1.3-1.5	n.a.	1.6	n.a.	1.7

a. Rice is included on a milled basis, except for World Bank.

Source: See text. Growth rates have been recalculated by Development Centre from their original base year to 1984. See also footnote to Table 2.5.

Table 3.7

Production, Area Harvested and Output per Hectare for Major Crops (Average Annual Growth Rates and Shares)

		Average Annual Growth Rate			Contribution to Production Increase	
		Produc-tion[a]	Area Harvested	Output per Hectare	Area Harvested	Output per Hectare
Developing countries	1961-70	3.6	1.1	2.5	30	70
	1971-80	2.9	0.6	2.3	20	80
(Excluding China)	1961-70	2.9	1.5	1.4	51	49
	1971-80	2.6	0.8	1.8	32	68
Asia	1961-70	3.8	0.5	3.4	13	87
	1971-80	3.3	0.5	2.8	16	84
(Excluding China)	1961-70	2.7	0.8	1.8	31	69
	1971-80	3.1	0.9	2.2	30	70
China[b]	1961-70	5.2	-0.1	5.4	..[c]	100
	1971-80	3.4	-0.2	3.6	..[c]	100
South Asia	1961-70	2.7	0.8	1.9	29	71
	1971-80	2.7	0.7	2.0	25	75
East and Southeast Asia	1961-70	2.7	1.1	1.6	40	60
	1971-80	3.9	1.7	2.2	44	56
North Africa/Middle East	1961-70	2.4	1.2	1.2	51	49
	1971-80	2.6	0.7	1.9	26	74
Sub-Saharan Africa	1961-70	2.2	2.4	-0.2	100	..[c]
	1971-80	1.6	0.8	0.8	50	50
Latin America	1961-70	4.2	2.8	1.4	66	34
	1971-80	1.8	0.6	1.2	33	47

a. The production data exclude bananas and plantains, for which area estimates are not available.

b. The data on area for China are for area planted.

c. Negative. The contribution to the production increase is assigned totally to the other source of increase.

Source: Paulino, Table 6. Based primarily on FAO data.

Table 3.8

Agricultural Resources and Input Use in Developing Countries

(1982-84 average — Excluding China)

	Arable land					Fertilizers		Cereals	
	Potential (million ha)	in use (million ha)	In use as % of potential	Irrigated as % of total	ha per agriculture worker	Total (mill.tons)	per ha (kg)	Harvested land as % of total	Yield (tons/ha)
Total developing countries	2 143	768	36	14	1.4	25.8	43	54	1.6
- of which:									
. low income	846	374	44	18	1.0	9.9	32	58	1.5
— (excl. India)	677	205	30	12	1.2	3.1	23	58	1.5
. middle income	1 297	394	30	11	2.2	15.9	56	50	1.9
- of which:									
. Latin America	890	195	22	7	4.9	6.5	53	43	2.0
. Sub-Saharan Africa	816	201	25	2	1.6	1.0	9	48	0.8
. Middle East/North Africa	95	92	97	20	2.8	4.6	72	67	1.4
. Other Asia	343	280	82	27	0.8	13.8	46	59	1.9
-of which:									
. India	169	169	100	25	0.9	6.8	38	58	1.5

Source: Alexandratos, Table 7.

Table 3.9
Average Crop Yields
(1983-85, tons per hectare)

	Wheat	Rice (Paddy)	Coarse grains	Cassava	Soybeans	Groundnuts
World	2.19	3.22	2.29	9.45	1.75	1.08
All developing countries	2.04	3.14	1.49	9.45	1.55	1.02
94 Developing countries	2.04	3.14	1.49	9.47	1.55	1.02
93 Developing countries	1.68	2.49	1.18	9.36	1.65	0.86
Africa (sub-Saharan)	1.31	1.44	0.76	7.34	0.67	0.68
Benin	n.a.	1.07	0.74	6.88	n.a.	0.70
Burundi	0.58	2.78	1.07	11.35	n.a.	1.23
Cameroon	1.38	3.26	0.94	1.60	0.55	0.40
Chad	0.94	0.45	0.50	4.16	n.a.	0.51
Côte d'Ivoire	n.a.	1.12	0.76	5.26	1.84	0.91
Ethiopia	1.12	n.a.	1.06	n.a.	4.58	0.91
Gabon	n.a.	1.92	1.46	5.99	n.a.	0.87
Ghana	n.a.	0.89	0.73	8.75	n.a.	0.99
Guinea	n.a.	0.76	0.60	7.05	n.a.	0.58
Kenya	1.59	4.06	1.43	8.97	n.a.	0.69
Liberia	n.a.	1.30	n.a.	3.68	0.40	0.67
Madagascar	1.50	1.81	1.03	6.08	1.10	0.95
Mali	1.00	0.96	0.73	8.90	n.a.	0.48
Mauritania	0.90	3.52	0.26	n.a.	n.a.	0.73
Niger	1.16	2.55	0.35	7.11	n.a.	0.36
Nigeria	2.44	2.01	0.66	9.65	0.31	0.86
Rwanda	1.08	4.55	1.25	10.06	0.71	0.98
Senegal	n.a.	1.99	0.62	2.70	1.05	0.70
Somalia	0.36	3.48	0.74	10.91	n.a.	0.80
Sudan	1.22	0.63	0.45	2.78	n.a.	0.58
Swaziland	3.25	6.21	1.42	n.a.	n.a.	0.43
Tanzania	1.35	1.34	1.03	12.22	0.24	0.60
Uganda	2.23	1.29	1.37	7.87	1.11	0.82
Zaire	0.87	0.87	0.97	7.07	1.11	0.72
Zambia	3.57	1.14	1.71	3.46	1.48	0.56
Zimbabwe	5.42	1.41	0.98	3.98	1.78	0.28
Near East/North Africa	1.41	3.94	1.34	n.a.	2.26	1.84
Algeria	0.71	3.11	0.76	n.a.	n.a.	n.a.
Egypt	3.67	6.10	4.04	n.a.	2.59	1.87
Iran	0.98	3.00	0.96	n.a.	2.06	1.89
Iraq	0.91	2.13	0.95	n.a.	1.57	2.29
Jordan	0.86	n.a.	0.50	n.a.	n.a.	n.a.
Morocco	1.13	3.37	0.76	n.a.	1.00	1.33
Saudi Arabia	3.32	n.a.	0.65	n.a.	n.a.	n.a.
Syria	1.35	5.00	0.59	n.a.	n.a.	2.03
Tunisia	0.95	n.a.	0.65	n.a.	n.a.	n.a.

Table 3.9 (cont)
Average Crop Yields
(1983-85, tons per hectare)

	Wheat	Rice (Paddy)	Coarse grains	Cassava	Soybeans	Groundnuts
Asia	2.32	3.25	1.74	12.39	1.23	1.14
Bangladesh	2.19	2.14	0.81	n.a.	n.a.	1.12
Burma	1.55	3.09	1.18	11.30	0.81	1.04
China	2.90	5.28	3.15	15.56	1.33	1.94
India	1.84	2.22	0.76	18.07	0.81	0.85
Indonesia	n.a.	3.91	1.77	10.62	0.92	1.55
S. Korea	3.90	6.34	2.53	n.a.	1.33	1.62
Malaysia	n.a.	2.72	1.53	10.76	1.63	3.47
Pakistan	1.59	2.47	0.84	n.a.	0.33	1.19
Philippines	n.a.	2.55	1.05	7.51	0.96	0.85
Sri Lanka	n.a.	2.99	0.91	12.35	0.60	0.56
Thailand	n.a.	2.07	2.34	15.76	1.38	1.36
Vietnam	n.a.	2.75	1.38	5.79	0.73	0.96
Latin America	1.99	2.24	2.00	11.14	1.81	1.47
Argentina	1.92	3.27	2.92	8.73	2.07	1.91
Bolivia	0.70	1.55	1.25	9.39	1.49	1.01
Brazil	1.36	1.69	1.78	11.56	1.75	1.57
Chile	2.05	4.02	3.54	n.a.	n.a.	n.a.
Colombia	1.59	4.77	1.73	8.98	1.95	1.52
Cuba	n.a.	3.41	1.23	6.52	n.a.	1.00
Ecuador	1.03	2.89	1.33	10.00	1.70	0.87
Guatemala	1.47	3.06	1.65	3.71	1.11	1.95
Honduras	0.67	2.29	1.39	17.84	n.a.	1.52
Jamaica	n.a.	3.39	1.29	11.13	n.a.	1.14
Mexico	4.10	2.94	1.90	17.55	1.69	1.27
Nicaragua	n.a.	3.88	1.54	4.03	1.67	1.67
Peru	1.04	4.41	1.72	10.76	1.61	1.89
Uruguay	1.47	4.64	1.45	n.a.	1.41	0.70
Venezuela	0.42	2.87	1.88	7.90	n.a.	1.92
Developing — Low-income	2.26	3.20	1.44	8.01	1.25	1.00
Low-income excl. China	1.73	2.25	0.79	7.71	0.81	0.80
Low-income excl. China/India	1.50	2.29	0.83	7.16	0.82	0.74
Developing — Middle-income	1.62	2.98	1.56	10.69	1.72	1.11

Note: The sign 'n.a.' indicates 'not available': in fact, in most cases national production is so small and data are so fragmentary that an estimate of 'average yields' could not be meaningful.

Source: Alexandratos, Table 8.

Table 3.10
Irrigated Area

	1970	1975	1980	1985	1970-75	1975-80	1980-85
	(million hectares)				(% change)		
Africa	7.6	8.2	9.3	10.6	7.2	14.3	13.8
North America	21.0	22.9	27.7	25.4	9.1	21.1	-8.3
South America	5.7	6.6	7.4	8.1	15.9	12.1	10.1
Asia	109.7	121.6	132.2	138.3	10.8	8.8	4.6
Europe	10.7	12.8	14.7	16.1	18.9	14.9	9.8
Oceania	1.6	1.6	1.7	1.9	2.5	4.0	11.1
USSR	11.1	14.5	17.5	20.0	30.5	20.7	14.1
World Total	167.4	188.0	210.4	220.3	12.3	11.9	4.7

Source: World Bank, 1989a, derived from FAO Production Yearbook.

Table 3.11
Agricultural Investment Requirements 1982/83 to Year 2000 (Cumulative)[a]

	Physical Units			Agricultural Investment 1982/84-2000 ($ billion)[b]	
	Units	Net Additions 1982/84-2000 (million)	Average Unit Cost ($)[b]	Net	Gross[c]
1. Investment in crop production					
Land development	ha	77.0	746/ha	57	57
Irrigation	ha	54.9	2 254/ha	124	236
Soil and water conservation	ha	171.2	176/ha	30	30
Flood control	ha	5.1	880/ha	12	15
Establishment of permanent crops	ha	11.6	1 760/ha	21	75
Tractors and equipment	units	3.2	13 173/tr	42	156
Draught animals	pairs	9.9	704/pair	7	7
Equipment for draught animals	set	9.9	325/set	3	51
Handtools	set	131.4	18/set	2	37
Increases in working capital	---	---	---	31	31
TOTAL CROP INVESTMENT				330	696
2. Investment in livestock production					
Increases in livestock numbers	---	---	---	80	89
Dairy production (on farm equipment)	tons milk	51.7	53/ton	3	3
Commercial pig and poultry production (structures and equipment)			1 000/sow, 8/bird	34	43
Grazing land development	ha	79.7	264/ha	21	21
TOTAL LIVESTOCK INVESTMENT				147	156
TOTAL PRIMARY INVESTMENT				477	851
SUPPORT INVESTMENT	---	---	---	430	635
GRAND TOTAL				907	1 486

a. Excluding China.
b. Constant 1980 dollars.
c. Including replacement expenditures.

Source: Alexandratos, Table 4.11.

Table 4.1
Major Seeds Groups and R&D Budgets ($ million)

Name of Group	Principal activity	Country of origin	Total sales	Seed sales	Seed sales as % of total sales	R&D budget	Research (% of sales)
CARDO	Agro-industries	Sweden	434.0	167.0	38.5	n.a.	n.a.
CARGILL	Agro-industries	USA	28 000.0	80-100	0.3	n.a.	n.a.
CLAEYS-LUCK	Seeds	France	153	79	51.6	3.2*	n.a.
CLAUSE	Seeds	France	125	43+	34.4	5.5*	n.a.
CIBA-GEIGY	Pharmaceuticals	Switzerland	6 802.0	135.5	1.99	579.0	8.5
DEKALB	Seeds	USA	577.3	151.6	26.3	17.6	3.0
KWS	Seeds	FRG	71.0	71	100.0	n.a.	n.a.
LUBRIZOL	Chemicals	USA	812.0	110.5	13.6	36.7	4.5
LIMAGRAIN	Seeds	France	184	150	81.5	11.5*	n.a.
PIONEER	Seeds	USA	557.0	526.4	94.5	19.0	3.4
ROYAL DUTCH/SHELL	Petroleum	GB/Netherlands	86 025.0	150-200	0.2	511.0	0.6
SANDOZ	Pharmaceuticals	Switzerland	2 981.0	292	9.8	271.0	9.1
SUIKER UNIE	Agro-industries	Netherlands	469.2	100	21.3	n.a.	n.a.
UPJOHN	Pharmaceuticals	USA	1 829.0	139	7.6	196.0	10.7

* 1984

Source: Ducos and Joly.

Table 6.1
Net Cereal Trade Projections in Year 2000
(million tons)

	1983-85	Year 2000 projections					
		Z&V	FAO	IFPRI	World Bank	IWC	IIASA
Developing countries							
Total	-61	n.a.	-95	-69	-201	-136	-181
(Excluding China)	-56	-173	-94	-76	-158	-108	-167
Asia	-15	n.a.	-19	+51	-140	-90	-160
(Excluding China)	-9	-30	-18	+44	-96	-62	-145
North Africa/ Middle East	-35	-86	-60	-64	n.a.	-32	n.a.
Sub-Saharan Africa	-9	-44	-17	-47	n.a.	-20	n.a.
Total Africa and Middle East	-44	-130	-77	-111	-53	n.a.	-16
Latin America	-2	-12	+1	-9	0	-6	-5
Developed countries							
OECD	+111		+142	-152	+271		+213
E. Europe & USSR	-42		-30	-40	-71		-32

Note: Minus sign indicates net imports.

Source: See text and footnote to Table 2.5.

Table 6.2

Long-Term Trends in Cereal Prices

(Constant 1985 $[a])

	Average								World Bank			IIASA[b]
	1960-69	1970-84	1980	1985	1986	1987	1988	1990	1995	2000	2000/1970-84 (per cent)	2000
Canadian wheat[c]	219.8	236.1	249.0	173.3	157.5	127.2	161.3	130.5	123.9	130.9	55.4	274.1
Thai rice[d]	517.4	509.2	566.2	215.9	206.4	219.4	277.6	208.4	200.8	193.1	37.9	511.9
US maize[e]	170.4	171.0	163.5	112.2	85.9	72.1	98.8	82.0	79.0	85.0	49.7	147.2
US sorghum[f]	153.7	161.3	168.2	103.0	80.8	69.4	91.8	75.5	71.9	79.3	49.2	151.4

a. Deflated by US GNP price deflator.
b. Calculated by Development Centre using IIASA's projected growth rates and WB historic series.
c. No. 1 Western Red Spring in store, Thunder Bay.
d. Thai 5% broken, f.o.b. Bangkok.
e. US No. 2 Yellow, f.o.b. Gulf ports.
f. Grain sorghum, US No. 2 Yellow, f.o.b. Gulf ports.

Source: World Bank, 1989a, and Parikh *et al.*

Table 6.3
Demand Price Elasticities[a]

	Argentina	Brazil	Mexico	China	S. Korea	India	Thailand	US	EC	SSA
Wheat										
Z&V	-0.04	-0.12	n.a.	n.a.	-0.36	-0.15	n.a.	-0.06	-0.09	-0.35
FAO	-1.48	-0.25	-0.05	-0.15	-0.15	-0.25	-0.50	n.a.	n.a.	n.a.
USDA	-0.40	-0.46	-0.30	-0.10	-0.40	-0.30	-0.75	0.06 [b]	n.a.	n.a.
IIASA	-0.15	-0.01	-0.35	n.a.	n.a.	-0.09	-0.11	-0.20	-0.12	n.a.
Rice										
Z&V	-0.19	-0.03	n.a.	n.a.	-0.18	-0.24	n.a.	-0.1	-0.68	-0.18
FAO	-0.20	-0.20	-0.40	-0.04	-0.30	-0.40	-0.05	n.a.	n.a.	n.a.
USDA	-0.40	-0.45	-0.30	-0.12	-0.20	-0.50	-0.10	-0.10 [b]	n.a.	n.a.
IIASA	n.a.	-0.07	-0.05	n.a.	n.a.	-0.04	-0.06	-0.07	-0.01	n.a.
Coarse grains										
Z&V	-0.19	-0.05	n.a.	n.a.	0.22	-0.02	n.a.	-0.21	-0.2	0.22
FAO	-0.35	-0.30	-0.20	-0.10	-0.50	-0.35	-0.05	n.a.	n.a.	n.a.
USDA	-0.50	-0.50	-0.40	-0.13	-0.50	-0.60	-0.30	-0.21 [b]	n.a.	n.a.
IIASA	-0.12	-0.47	-0.11	n.a.	n.a.	-0.31	-0.50	-0.03	-0.35	n.a.

a. Medium-term "own" price elasticities in physical terms: A 1 per cent change in the international price of the product would lead over 5-10 years to the indicated percentage change in the quantity consumed. See also footnote to Table 2.5.

b. Human and industrial uses.

Sources: OECD, 1989a, for FAO and USDA.
Fischer for IIASA.

Table 6.4
Supply Price Elasticities[a]

	Argentina	Brazil	Mexico	China	S. Korea	India	Thailand	US
Wheat								
FAO	0.63	0.37	0.47	0.07	0.23	0.13	0.05	n.a.
USDA	0.60	0.45	0.55	0.15	0.40	0.45	0.10	0.50
IIASA	0.20	0.26	0.31	n.a.	n.a.	0.04	n.a.	n.a.
Rice								
FAO	0.53	0.55	0.59	0.09	0.23	0.23	0.27	n.a.
USDA	0.70	0.40	0.65	0.15	0.35	0.40	n.a.	0.37
IIASA	0.00	0.26	0.15	n.a.	n.a.	0.01	0.45	n.a.
Coarse grains								
FAO	0.27	0.10	0.45	0.08	0.25	0.20	0.55	n.a.
USDA	0.55	0.35	0.61	0.17	0.36	0.37	0.75	0.43
IIASA	0.04	0.30	0.56	n.a.	n.a.	0.34	0.60	n.a.

a. Medium-term "own" price elasticities in physical terms.

Source: OECD, 1989a, for FAO and USDA. Fischer for IIASA.

Table 7.1
PSEs/CSEs in Developing Countries [a]

	Egypt	Korea	NA/ME	Argentina	Brazil	India	Nigeria	Pakistan	Rest of Asia	Rest of SSA	Rest of LA
PSE											
Wheat	-0.28	0.62	-0.18	-0.32	-0.14	-0.27	-0.24	-0.24	0.08	0.13	0.05
Coarse grains	-0.28	0.54	-0.18	-0.32	-0.26	-0.27	-0.35	-0.24	-0.31	-0.22	-0.22
Rice	-0.28	0.68	-0.18	-0.32	-0.14	-0.30	-0.51	-0.24	-0.31	0.15	0.05
Beef	-0.28	0.77	-0.18	-0.32	-0.26	-0.21	-0.35	-0.38	0.08	0.15	0.05
Sugar	-0.28	0.00	-0.18	-0.32	-0.14	-0.21	-0.10	-0.38	-0.31	-0.22	-0.22
Soya	-0.28	0.76	-0.18	-0.32	-0.26	-0.12	-0.35	-0.38	0.08	-0.22	-0.22
CSE											
Wheat	0.21	0.20	0.08	0.13	0.07	0.16	1.60	0.07	-0.21	-0.41	-0.18
Coarse grains	0.21	-0.65	0.08	0.13	0.19	0.16	1.60	0.07	0.19	-0.07	0.12
Rice	0.21	-0.66	0.08	0.13	0.07	0.12	0.35	0.07	0.19	-0.41	-0.18
Beef	0.21	-0.76	0.08	0.13	0.19	0.11	0.63	0.21	-0.21	-0.41	-0.18
Sugar	0.21	-0.68	0.08	0.13	0.07	0.11	1.60	0.21	0.19	-0.07	0.12
Soya	0.21	-0.74	0.08	0.13	0.19	0.45	0.63	0.21	-0.21	-0.07	0.12

a. PSE = Product Subsidy Equivalent; CSE = Consumer Subsidy Equivalent. See text.

Source: Zietz & Valdés, 1989.

Table 7.2
Changes in World Price Resulting from Trade Liberalisation in Industrialised Countries

Percentage Reduction in PSEs and CSEs	Wheat	CGs	Rice	Beef	Sugar	Soya
Present Study						
10 per cent	0.4	-0.1	0.2	.9	1.5	-0.3
50 per cent	2.0	-0.3	0.9	4.9	7.6	-1.5
100 per cent	3.5	-2.8	1.7	10.5	15.0	-4.0
Other Studies						
OECD-1987 (10%)	-0.1	-0.3	0.1	1.5	1.0	-1.0
Valdés/Zietz-80 (50%)	4.9	2.1[a]	0.4	6.8	7.7[b]	1.0
IIASA (100%)	18.0	11.0	21.0	17.0	n.a.	n.a.
T/A-87[c] (100%)	9.9	3.0	18.0	43.0	22.0	n.a.
T/A-87[d] (100%)	25.0	3.0	18.0	43.0	22.0	n.a.
Roningen (100)%	25.9	18.8	18.1	17.3	31.0	6.8
Zietz/V-86[e] (100%)	12.1	11.0	n.a.	17.4	18.2	n.a.

a. Maize.
b. Raw sugar.
c. Based on protection levels of 1980-82.
d. Based on projected protection levels for 1988.
e. The reported price increases are simple averages of the various alternative model simulations reported in Table 1 of Zietz and Valdés (1986); the estimates are based on 1979-81 protection levels.

Source: Zietz & Valdés (1989), Table 8.

Table 7.3
Changes in World Price Resulting from Liberalisation in LDCs and All Countries

100 per cent reduction in PSEs and CSEs	Wheat	CGs	Rice	Beef	Sugar	Soya
Present Study						
LDCs	-13.6	-20.9	-21.8	2.9	-12.1	-11.5
All countries	-11.7	-24.4	-21.1	13.3	0.8	-15.9
IIASA						
Developing countries	5.0	4.0	1.0	-3.0	n.a.	n.a.
All countries	23.0	13.0	16.0	11.0	n.a.	n.a.
Tyers/Anderson-87						
All countries	10.0	2.0	-8.0	13.0	-1.0	n.a.

Source: Zietz & Valdés (1989), Table 9.

Table 7.4
Absolute Change in LDC Net Exports under Various Liberalisation Scenarios
(million tons)

	Wheat	CGs	Rice	Beef	Sugar	Soya
Present Study						
ICs liberalise	8.8	-11.6	4.0	0.8	5.1	-0.9
LDC liberalise	0	16.1	2.5	-1.8	2.5	-4.0
All liberalise	8.9	1.7	6.4	-0.7	7.8	-5.3
IIASA						
ICs liberalise	11.1	1.3	9.1	1.8	n.a.	n.a.
LDCs liberalise	-11.0	-10.0	-0	0.3	n.a.	n.a.
Tyers/Anderson-87						
ICs liberalise	4.9	-2.3	4.0	2.9	2.9	n.a.

Note: Liberalisation means complete removal of all PSEs and CSEs as given in Table 7.1. Liberalisation is superimposed on the base line results.

Source: Zietz & Valdés (1989), Table 10.

Table 7.5

Imports of LDCs in the Year 2000 under Various Liberalisation Scenarios

(million tons)

	Base-Line Run	Liberalisation by		
		ICs	LDCs	All
Wheat	86.8	78.1	86.8	77.9
Coarse grains	82.4	93.7	66.3	80.7
Rice	3.5	-0.5	1.0	-2.9
Beef	2.5	1.7	4.3	3.2
Sugar	9.7	4.6	7.2	1.9
Soybeans	-6.8	-5.9	-2.8	-1.5

Note: The figures exclude China. Liberalisation means complete removal of all PSEs and CSEs as given in Table 7.1. Liberalisation is superimposed on the base-line results.

Source: Zietz & Valdés (1989), Table 11.

Table 7.6

Self-Sufficiency of ICs and LDCs, 1981-83, and Year 2000 (per cent)

	Cereals	Wheat	CG	Rice	Beef	Sugar	Soya
1981-83							
Industrialised countries	124	178	107	108	100	102	100
Developing countries	92	76	95	100	100	115	194
Year 2000							
Base-line results							
Industrialised countries	137	189	122	128	109	167	106
Developing countries	82	68	76	99	88	90	132
Industrialised countries liberalise							
Industrialised countries	136	185	124	104	106	143	107
Developing countries	82	71	73	100	92	95	127
Developing countries liberalise							
Industrialised countries	134	195	118	113	115	155	112
Developing countries	84	69	81	100	82	93	111
All liberalise							
Industrialised countries	134	190	121	91	112	133	113
Developing countries	84	72	77	101	86	98	106

Note: The figures exclude China. Liberalisation means complete removal of all PSEs and CSEs as given in Table 7.1. Liberalisation is superimposed on the base-line results.

Source: Zietz & Valdés (1989), Table 12.

Table 7.7
Self-Sufficiency of LDCs by Region, 1981-83, and Year 2000 (per cent)

	Cereals	Wheat	CG	Rice	Beef	Sugar	Soya
1981-83 averages							
Asia	97	86	94	102	97	105	49
North Africa/ME	70	67	75	69	78	46	24
Sub-Saharan Africa	84	29	95	66	97	109	83
Latin America	99	83	106	97	106	162	353
Year 2000							
Base-line run							
Asia	94	87	77	104	77	80	38
North Africa/ME	51	52	46	77	65	30	16
Sub-Saharan Africa	55	18	64	40	86	62	131
Latin America	92	63	102	95	99	157	270
Industrialised countries liberalise							
Asia	94	89	72	105	85	86	37
North Africa/ME	52	55	43	79	67	32	15
Sub-Saharan Africa	54	19	63	41	89	65	128
Latin America	92	66	100	96	102	164	261
Developing countries liberalise							
Asia	98	87	87	107	44	83	25
North Africa/ME	54	58	46	75	72	32	17
Sub-Saharan Africa	53	14	66	33	83	64	130
Latin America	92	58	107	82	104	160	299
All liberalise							
Asia	98	89	81	108	49	89	24
North Africa/ME	54	61	42	76	75	34	16
Sub-Saharan Africa	52	15	64	34	86	66	126
Latin America	91	60	105	83	107	167	287

Note: The figures exclude China. Liberalisation means complete removal of all PSEs and CSEs. The figures for the base-line results and the various liberalisation scenarios are predictions for the year 2002, i.e. 20 years from the base year.

Source: Zietz & Valdés (1989), Table 13.

Table 7.8

Cereal Import Needs in Year 2000 under Various Liberalisation Scenarios[a]

	All LDCs	Asia	NA/ME	Sub-Sah. Africa	Latin America
Base-line run					
Import level (million tons)	173	30	86	44	12
Cereal import bill (% change)	174	29	143	350	293
Industrialised countries liberalise					
Import level (million tons)	171	29	85	45	13
Cereal import bill (% change)	157	-56	137	352	287
Developing countries liberalise					
Import level (million tons)	154	11	81	48	14
Cereal import bill (% change)	106	-204[b]	88	322	384
All liberalise					
Import level (million tons)	156	10	81	49	14
Cereal import bill (% change)	93	-267[b]	81	323	383

a. The figures exclude China. The percentage change in the cereal import bill is calculated with reference to the cereal import bill of 1981-83.

b. Export earnings exceed the import bill in the reference period.

Source: Zietz & Valdés (1989), Table 14.

Table 8.1

Indexes of "Revealed" Comparative Advantage in East Asia[a]

		Agriculture	Textiles and clothing
Japan			
	1899	>1.0	1.5
	1913	0.7	2.6
	1929	0.7	2.9
	1937	0.5	4.1
	1954-56	0.4	5.5
	1964-66	0.3	2.7
	1971-73	0.2	1.7
	1976-78	0.2	1.0
	1982-84	0.1	0.7
	1985-86	0.1	0.5
Hong Kong			
	1954-56	n.a.	5.4
	1964-66	n.a.	7.0
	1971-73	n.a.	7.6
	1976-78	n.a.	9.2
	1982-84	n.a.	7.2
	1985-86	n.a.	6.9
Korea, Rep.			
	1954-56	2.7	n.a.
	1964-66	1.6	4.3
	1971-73	0.7	6.3
	1976-78	0.6	6.6
	1982-84	0.5	4.8
	1985-86	0.3	4.1
Taiwan			
	1954-56	2.6	n.a.
	1964-66	2.1	2.2
	1971-73	0.8	4.8
	1976-78	0.7	5.0
	1982-84	0.6	4.1
	1985-86	0.5	3.3

a. Share of an economy's exports due to these commodities relative to those commodities' share in total world exports, following Balassa (1965). Agriculture is defined as SITC sections 0, 1, 2 (excluding 27, 28) and 4; textiles and clothing include SITC division, 65 and 84.

Source: Anderson 1990, Table 3.8.

BIBLIOGRAPHY

ABBOTT, P. and R. THOMPSON (1987), "Changing Agricultural Comparative Advantage", *Agricultural Economics*, No. 1, pp. 97-112.

ADELMAN, Irma and Edward TAYLOR (1990), *Changing Comparative Advantage in Food and Agriculture: Lessons from Mexico*, Development Centre Studies, OECD, Paris.

AHMED, R. and John MELLOR (1988), "Agricultural Price Policy: The Context and the Approach" in J. Mellor and R. Ahmed (eds.), *Agricultural Price Policy for Developing Countries*, Johns Hopkins for IFPRI.

ALDERMAN, Harold (1986), *The Effect of Food Price and Income Changes on the Acquisition of Food by Low-Income Households*, IFPRI, Washington, May.

ALEXANDRATOS, N. (ed.) (1988), *World Agriculture: Towards 2000, An FAO Study*, Belhaven Press, London.

ALI, I. (1986), *Rice in Indonesia: Price Policy and Comparative Advantage*, Asian Development Bank, Manila.

ANDERSON, Kym (1988), *Rent Seeking and Price-distorting Policies in Rich and Poor Countries*, Department of Economics Working Paper 88-10, University of Adelaide.

ANDERSON, Kym (1990), *Changing Comparative Advantages in China: Effects on Food, Feed and Fibre Markets*, Development Centre Studies, OECD, Paris.

ANTONELLI, G. and A. QUADRIO-CURZIO, (eds.) (1988), *The Agro-Technological System towards 2000: A European Perspective*, Elsevier Science Publishers B.V. (North-Holland), Amsterdam.

ASIAN DEVELOPMENT BANK (1988), *Evaluating Rice Market Intervention Policies: Some Asian Examples*, ADB, Manila.

AZIZ, Sartaj (1990), *Agricultural Policies for the 1990s*, Development Centre Studies, OECD, Paris.

BALASSA, B. (1977), *Trade Liberalization and Revealed Comparative Advantage*, The Manchester School of Economics and Social Studies, Vol. 33, No. 256, May.

BALASSA, B. (1977), *A Stages' Approach to Comparative Advantage*, World Bank Staff Working Paper No. 256, May.

BALDWIN, R. and R.S. HILTON (1984), "A Technique for Indicating Comparative Costs and Predicting Changes in Trade Ratios", *The Review of Economics and Statistics*, Vol. LXVI, No. 1, pp. 105-10, February.

BARDHAN, P. (1965), "International Differences in Production Functions, Trade and Factor Prices", *The Economic Journal*, Vol. LXXV, No. 297, pp. 81-7, March.

BARKER, R. *et al.* (1985), *The Rice Economy of Asia*, Resources for the Future, Washington, D.C.

BEHRMAN, Jere, Anil DEOLALIKAR and Barbara WOLFE (1988), "Nutrients: Impacts and Determinants", *World Bank Economic Review*, Vol. 2, No. 3, September.

BELL, Daniel (1976), *The Coming of Post-Industrial Society*, Basic Books, New York.

BRENNER, Carliene (1991), *Biotechnology and Developing Country Agriculture: The Case of Maize*, Development Centre Studies, OECD, Paris.

BROWN, Lester (1988), *The Changing World Food Prospect: The Nineties and Beyond*, Worldwatch, Paper 85, Washington, October.

BROWN, Lester *et al.* (1989), *State of the World 1989: A Worldwatch Institute Report on Progress toward a Sustainable Society*, Norton, New York.

BROWN, Lester *et al.* (1990), *State of the World 1990: A Worldwatch Institute Report on Progress toward a Sustainable Society*, Norton, New York.

BROWN, Martin (1988), *World Phosphates Supply to the Year 2000*, Development Centre Studies, OECD, Paris.

BRUNO, M. (1970), "Development Policy and Dynamic Comparative Advantage" in R. Vernon (ed.), *The Technology Factor in International Trade*, Columbia University Press, New York.

BURNIAUX, Jean-Marc (1987), *Le Radeau de la Méduse : Analyse des dilemmes alimentaires*, Economica, Paris.

BURNIAUX, Jean-Marc, François DELORME, Ian LIENERT, John P. MARTIN, and Peter HOELLER (1988), *Quantifying the Economy-wide Effects of Agricultural Policies: a General Equilibrium Approach*, OECD Department of Economics and Statistics Working Papers No. 55, July.

BURNIAUX, Jean-Marc and Dominique van der MENSBRUGGHE (1990), *The RUNS Model: A Rural-Urban North-South General Equilibrium Model for Agricultural Policy Analysis*, OECD Development Centre, Technical Paper No. 33, OECD, Paris, December.

BUTLER, Nick (1988), *The International Grain Trade: Problems and Prospects*, Croom Helm for the Royal Institute of International Affairs, London.

CARTER, Colin, Alex F. McCALLA and Andrew SCHMITZ (1989), *Canada and International Grain Markets: Trends, Policies and Prospects*, Canadian Government Publishing Centre for the Economic Council of Canada, Ottawa.

CENTRE FOR INTERNATIONAL ECONOMICS (1988), *Macroeconomic Consequences of Farm-support Policies*, Canberra.

CHARVET, Jean Paul (1985), *La Guerre du blé. Bases et stratégies des grands exportateurs*, Editions Economica, Paris.

CHENERY, H. (1979), *Structural Change and Development Policy*, Oxford University, Oxford.

CLARK, William C. and R.E. MUNN (eds.) (1986), *Sustainable Development of the Biosphere*, Cambridge University Press for IIASA, Cambridge.

CONTRÉ, Florence and Ian GOLDIN (1990), *Agriculture and the Economic Cycle: An Economic and Econometric Analysis with Special Reference to Brazil*, OECD Development Centre, Technical Paper No. 15, OECD, Paris, June.

DAVIS, Ted J. and Isabelle A. SCHIRMER (eds.) (1987), *Sustainability Issues in Agricultural Development*, World Bank, Washington, D.C.

DEARDORFF, A. (1975), "Weak Links in the Chain of Comparative Advantage", *Journal of International Economics*, Vol. 5, pp. 153-65.

DEARDORFF, A. (1984), "Testing Trade Theories and Predicting Trade Flows", Chapter 10 in R.W. Jones and P.B. Denen (eds.), *Handbook of International Economics*, North Holland, Amsterdam.

DOSI, G. (1982), "Technological Paradigms and Technological Trajectories", *Research Policy*, Vol. 11, pp. 147-63.

DUCOS, Chantal and Pierre-Benoit JOLY (1978), *L'industrie des semences face aux biotechnologies*, Doctoral thesis presented in March 1987 at Université des Sciences de Toulouse, France.

FAO (1987a), *The Fifth World Food Survey*, FAO, Rome.

FAO (1987b), *Transnational Corporations in Food and Agriculture, Forestry and Fishery Sectors in Developing Countries*, ESC/Misc/87/1, Rome.

FAO (1988), *European Agriculture: Policy Issues and Options to 2000*, ERC/88/INF/4 May.

FISCHER, G., K. FROHBERG, M.A. KEYZER and K.S. PARIKH (1988), *Linked National Models: A Tool for International Food Policy Analysis*, Kluwer for IIASA, Dordrecht.

FLICHMAN, Guillermo (1990), *International Comparisons of Efficiency in Agricultural Production*, OECD Development Centre, Technical Paper No. 21, OECD, Paris, July.

FOOD RESEARCH INSTITUTE STUDIES (1976), Vol. 15, No. 2. (This issue contains six articles relating to measuring comparative advantage in rice production.)

FRY, J. (1986), "Methodological Problems Encountered in the Estimation of Sugar Production Costs", *Zuckerind*, 111.

GERMAN BUNDESTAG (ed.) (1989), *Protecting the Earth's Atmosphere: An International Challenge*, German Bundestag Publ. Sect., Bonn.

GOLDIN, Ian and Odin KNUDSEN (1990a), *Agricultural Trade Liberalisation: Implications for Developing Countries*, OECD Development Centre/World Bank, Paris.

GOLDIN, Ian and Gervasio Castro de REZENDE (1990b), *Agriculture and Economic Crisis: Lessons from Brazil*, Development Centre Studies, OECD, Paris.

GOLDIN, Ian (1990c), *Comparative Advantage: Theory and Application to Developing Country Agriculture*, OECD Development Centre, Technical Paper No. 16, OECD, Paris, June.

GOODMAN, David, Bernado SORJ and John WILKINSON (1987), *From Farming to Biotechnology: A Theory of Agro-Industrial Development*, Blackwell, Oxford.

GRIFFIN, Keith (1987), *World Hunger and World Economy*, Macmillan, London.

GRIFFIN, Keith (1989), *Alternative Strategies for Economic Development*, Macmillan for the OECD Development Centre, London.

HABERLER G. (1977), "Survey of the Circumstances Affecting the Location of Production", in B. Ohlin *et. al.* (eds.), *The International Allocation of Economic Activity: Proceedings of a Nobel Symposium*, Holmes and Meier, New York.

HALEY, S. and P. ABBOTT (1986), *An Investigation of the Determinants of Agricultural Comparative Advantage*, Purdue University, Research Bulletin 984, September.

HAMID, Naved and Wouter TIMS (1990), *Agricultural Growth and Economic Development: The Case of Pakistan*, OECD Development Centre, Technical Paper No. 13, OECD, Paris, April.

HARKNESS, I. (1978), "Factor Abundance and Comparative Advantage", *The American Economic Review*, Vol. 65, No. 5, pp. 784-800, December.

HAYAMI, Yujiro and Vernon W. RUTTAN (1971), *Agricultural Development: An International Perspective*, John Hopkins, Baltimore.

HECKSCHER, E. (1965), "The Effect of Foreign Trade on the Distribution of Income", in Ellis and Metzler (eds.), *Readings in the Theory of International Trade*, Duckworth, London.

INSTITUT AGRONOMIQUE MÉDITERRANÉEN DE MONTPELLIER (IAMM) (1987), *Les Cent Premiers Groupes Agro-Industriels Mondiaux*, Montpellier.

INTERNATIONAL WHEAT COUNCIL (1988), *Long Term Outlook for Grain Imports by Developing Countries*, Secretariat Paper No. 17, London, July.

IPCC (International Panel on Climate Change) (1990), Working Group Reports, July, mimeo.

KILBY, Peter, and Carl LIEDHOLM (1986), *The Role of Nonfarm Activities in the Rural Economy*, EEPA Discussion Paper No. 7, USAID, Washington, November.

KRUEGER, A. (1984), "Comparative Advantage and Development Policy — Twenty Years Later" in M. Syrquin, L. Taylor and L. Westphal (eds.), *Economic Structure and Performance: Essays in Honor of Hollis B. Chenery*, Academic Press, Orlando.

KRUEGER, Anne O., Maurice SCHIFF and Alberto VALDÉS (1988), "Agricultural Incentives in Developing Countries: Measuring the Effect of Sectoral and Economywide Policies", *World Bank Economic Review*, Vol. 2, No. 3.

KRUGMAN, P. (1990), *Rethinking International Trade*, MIT Press, Cambridge, Mass.

LANGLEY, J. (1986), *Wheat Competitiveness Conference Summary*, Paper 1598J, USDA, ERS, Washington, D.C.

LEAMER, E. (1984), *Sources of Comparative Advantage*, MIT, Cambridge, Mass.

LEONTIEFF, W. (1965), "Factor Proportions and the Structure of American Trade" in *Review of Economics and Statistics*, Vol. 38, pp. 437-60.

LERNER, A. (1952), "Factor Prices and International Trade", *Economica*, February.

LIPSEY, R. (1979), *Shaping Comparative Advantage*, Prentice Hall, Scarborough.

LYONS, Thomas (1988), "Concentration and Specialisation in Chinese Agriculture, 1979-85", *Journal of Developing Areas*, Vol. 22, July.

MATUS GARDEA, Jaime A., Arturo PUENTE GONZÁLEZ and Cristina LÓPEZ PERALTA (1990), *Biotechnology and Developing Country Agriculture: Maize in Mexico*, OECD Development Centre, Technical Paper No. 19, OECD, Paris, June.

MAUNDER, Allen and Ulf RENBORG (eds.) (1986), *Agriculture in a Turbulent World Economy*, Proceedings of the 19th International Conference of Agricultural Economists, Gower for the IAAE, Aldershot.

MELLOR, John (1988a), "Food Policy, Food Aid and Structural Adjustment Programmes", *Food Policy*, Vol. 3, No. 1, February.

MELLOR, John (1988b), "Global Food Balances and Food Security", *World Development*, Vol. 16, No. 9, September.

MELLOR, John (1988c), *Ending Hunger: An Implementable Program for Self-Reliant Growth*, draft, IFPRI, 29 November.

MELLOR, John (1990), "Global Food Supply: Sustainable Agriculture and Natural Resource Base", in NAVF.

MELLOR, John and Gunvant DESAI (eds.) (1985), *Agricultural Change and Rural Poverty*, Johns Hopkins for IFPRI, Baltimore.

MINHAS, B. (1963), *An International Comparison of Factor Costs and Factor Use*, North Holland, Amsterdam.

MORRIS, Cynthia Taft and Irma ADELMAN (1988), *Comparative Patterns of Economic Development 1850-1914*, Baltimore, Johns Hopkins.

MUNDLAK, Yair, Domingo CARVALLO and Roberto DOMENECH, *Economic Policies and Sectoral Growth: Argentina, 1913-1984*, OECD Development Centre, Technical Paper No. 18, OECD, Paris, June.

NAVF (Norwegian Research Council for Science and the Humanities) (1990), *Sustainable Development, Science and Policy*, NAVF, Oslo.

OECD (1987), *National Policies and Agricultural Trade*, Paris, May.

OECD (1989a), *Agricultural Policies, Markets and Trade: Monitoring and Outlook*, Paris.

OECD (1989b), *Bio-technology: Economic and Wider Impacts*, Paris.

OECD (1990), *Economic Studies*, No. 13, Winter 1989-90, Paris.

OHLIN, B. *et al.* (eds.), *The International Allocation of Economic Activity: Proceedings of a Noble Seminar*, Holmes and Meier, New York.

OMAN, Charles *et al.* (1989), *New Forms of Investment in Developing Country Industries: Mining, Petrochemicals, Automobiles, Textiles, Food*, Development Centre Studies, OECD, Paris.

ONIKI, H. and M. UZAWA (1965), "Patterns of Trade and Investment in a Dynamic Model of International Trade", *Review of Economic Studies*, January.

OTA (1986), *Technology, Public Policy, and the Changing Structure of American Agriculture*, US Government Printing Office, Washington, D.C.

PARIKH, K.S., G. FISCHER, K. FROHBERG and O. GULBRANDSEN (1988a), *Towards Free Trade in Agriculture*, Nijhoff for IIASA, Dordrecht.

PARIKH, J.K. (ed.) (1988b), *Sustainable Development in Agriculture*, Nijhoff for IIASA, Dordrecht.

PARRY, M.L., T.R. CARTER and N.T. KONIJN (eds.) (1988), *The Impact of Climatic Variations on Agriculture*, Kluwer for IIASA and UNEP, Dordrecht.

PAULINO, L. (1986), "Food in the Third World: Past Trends and Projections to 2000", *Research Report 52*, IFPRI, June.

PICKETT, James (1989), "Reflections on the Market and the State in Sub-Saharan Africa", *African Development Review*, Vol. 1, No. 1, June.

PICKETT, James (1991), *Agriculture, the Market and the State: Economic Development in Ethiopia*, Development Centre Studies, OECD, Paris.

PICKETT, James and E. SHAEELDIN (1990), *Comparative Advantage in Agriculture in Ghana*, OECD Development Centre, Technical Paper No. 31, OECD, Paris, October.

RICARDO, D. (1817), *On the Principles of Political Economy and Taxation*, John Murray, London.

ROBINSON, R. (1956), "Factor Proportions and Comparative Advantage", *Quarterly Journal of Economics*, May.

SAMUELSON, P. (1948 and 1949), "International Trade and the Equalisation of Factor Prices", *Economic Journal*, June and June.

SCHUMPETER, J. (1939), *Business Cycles*, 2 volumes, McGraw Hill, New York.

SEN, Amartya (1981), *Poverty and Famines*, Oxford University Press, Oxford.

SEN, Amartya (1986), *Food, Economics and Entitlements*, WIDER Working Papers, UN University, Helsinki, February.

SEN, Amartya (1989), "Food and Freedom", *World Development*, Vol. 17, No. 6, pp. 769-81.

SETBOONSARNG, Suthad (1990), *Biotechnology and Developing Country Agriculture: Maize in Thailand*, OECD Development Centre, Technical Paper No. 20, OECD, Paris, July.

SHAW, John and Hans SINGER (1988), "Introduction: Food Policy, Food Aid and Economic Adjustment", *Food Policy*, Vol. 13, No. 1, February.

SIAMWALLA, Ammar, Suthad SETBOONSARNG and Prasong WERAKARNJANAPON GS (forthcoming), *Changing Comparative Advantage in Thai Agriculture*, OECD, Paris.

SINGER, Hans, John WOOD and Tony JENNINGS (1987), *Food Aid: The Challenge and the Opportunity*, Oxford University Press, Oxford.

SORJ, Bernardo and John WILKINSON (1990), *Biotechnology and Developing Country Agriculture: Maize in Brazil*, OECD Development Centre, Technical Paper No. 17, OECD, Paris, June.

STANTON, B. (1986), *Production Costs for Cereals in the European Community: Comparisons with the United States, 1977-1984*, Report A.E. Res 86-2, Cornell University, Ithaca.

STREETEN, Paul (1987), *What Price Food? Agricultural Price Policies in Developing Countries*, Macmillan, London.

SUNDQUIST, W. Burt (1989), *Emerging Maize Biotechnologies and Their Potential Impact*, OECD Development Centre, Technical Paper No. 8, OECD, Paris, October.

SUNDQUIST, W. Burt, K. MENZ and C. NEUMEYER (1982), *A Technology Assessment of Commercial Corn Production in the US*, Station Bulletin 546-1982, University of Minnesota, Agricultural Experiment Station.

TYERS, Rodney and Kym ANDERSON (1987), *Liberalising OECD Agricultural Policies in the Uruguay Round: Effects on Trade and Welfare*, Australian National University, Working Papers in Trade and Development, No. 87/10, Canberra, June.

UNITED STATES CONGRESS, OFFICE OF TECHNOLOGY ASSESSMENT (1986), *A Review of US Competitiveness in Agricultural Trade: A Technical Memorandum*, Washington, D.C., October.

UNITED STATES, DEPARTMENT OF AGRICULTURE (1986), *Department of Agriculture, Conceptual Framework Overview and Summaries of Contributing Projects to US Competitiveness in the World Wheat Market: A Prototype Study*, ERS, Washington, D.C., June.

UNITED STATES, DEPARTMENT OF AGRICULTURE (1987), *Government Intervention in Agriculture*, USDA Economic Research Service FAER-229, April.

UNITED STATES, DEPARTMENT OF AGRICULTURE (1988), *Estimates of Producer and Consumer Subsidy Equivalents: Government Intervention in Agriculture 1982-1986*, ERS Staff Report AGE5880127, Washington, D.C., April.

UNITED STATES, DEPARTMENT OF AGRICULTURE (1989), *Economic Indicators of the Farm Sector: Costs of Production*, ERS, Washington, D.C.

UNITED STATES, INTERNATIONAL TRADE COMMISSION (1987), *US Global Competitiveness: Oilseeds and Oilseed Products*, USITC Publication 2045, December.

VINER, J. (1937), *Studies in the Theory of International Trade*, Harper, New York.

VOLLRATH, Thomas L. (1989), "Competitiveness and Protection in World Agriculture", *Agriculture Information Bulletin*, No. 567, ERS, USDA, July.

VOLLRATH, T. and D. HUU VOO (1988), *Investigating the Nature of Agricultural Competitiveness*, USDA, ERS, Washington, D.C.

WAHREN, Carl (1988), "Can AIDS Be Contained?", *OECD Observer*, October-November.

WINTERS, L. Alan (1987), "The Economic Consequences of Agricultural Support: Survey", *OECD Economic Studies*, No. 9, Autumn.

WINTERS, L. Alan (1988), "The So-called 'Non-economic' Objectives of Agricultural Policy", OECD Department of Economics and Statistics Working Papers No. 52, April.

WORLD BANK (1986a), *Poverty and Hunger: Issues and Options in Food Security in Developing Countries*, Washington, D.C., February.

WORLD BANK (1986b), *World Development Report 1986*, Washington, D.C.

WORLD BANK (1989a), *Price Prospects for Major Primary Commodities*, Washington, D.C.

WORLD BANK (1989b), *World Development Report 1989*, Washington, D.C.

WORLD BANK (1990), *World Development Report 1990*, Washington, D.C.

WORLD COMMISSION ON ENVIRONMENT AND DEVELOPMENT (1987), *Our Common Future*, Oxford University Press, Oxford.

WORLD FOOD COUNCIL (1984), *The World Food and Hunger Problem: Changing Perspectives and Possibilities, 1974-84*, WFC/1984/6, Rome, 10 February.

WORLD FOOD COUNCIL (1989), *The Cyprus Initiative against Hunger in the World*, WFC/1989/2, Rome, 22 March.

YANG, Yongzheng and Rodney TYERS (1989), "The Economic Costs of Food Self-Sufficiency in China", *World Development*, Vol. 17, No. 2.

ZIETZ, Joachim and Alberto VALDÉS (1986), *The Costs of Protectionism to Developing Countries: An Analysis for Selected Agricultural Products*, World Bank Staff Working Papers 769, Washington, D.C./IBRD, January.

ZIETZ, Joachim and Alberto VALDÉS (1989), *International Interactions in Food and Agricultural Policies: The Effect of Alternative Policies*, OECD Development Centre, Technical Paper No. 2, OECD, Paris, April.

MAIN SALES OUTLETS OF OECD PUBLICATIONS – PRINCIPAUX POINTS DE VENTE DES PUBLICATIONS DE L'OCDE

Argentina – Argentine
Carlos Hirsch S.R.L.
Galería Güemes, Florida 165, 4° Piso
1333 Buenos Aires Tel. (1) 331.1787 y 331.2391
Telefax: (1) 331.1787

Australia – Australie
D.A. Book (Aust.) Pty. Ltd.
648 Whitehorse Road, P.O.B 163
Mitcham, Victoria 3132 Tel. (03) 873.4411
Telefax: (03) 873.5679

Austria – Autriche
OECD Publications and Information Centre
Schedestrasse 7
D-W 5300 Bonn 1 (Germany) Tel. (49.228) 21.60.45
Telefax: (49.228) 26.11.04

Gerold & Co.
Graben 31
Wien I Tel. (0222) 533.50.14

Belgium – Belgique
Jean De Lannoy
Avenue du Roi 202
B-1060 Bruxelles Tel. (02) 538.51.69/538.08.41
Telefax: (02) 538.08.41

Canada
Renouf Publishing Company Ltd.
1294 Algoma Road
Ottawa, ON K1B 3W8 Tel. (613) 741.4333
Telefax: (613) 741.5439

Stores:
61 Sparks Street
Ottawa, ON K1P 5R1 Tel. (613) 238.8985
211 Yonge Street
Toronto, ON M5B 1M4 Tel. (416) 363.3171

Federal Publications
165 University Avenue
Toronto, ON M5H 3B8 Tel. (416) 581.1552
Telefax: (416)581.1743

Les Éditions La Liberté Inc.
3020 Chemin Sainte-Foy
Sainte-Foy, PQ G1X 3V6 Tel. (418) 658.3763
Telefax: (418) 658.3763

China – Chine
China National Publications Import
Export Corporation (CNPIEC)
P.O. Box 88
Beijing Tel. 44.0731
Telefax: 401.5661

Denmark – Danemark
Munksgaard Export and Subscription Service
35, Nørre Søgade, P.O. Box 2148
DK-1016 København K Tel. (33) 12.85.70
Telefax: (33) 12.93.87

Finland – Finlande
Akateeminen Kirjakauppa
Keskuskatu 1, P.O. Box 128
00100 Helsinki Tel. (358 0) 12141
Telefax: (358 0) 121.4441

France
OECD/OCDE
Mail Orders/Commandes par correspondance:
2, rue André-Pascal
75775 Paris Cédex 16 Tel. (33-1) 45.24.82.00
Telefax: (33-1) 45.24.85.00
or (33-1) 45.24.81.76
Telex: 620 160 OCDE

Bookshop/Librairie:
33, rue Octave-Feuillet
75016 Paris Tel. (33-1) 45.24.81.67
(33-1) 45,24.81.81

Librairie de l'Université
12a, rue Nazareth
13100 Aix-en-Provence Tel. 42.26.18.08
Telefax: 42.26.63.26

Germany – Allemagne
OECD Publications and Information Centre
Schedestrasse 7
D-W 5300 Bonn 1 Tel. (0228) 21.60.45
Telefax: (0228) 26.11.04

Greece – Grèce
Librairie Kauffmann
Mavrokordatou 9
106 78 Athens Tel. 322.21.60
Telefax: 363.39.67

Hong Kong
Swindon Book Co. Ltd.
13 - 15 Lock Road
Kowloon, Hong Kong Tel. 366.80.31
Telefax: 739.49.75

Iceland – Islande
Mál Mog Menning
Laugavegi 18, Pósthólf 392
121 Reykjavik Tel. 162.35.23

India – Inde
Oxford Book and Stationery Co.
Scindia House
New Delhi 110001 Tel.(11) 331.5896/5308
Telefax: (11) 332.5993

17 Park Street
Calcutta 700016 Tel. 240832

Indonesia – Indonésie
Pdii-Lipi
P.O. Box 269/JKSMG/88
Jakarta 12790 Tel. 583467
Telex: 62 875

Ireland – Irlande
TDC Publishers – Library Suppliers
12 North Frederick Street
Dublin 1 Tel. 74.48.35/74.96.77
Telefax: 74.84.16

Israel
Electronic Publications only
Publications électroniques seulement
Sophist Systems Ltd.
71 Allenby Street
Tel-Aviv 65134 Tel. 3-29.00.21
Telefax: 3-29.92.39

Italy – Italie
Libreria Commissionaria Sansoni
Via Duca di Calabria 1/1
50125 Firenze Tel. (055) 64.54.15
Telefax: (055) 64.12.57

Via Bartolini 29
20155 Milano Tel. (02) 36.50.83
Editrice e Libreria Herder
Piazza Montecitorio 120
00186 Roma Tel. 679.46.28
Telex: NATEL I 621427

Libreria Hoepli
Via Hoepli 5
20121 Milano Tel. (02) 86.54.46
Telefax: (02) 805.28.86

Libreria Scientifica
Dott. Lucio de Biasio 'Aeiou'
Via Meravigli 16
20123 Milano Tel. (02) 805.68.98
Telefax: (02) 80.01.75

Japan – Japon
OECD Publications and Information Centre
Landic Akasaka Building
2-3-4 Akasaka, Minato-ku
Tokyo 107 Tel. (81.3) 3586.2016
Telefax: (81.3) 3584.7929

Korea – Corée
Kyobo Book Centre Co. Ltd.
P.O. Box 1658, Kwang Hwa Moon
Seoul Tel. 730.78.91
Telefax: 735.00.30

Malaysia – Malaisie
Co-operative Bookshop Ltd.
University of Malaya
P.O. Box 1127, Jalan Pantai Baru
59700 Kuala Lumpur
Malaysia Tel. 756.5000/756.5425
Telefax: 757.3661

Netherlands – Pays-Bas
SDU Uitgeverij
Christoffel Plantijnstraat 2
Postbus 20014
2500 EA's-Gravenhage Tel. (070 3) 78.99.11
Voor bestellingen: Tel. (070 3) 78.98.80
Telefax: (070 3) 47.63.51

New Zealand – Nouvelle-Zélande
GP Publications Ltd.
Customer Services
33 The Esplanade - P.O. Box 38-900
Petone, Wellington Tel. (04) 5685.555
Telefax: (04) 5685.333

Norway – Norvège
Narvesen Info Center - NIC
Bertrand Narvesens vei 2
P.O. Box 6125 Etterstad
0602 Oslo 6 Tel. (02) 57.33.00
Telefax: (02) 68.19.01

Pakistan
Mirza Book Agency
65 Shahrah Quaid-E-Azam
Lahore 3 Tel. 66.839
Telex: 44886 UBL PK. Attn: MIRZA BK

Portugal
Livraria Portugal
Rua do Carmo 70-74
Apart. 2681
1117 Lisboa Codex Tel.: (01) 347.49.82/3/4/5
Telefax: (01) 347.02.64

Singapore – Singapour
Information Publications Pte. Ltd.
Pei-Fu Industrial Building
24 New Industrial Road No. 02-06
Singapore 1953 Tel. 283.1786/283.1798
Telefax: 284.8875

Spain – Espagne
Mundi-Prensa Libros S.A.
Castelló 37, Apartado 1223
Madrid 28001 Tel. (91) 431.33.99
Telefax: (91) 575.39.98

Libreria Internacional AEDOS
Consejo de Ciento 391
08009 - Barcelona Tel. (93) 488.34.92
Telefax: (93) 487.76.59

Llibreria de la Generalitat
Palau Moja
Rambla dels Estudis, 118
08002 - Barcelona Tel. (93) 318.80.12 (Subscripcions)
(93) 302.67.23 (Publicacions)
Telefax: (93) 412.18.54

Sri Lanka
Centre for Policy Research
c/o Colombo Agencies Ltd.
No. 300-304, Galle Road
Colombo 3 Tel. (1) 574240, 573551-2
Telefax: (1) 575394, 510711

Sweden – Suède
Fritzes Fackboksföretaget
Box 16356
Regeringsgatan 12
103 27 Stockholm Tel. (08) 23.89.00
Telefax: (08) 20.50.21

Subscription Agency/Abonnements:
Wennergren-Williams AB
Nordenflychtsvägen 74
Box 30004
104 25 Stockholm Tel. (08) 13.67.00
Telefax: (08) 618.62.32

Switzerland – Suisse
OECD Publications and Information Centre
Schedestrasse 7
D-W 5300 Bonn 1 (Germany) Tel. (49.228) 21.60.45
Telefax: (49.228) 26.11.04

Suisse romande

Maditec S.A.
Chemin des Palettes 4
1020 Renens/Lausanne Tel. (021) 635.08.65
Telefax: (021) 635.07.80

Librairie Payot
6 rue Grenus
1211 Genève 11 Tel. (022) 731.89.50
Telex: 28356

Subscription Agency – Service des Abonnements
Naville S.A.
7, rue Lévrier
1201 Genève Tél.: (022) 732.24.00
Telefax: (022) 738.87.13

Taiwan – Formose
Good Faith Worldwide Int'l. Co. Ltd.
9th Floor, No. 118, Sec. 2
Chung Hsiao E. Road
Taipei Tel. (02) 391.7396/391.7397
Telefax: (02) 394.9176

Thailand – Thaïlande
Suksit Siam Co. Ltd.
113, 115 Fuang Nakhon Rd.
Opp. Wat Rajbopith
Bangkok 10200 Tel. (662) 251.1630
Telefax: (662) 236.7783

Turkey – Turquie
Kültur Yayinlari Is-Türk Ltd. Sti.
Atatürk Bulvari No. 191/Kat. 21
Kavaklidere/Ankara Tel. 25.07.60
Dolmabahce Cad. No. 29
Besiktas/Istanbul Tel. 160.71.88
Telex: 43482B

United Kingdom – Royaume-Uni
HMSO
Gen. enquiries Tel. (071) 873 0011
Postal orders only:
P.O. Box 276, London SW8 5DT
Personal Callers HMSO Bookshop
49 High Holborn, London WC1V 6HB
Telefax: 071 873 2000
Branches at: Belfast, Birmingham, Bristol, Edinburgh, Manchester

United States – États-Unis
OECD Publications and Information Centre
2001 L Street N.W., Suite 700
Washington, D.C. 20036-4910 Tel. (202) 785.6323
Telefax: (202) 785.0350

Venezuela
Libreria del Este
Avda F. Miranda 52, Aptdo. 60337
Edificio Galipán
Caracas 106 Tel. 951.1705/951.2307/951.1297
Telegram: Libreste Caracas

Yugoslavia – Yougoslavie
Jugoslovenska Knjiga
Knez Mihajlova 2, P.O. Box 36
Beograd Tel. (011) 621.992
Telefax: (011) 625.970

Orders and inquiries from countries where Distributors have not yet been appointed should be sent to: OECD Publications Service, 2 rue André-Pascal, 75775 Paris Cédex 16, France.

Les commandes provenant de pays où l'OCDE n'a pas encore désigné de distributeur devraient être adressées à : OCDE, Service des Publications, 2, rue André-Pascal, 75775 Paris Cédex 16, France.

OECD PUBLICATIONS, 2 rue André-Pascal, 75775 PARIS CEDEX 16
PRINTED IN FRANCE
(41 92 02 1) ISBN 92-64-13628-2 - No. 45941 1992